The Healthy Male

The Healthy Male

A COMPREHENSIVE HEALTH GUIDE FOR MEN (AND THE WOMEN WHO CARE ABOUT THEM)

by Maureen Mylander

Foreword by Robert N. Butler, M.D.

LITTLE, BROWN AND COMPANY
BOSTON   TORONTO

FIRST EDITION

The table on page 60 is reprinted by permission from Dr.
Robert E. Johnson, Professor Emeritus of Physiology,
University of Illinois, and colleagues, *Physiological Measure-
ments of Metabolic Functions in Man* (New York; McGraw-
Hill, 1963).

The excerpt on page 66 from "Don't the Girls All Get
Prettier at Closing Time?" by Mickey Gilley and Baker
Knight is reprinted by permission of Merit Music Corpora-
tion. Copyright © 1975 by Singletree Music (A Division of
Merit Music Corporation), 815 18th Ave., So. Nashville,
TN 37203.

The Holmes-Rahe Stress Scale on pages 124–125 is reprinted from *The Journal of Psychosomatic Research*, Vol. 2,
pages 213–218, Thomas H. Holmes and Richard H. Rahe,
"The Social Readjustment Rating Scale," 1967, Pergamon
Press, Ltd.

Library of Congress Cataloging-in-Publication Data

Mylander, Maureen.
  The healthy male.

  Includes index.
  1. Men — health and hygiene. 2. Longevity. I. Title.
[DNLM: 1. Health. 2. Longevity — popular works.
3. Medicine — popular works. 4. Men — popular
works. WB 120 M997h]
RA777.8.M95 1987   613'.0423   87-2808
ISBN 0-316-59368-0

10 9 8 7 6 5 4 3 2

RRD VA

*Published simultaneously in Canada
by Little, Brown & Company (Canada) Limited*

PRINTED IN THE UNITED STATES OF AMERICA

To Willard G. Root,
Michael J. Halberstam, and
Donald S. Jewell

I felt the presence of these three men almost constantly during the two years I wrote this book. The first, my father, died at age fifty-one of heart disease. He might have lived many years longer had the other two been taking care of him.

Dr. Michael J. Halberstam, an internist and cardiologist with whom I collaborated in writing health advice columns for several years, died tragically at age forty-eight of gunshot wounds inflicted by a burglar.

Dr. Donald S. Jewell, a clinical psychologist, is lively and well in Washington, D.C., where he helps many others be the same. I wish him a long and happy life.

Contents

Acknowledgments

For their help with the launching of *The Healthy Male*, I wish to thank Fred Schellenberg; Gary Hammer; my original editor, Beth Rashbaum; my final editor, Christina Coffin; and my agent, Carl Brandt. For the time they spent reading and commenting on the manuscript, I would like to thank Clarissa Wittenberg, Ken Roberts, and Jim Sheaks, as well as Jim Walker, Richard McManus, and Loring Henderson. For research assistance, I thank Laurie Doepel, Marcia Doniger, Winnie Adams, and countless Fairfax County Public Library reference librarians; and for help with manuscript preparation, Cynthia Phelps and Bruce Birnbaum.

Special thanks also go to the many experts who reviewed various parts of the manuscript:

John T. Hagenbucher, M.D., Internal Medicine, Washington, D.C. (chapters 6 and 11)

Ms. Karen Donato, formerly of the National Institutes of Health Nutrition Coordinating Committee (chapter 1)

Ms. Anne Thomas, Director of Public Information, National Institutes of Health (chapters 1 and 2)

Mr. York Onnen, Director of Program Development, President's Council on Physical Fitness and Sports (chapter 2)

Ms. Janet Vizard and Mr. Tom Klein, National Institutes of Health Fitness Center (chapter 2)

Ms. Susan J. Kalish, Director of Communications, American Running and Fitness Association (chapter 2)

Ms. Esther McBride, Public Affairs Specialist, Office of Communications, National Institute of Allergy and Infectious Diseases (chapter 3)

Ms. Maureen Gardner, Public Affairs Specialist, Office of Research Reporting, National Institute of Child Health and Human Development (chapter 3, sections on infertility, vasectomy, and contraceptives)

Michael McClure, Ph.D., Reproductive Sciences Branch, National Institute of Child Health and Human Development (chapter 3, section on infertility)

Jeffrey Perlman, Ph.D., Chief, Contraceptive Evaluation Branch, National Institute of Child Health and Human Development (chapter 3, sections on contraceptives and vasectomy)

Gabriel Bialy, M.D., Chief, Contraceptive Development Branch, National Institute of Child Health and Human Development (chapter 3, sections on contraceptives and vasectomy)

Michael J. Free, Ph.D., Director, Product Development, Program for Appropriate Technology in Health, Seattle, Washington (chapter 3, section on condoms)

Mr. Robert N. Kohmescher, Education Specialist, and Susan Schultz, Division of Sexually Transmitted Diseases, Centers for Disease Control (chapter 3, section on sexually transmitted diseases)

Stephen E. Straus, M.D., Head, Medical Virology Section, Laboratory of Clinical Investigation, National Institute of Allergy and Infectious Diseases (chapter 3, section on herpes)

Ms. Lynne Lamberg, author, *The American Medical Association Guide to Better Sleep* (chapter 4)

David N. Fairbanks, M.D., otolaryngologist, Washington, D.C. (chapter 4, sections on snoring)

Donald S. Jewell, Ph.D., clinical psychologist, Washington, D.C. (chapters 5 and 9)

Molly Jones, Ph.D., clinical psychologist, Washington, D.C. (chapter 5)

George P. Chrousos, Ph.D., Senior Investigator, Developmental Endocrinology Branch, National Institute of Child Health and Human Development (chapter 5)

Stephen M. Weiss, Ph.D., Chief, Behavioral Medicine Branch; National Heart, Lung, and Blood Institute (chapter 5)

Mr. Larry Blaser, Chief, Research Reporting Section; Office of Prevention, Education, and Control; National Heart, Lung, and Blood Institute (chapter 6, section on heart disease)

Mr. Bowen Hosford, author, Vienna, Virginia (chapter 6, section on heart disease)

Ms. Patricia Newman, Chief, Reports Section, Office of Cancer Communications, National Cancer Institute (chapter 6, section on cancer, and chapter 1, section on diet and cancer)

Rosemary Romano, Linda Anderson, Eleanor Nealon, and Joyce Doherty, Office of Cancer Communications, National Cancer Institute (chapter 6, section on cancer)

Ritva Butrum, Ph.D., Chief, Diet and Cancer Branch, Division of Cancer Prevention and Control, National Cancer Institute (chapter 6, section on cancer, and chapter 1, section on diet and cancer)

Mr. Ernst Meyer, Research Scientist, U.S. Department of Transportation (chapter 7, section on accidents)

John R. Marler, M.D., Medical Officer, Stroke and Trauma Program, National

Institute of Neurological and Communicative Disorders and Stroke (chapter 7, section on stroke)

Hannah H. Peavy, M.D., Airways Diseases Branch, Division of Lung Diseases; National Heart, Lung, and Blood Institute (chapter 7, section on chronic obstructive pulmonary diseases)

William Jordan, M.D., Director, Microbiology and Infectious Diseases Program, National Institute of Allergy and Infectious Diseases (chapter 7, section on influenza)

Ms. Connie Raab, Deputy Information Officer, National Institute of Diabetes and Digestive and Kidney Diseases (chapter 7, sections on cirrhosis and diabetes)

Kenneth R. Warren, Ph.D., National Institute of Alcohol Abuse and Alcoholism (chapter 7, section on cirrhosis)

Mr. Thomas Lalley, Deputy Chief, Antisocial and Violent Behavior Branch, National Institute of Mental Health (chapter 7, section on homicide)

Robert E. Silverman, M.D., Ph.D., Chief, Diabetes Program Branch, National Institute of Diabetes and Digestive and Kidney Diseases (chapter 7, section on diabetes)

Laurence H. Miller, M.D., dermatologist, Washington, D.C. (chapter 8, sections on baldness and various skin conditions)

Nancy B. Cummings, M.D., Associate Director, Research and Assessment, National Institute of Diabetes and Digestive and Kidney Diseases (chapter 8, section on prostate problems)

Ms. Susan Lachter, Division of Prevention and Communications, National Institute on Drug Abuse (chapter 9)

Victor Cohn, Ph.D., Professor of Pharmacology, George Washington University Medical Center, Washington, D.C. (chapter 9)

Mr. Richard J. Bast, Director, Quality Assurance, National Clearinghouse for Alcohol Information (chapter 7, section on drinking and driving, and chapter 9, section on alcoholism)

Lon R. White, M.D., Chief, Epidemiology Office; Epidemiology, Demography and Biometry Program; National Institute on Aging (chapters 10 and 11)

Ms. Barbara Katzman, Public Affairs Specialist, Public Information Office, National Institute on Aging (chapter 10)

Robert N. Butler, M.D., Brookdale Professor of Geriatrics and Adult Development, Mount Sinai Medical Center, New York (chapter 3, section on sex after sixty, and chapter 10)

William E. Wright, D.D.S., Senior Staff Periodontist, Dental Clinic, National Institute of Dental Research (chapter 10, section on tooth loss)

Ms. Sally Wilberding, Public Affairs Specialist, Public Inquiries and Reports Section, National Institute of Dental Research (chapter 10, section on tooth loss)

Robert Sperduto, M.D., Medical Officer, Biometry and Epidemiology Program, National Eye Institute (chapter 10, section on eyesight)

Ms. Mary Lynn Hendrix, Public Affairs Specialist, Office of Scientific Reporting, National Eye Institute (chapter 10, section on eyesight)

Buckminster Ranney, Ph.D., Deputy Director, Communicative Disorders Program, National Institute of Neurological and Communicative Disorders and Stroke (chapter 10, section on hearing)

Ingrid Waldron, Ph.D., Associate Professor of Biology, University of Pennsylvania (chapter 11)

Estelle Ramey, Ph.D., Professor of Physiology and Biophysics, Georgetown University (chapter 11)

Mr. Jules Asher, Public Affairs Specialist, Intramural Research Program, National Institute of Mental Health (chapter 5, section on depression, and chapter 7, section on suicide)

Mr. Ed Long, Acting Deputy Director, Office of Scientific Information, National Institute of Mental Health (chapter 5, section on depression, and chapter 7, sections on suicide and homicide)

Ms. Lynn Cave, Writer-Editor, Office of Scientific and Health Reports, National Institute of Neurological and Communicative Disorders and Stroke (chapter 7, section on stroke, and chapter 10, section on hearing)

Ms. Judy Murphy, Deputy Chief, Office of Communications, National Institute of Allergy and Infectious Diseases (chapter 7, section on influenza, and chapter 9, section on smoking).

Foreword

The Healthy Male by Maureen Mylander is the first comprehensive book I know of devoted to health promotion and disease prevention in men. Reviewed extensively by dozens of experts in a variety of institutions, including the National Institutes of Health, the Centers for Disease Control, and the President's Council on Physical Fitness and Sports, the book covers nutrition, exercise, sexuality, rest, sleep, stress, heart disease, cancer, and other "leading man-killers," including accidents, suicide, and addiction.

The special characteristics of growing older are also covered. There is a significant difference in life expectancy between the sexes: 71.2 for American men as compared with 78.2 for women. But the fact that women live longer than men can be a mixed blessing. Surviving women are often left economically bereft and suffering from many chronic illnesses as well as emotional and social problems. It is obviously important to both sexes to focus on this extraordinary difference in life expectancy and confront the problem of how to minimize that difference by increasing the longevity of men. *The Healthy Male* addresses such questions as: To what extent is the gap in life expectancy between the sexes modifiable? Is the difference predominantly a consequence of genes or the greater strength of the female's hormonal or immune system as compared with the male's? How much is it a function of behavior? How much will it be changeable in the near future, and how much will it require long-term changes in society? We do have some information, but the gender difference in life expectancy is still not the active topic of research it should be.

The great antecedents of disease are genes, aging, and the environment broadly defined to include external pathogens and our health-related behavior — what we eat and how we take care of ourselves. Genes and aging are powerful factors over which we are only now beginning to gain some control. But about 50 percent of disease and longevity is due to environmental factors. Perhaps a third of the longevity gap between men and women, for example, is accounted for by the greater tobacco consumption of men. This is a rare occasion in which prejudice against women was helpful, i.e., the negative view toward women's smoking that was held through the first third of the twentieth century. While overall tobacco use has declined remarkably since the 1964 report of the Surgeon General of the United States, young women are now increasing their rate of smoking to a greater extent than young men with the same socioeconomic background as the young women.

If cessation of tobacco intake could be the single most important factor that would close the life expectancy gap between males and females, some other culprits of a more social character — hazardous occupations, exposure to toxic environments, "macho behavior," and alcohol abuse — may be even more difficult to control than smoking. As Betty Friedan has said, perhaps men could learn from women how to alter their behavior and extend their life.

People should not assume that there is nothing they can do about their aging and longevity. One of the great transforming events of modern-day medicine, gerontology, and geriatrics is the realization that it is possible to intervene through a variety of social, behavioral, and environmental manipulations to extend life and make it more active, vigorous, and healthy.

Robert N. Butler, M.D.
New York City
April 1987

Preface

The Healthy Male is a book about bodybuilding — not the Arnold Schwarzenegger type, but the type that fends off diseases that kill men in their prime, extends life expectancy, and makes men well and fit. A good working definition of fitness comes from the President's Council on Physical Fitness and Sports:

> . . . the ability to carry out daily tasks with vigor, safety, and alertness, without undue fatigue, and with ample energy to enjoy leisure time pursuits and to meet unforeseen emergencies.

This definition encompasses running marathons or enjoying an evening with your wife, girlfriend, kids, or friends, or with yourself.

"You," as used herein, refers to men of all ages. This book might appeal to women on behalf of their husbands, lovers, boyfriends, fathers, brothers, sons, grandfathers, uncles, and other men in their lives. Women might even be interested on their own behalf, since many men's health issues are women's issues as well. But this book is for and about men.

There are two reasons for such targeting. First, no comprehensive health guide for men has ever been written. Single-subject books about male sexual health, vasectomy, prostate problems, mid-life crisis, diet, fitness, and bodybuilding line the bookshelves of America. But no complete health guide for men exists, even though more than 150 health books — not including dozens on physical fitness and beauty — have been written for women. Second, the average man lives seven years fewer than the average woman. In 1984 men had a life expectancy of 71.2 years, while women had a life expectancy of 78.2. The gap in life expectancy — which had been widening from 1900 to 1972 — has narrowed by one year since 1979. Still, men continue to die prematurely, primarily of heart disease, cancer, accidents, stroke, chronic obstructive lung disease, pneumonia and influenza, suicide, liver disease, homicide, and diabetes, in that order. Specifically, men succumb to

- heart disease at 2 times the death rate of women
- cancer at 1.5 times the rate of women
- accidents at 2.8 times the rate of women
- stroke at 1.2 times the rate of women
- chronic obstructive lung disease, including emphysema, at 2.4 times the rate of women
- pneumonia/influenza at 1.8 times the rate of women
- suicide at 3.6 times the rate of women, the greatest sex difference in mortality
- cirrhosis of the liver and chronic liver disease at 2.2 times the rate of women
- homicide at 3.3 times the rate of women
- diabetes at 1.1 times the rate of women, the smallest sex difference in mortality

Why do men die earlier and at two to more than three times the rate of women from nearly every leading cause of death? Genetic influences and hormonal differences partially explain the longevity gap. But the most compelling reason women outlive men, and the main message of this book, is that men's lifestyles account for much of the longevity gap — and that they need not die "young." The *potential life expectancy* of the American male is far greater than his *actual life expectancy*. This means that you — a man and not a statistic — can live not only longer, but also more energetically and enjoyably, by getting involved in your own health care and making certain lifestyle changes that will lower your risk of dying prematurely of a heart attack or some other man-killer. It is not too late to start.

Part 1 presents chapters on basic lifestyle practices that affect health: better diet, exercise, sexual health, sleep and rest, and better management of stress. Part 2 covers the ten most likely causes of premature death. Three of these — accidents, suicide, and homicide — are seldom covered in traditional health guides. Part 2 also covers special health concerns of men, including baldness, jock itch, vasectomies, and prostate problems, and addictions to alcohol, drugs, and unhealthy relationships. Part 3 explores the best antiaging remedies, "inner listening" to your body's signals and warnings, the dangers of overreliance on doctors, and checkpoints for choosing your own (not your wife's or girlfriend's) physician. Throughout, *The Healthy Male* explores how men can extend their lives, not by attending to one health risk factor such as diet or exercise while ignoring all the others, not by quick-fix approaches, but by basic attitude changes from which health-seeking decisions and actions will naturally evolve.

Dr. Herb Goldberg, in *The New Male*, wrote that if men are to rid themselves of outdated roles and burdensome patterns of behavior that are self-limiting and destructive, they might well begin by taking better care of themselves physically. This book is a step in that direction. It does not guarantee good health. Nor will it substitute for a physician's care when you need it. But it can help you decide when to seek professional medical help and, better still, keep you from needing it.

A final point: why is a woman writing a book about men's health? Women have always taken a greater interest than men in health matters, and have traditionally learned about their own and their children's bodies through childbearing and family and child care.

During two decades as a medical writer, I have watched research scientists — most of them male — study, and find answers to, men's health problems. But men in the general population are missing the full benefit of these studies because nobody has yet presented the findings to them in a comprehensive and readable form.

There is a deeper reason why I have written this book. My father died when he was fifty-one, after more than a decade of physical decline from heart disease. His illness was a well-kept secret in our family. He never said much about how sick, or how frightened, he felt. My mother followed his lead and kept silent. My sister and I, barely aware that he was seriously ill, thought that his remoteness and passivity were caused by something we had done wrong. So we, like both our parents in their differing ways, suffered because of the secrecy surrounding his illness.

How many people — women, men, the health establishment — look the other way when fathers, husbands, or lovers fall ill? How many women rehearse for widowhood rather than for growing old with their husbands at their sides? How many men, especially those whose fathers died early, worry that the same fate awaits them?

Many men are no longer content to worry. Since 1964, when the Surgeon General first warned against the health dangers of smoking, the number of male smokers has decreased by 27 percent, while the number of female smokers has decreased by only 14 percent. Some seven million Americans — most of them men — run at least three miles a week. Additional millions of men work out in other sports. The sheer numbers suggest that men are keenly interested in their health and, having attended to two health risks (smoking and sedentary living), are well down the road toward eliminating the others. Armed with the kind of information *The Healthy Male* provides, men who have invested so heavily in families and careers can now invest in themselves in terms of fitness, health, and — above all — living longer and better.

Maureen Mylander
Vienna, Virginia
April 1987

I

LIFESTYLES FOR MEN

❧ 1

Safe at the Plate: Nutrition

Dietary Guidelines for Americans

Few topics capture public attention more than what to eat, what not to eat, how much to eat, and even when and how to eat. American diets have greatly changed during the past fifty years. During the 1920s and 1930s, there was none of the variety of foods available today. Yesteryear's staples were potatoes, turnips, boiled cabbage, and, occasionally, meat. Fresh fruits were served at Christmas, if then. Dairy products and salads were scarce, and rickets from lack of vitamin D was common.

Today Americans eat a greater variety of food than ever before. But the fare includes unhealthy amounts of red meat, fats, dairy products, sugar, white bread, and other highly processed, low-fiber foods. In 1977 a Senate Select Committee on Nutrition and Human Needs, headed by Senator George McGovern, reported that six of the ten leading causes of death in the United States are linked to diet. Americans, the committee concluded, are risking their health by eating too much fat, sugar, cholesterol, and salt, and not enough fruit, vegetables, grain products, and other complex carbohydrates.

The McGovern committee's report and recommendations seemed revolutionary at the time. Today they are widely accepted in theory, if not in practice. The typical American diet continues to invite obesity, atherosclerosis (fatty deposits along the inner walls of arteries), high blood pressure, heart disease, and cancer. Accordingly, the federal government published formal *Dietary Guidelines for Americans* in 1980. These guidelines were reissued in 1985 virtually unchanged.

Dietary Guidelines for Americans

1. Eat a variety of foods: fruits, vegetables, whole grains, legumes, dairy products, meats, poultry, and fish.
2. Maintain desirable weight. (See weight table on p. 26.)
3. Avoid too much fat, saturated fat, and cholesterol by eating less fatty meat, cream, butter, eggs, fried food, and milk, and more skim milk, lean meat, poultry, and fish.
4. Eat foods with adequate starch and fiber: whole grain breads and cereals, fruits and vegetables, peas, and nuts.
5. Avoid too much sugar: white sugar, brown sugar, raw sugar, honey, *and* syrups, candy, soft drinks, ice cream, cakes, and cookies.
6. Avoid too much sodium in salty foods, such as potato chips, pretzels, salted nuts and popcorn, soy sauce, steak sauce, garlic salt, cheese, and pickled foods; and in cured meats like bacon, sausage, and salami.
7. If you drink alcohol, do so in moderation: no more than two drinks daily.

SOURCE: *Nutrition and Your Health: Dietary Guidelines for Americans,* U.S. Department of Agriculture and U.S. Department of Health and Human Services, 1985.

Men's Special Nutrition Needs

These dietary guidelines apply to men and women alike. But men have specific nutrition needs that differ from women's. Men need more calories: 1,200 to 1,500 a day for the average adult male at rest, compared to 1,000 to 1,300 for the average woman at rest. Men need more calories mainly because they are larger than women. When men and women are of similar age, weight, height, and body composition, and are equally active, their daily calorie needs are similar.

Men also have different needs from women for certain nutrients, as reflected in the recommended dietary allowances (RDAs). These state levels — according to age and sex — of certain vitamins, minerals, and other nutrients needed to maintain good nutrition in healthy individuals. The RDAs — first developed during World War II to encourage production of nutritious foods — are used to plan menus in the armed services, schools, and hospitals; for nutritional labeling of food; in nutrition surveys; and in developing new food products and diet supplements.

In addition to their greater caloric requirements, men of all ages need more protein, vitamins A, E, B-1, B-3, B-6, and magnesium than do

women. For example, an adult man needs 56 grams of protein compared with an adult woman's daily requirement of 44 grams. The only
minerals women need more of are iron — mainly during the childbearing years — and calcium. Deficiencies of this mineral can cause
osteoporosis, a disease that afflicts mainly postmenopausal women,
but also many men over age sixty-five. Women's bones in particular
lose density and become prone to hip and other fractures. Although
the RDA for adult men and women is 800 milligrams of calcium, the
National Institutes of Health urges men to consume 1,000 milligrams
and women from 1,000 to 1,500 milligrams of calcium daily from foods
when possible, and otherwise from calcium tablets. These recommendations are based on current scientific evidence and may change as
research continues. Men and women of all ages need the same amounts
of phosphorus, zinc, and iodine (see table on p. 6).

RDAs represent the average daily amounts of nutrients that population groups should consume over a period of time, not on a daily
basis. RDAs exceed the daily nutrient levels most people need to function normally because the RDAs include a margin of safety and take
into account individual differences in food intake, ability to absorb
nutrients, and other factors.

RDAs are reviewed and usually revised every five years. But in
October 1985 the National Academy of Sciences declined to issue expected new RDAs because of scientific differences of opinion about the
levels of certain vitamins and minerals needed to maintain health.
According to a report in the February 7, 1986, *Science,* the 1985 revisions
were postponed because they would have lowered levels of vitamins A
and C, magnesium, iron, and zinc, and raised the allowance for calcium. The National Cancer Institute emphasizes the value of vitamins
A and C in food as anticancer agents. (See p. 8.)

Vitamin Supplements

Between 35 and 40 percent of American adults take vitamin supplements, but only about 7 percent of these users take vitamins under a
doctor's orders. A daily multivitamin tablet may benefit some people,
especially those who eat an unbalanced diet or who overcook the nutrients out of their food. Vitamin supplements will not change a poor
diet into good nutrition, even though they may help make up for some
deficiencies. The bottom line is that you probably do not need vitamin
supplements if you eat a well-balanced, varied diet.

Many people spend a lifetime ignoring what they learned in grade

RECOMMENDED DIETARY ALLOWANCES (RDAs) FOR MEN

Nutrient	Daily requirement for men
*Fat-Soluble Vitamins**	
Vitamin A (liver, eggs, fortified milk, carrots, tomatoes, apricots, cantaloupe, fish)	1,000 micrograms (mcg)
Vitamin D (fortified milk, fish; also produced by the body in response to sunlight)	5 mcg
Vitamin E (nuts, vegetable oils, whole grains, olives, asparagus, spinach)	10 milligrams (mg)
*Water-Soluble Vitamins**	
Vitamin C/ascorbic acid (citrus fruits, strawberries, tomatoes)	60 mg
Vitamin B-1/thiamin (whole grains, dried beans, lean meats [especially pork], fish)	1.2–1.4 mg
Vitamin B-2/riboflavin (milk, cheese, other dairy products)	1.4–1.6 mg
Vitamin B-3/niacin (nuts, dairy products, liver)	16–18 mg
Vitamin B-6/pyridoxine (wheat germ, brown rice, yeast)	2.2 mg
Vitamin B-12 (liver, beef, eggs, milk, shellfish)	3 mcg
Folacin (liver, wheat bran, leafy green vegetables, beans, grains)	400 mcg
Minerals	
Calcium (Swiss cheese, low-fat plain yogurt, cheddar cheese, part-skim mozzarella cheese, American cheese, skim milk)	800 mg
Phosphorus (present in nearly all foods)	800 mg
Magnesium (nuts, peanuts, beans, whole grains, blackstrap molasses)	350 mg
Iron (beef liver, clams, chicken liver, black beans, chick-peas, raw spinach)	10 mg
Zinc (shellfish, fish, meat, poultry, eggs, cheese, liver)	15 mg
Iodine (iodized salt)	150 mcg

* The body stores fat-soluble vitamins in the liver for relatively long periods, but generally stores water-soluble vitamins only for short periods.
SOURCE: National Academy of Sciences/National Research Council, *Recommended Dietary Allowances*, 9th ed., 1980.

school about a healthy diet. Yet the principles of good nutrition are as simple as they were in fourth grade. You will get all the vitamins and minerals you need if you eat

- fruits and vegetables, including citrus fruit or juice and a dark green, leafy vegetable: 4 servings daily*
- whole grain and enriched breads, cereals, rice, spaghetti, and other pasta: 4 servings daily
- low-fat milk, cheese, and yogurt: 2 servings daily
- lean meat, poultry, fish, eggs, beans, nuts, or peanut butter: 2 servings daily

* Vegetables cooked to the soft mushy state will lose their vitamin content.

Belief in "vitamin power" probably originated in the ancient search for vitality and the "life force" that foods supposedly contain. Indeed, the word vitamin means "chemical essential to life." Today people take vitamins because they hope to prevent or cure diseases, improve sex life, enhance appearance, bolster energy levels, and even live longer. But there is little scientific evidence to substantiate most of these claims. Scientists know that the thirteen vitamins discovered thus far help your body produce and maintain healthy bones, skin, teeth, blood cells, eyes, and organs; in short, they are absolutely essential to life.

Many men, especially athletes and bodybuilders, load up on meats and other high-protein foods and supplements in hope of developing bigger muscles. Sports nutritionist Dr. Robert Haas says in *Eat to Win: The Sports Nutrition Bible* that Americans consume up to five times the amount of protein they need daily. Exercise, not diet, builds muscles. (See the section on nutrition for athletes, pp. 11–13.) Excess protein serves no useful purpose; the body either uses it for energy or converts it into fat. If your diet consists of 50 to 60 percent carbohydrate, 30 to 35 percent unsaturated fat, and 10 to 15 percent protein, it will follow the Dietary Guidelines and provide all the vitamins and minerals you need.

The Megavitamin Theory

The megavitamin theory maintains that if something is good, more must be better. Megavitamin enthusiasts claim that you routinely need vitamin and mineral supplements to prevent a variety of illnesses, and extra-large doses when things actually go wrong with your body. Megavitamins are ordinary vitamins taken in megadoses of ten or more times the recommended dietary allowance. At this level, vitamins are no longer nutrients but drugs, and few drugs are free of adverse effects when taken in large doses for long periods.

Megavitamins have received a boost from Dr. Linus Pauling, twice a winner of the Nobel Prize in chemistry. Dr. Pauling recommends vitamin C in amounts from 250 to 10,000 milligrams (or 4 to 166 times the RDA) as a remedy for the common cold. He also recommends vitamin C at 100 to 166 times the RDA to prevent heart disease and cancer and to prolong life. Yet no scientific evidence substantiates the benefits of such megadoses.

For years physicians have prescribed high doses of vitamin D combined with calcium for people with osteomalacia (adult rickets), and high doses of vitamin B-6 for children with a rare congenital disease called homocystinuria. Large doses of niacin have reduced cholesterol in some heart patients, although it is better to avoid foods with high cholesterol content. Scientists have found that lack of vitamin A or C may be related to cancer and that the presence of these vitamins in your diet may help protect against some types of cancer. But you do not need supplements. You can get all the vitamins A and C your body can use from four servings daily of fruits and vegetables that contain natural amounts of these vitamins.

Indeed, megadoses above the RDA of some vitamins can be harmful. Too much vitamin A can cause headaches, nausea, diarrhea, and, eventually, liver damage and retarded growth in children. Overdoses of vitamin D can cause kidney damage in adults. Even vitamin C, once regarded as safe, can cause kidney stones and other problems when taken in large doses for long periods of time. At best, excess amounts of such vitamins are excreted, giving Americans the most valuable urine in human history.

Vitamin E is another supplement that some people take in hope of preventing cancer and other diseases. There is no evidence that vitamin E prevents cancer in humans. Nor do you need vitamin E supplements. You get enough of this nutrient in a well-balanced diet.

Some scientists believe zinc is indispensable in maintaining the immune system's ability to protect the body against disease. Zinc is used to treat many medical conditions, including skin conditions and impotence in men undergoing kidney dialysis. But this does not mean you need zinc supplements.

Some nutrients — the amino acids tryptophan, phenylalanine, and arginine — are readily available in foods. Some supplements — such as bioflavonoids, para-aminobenzoic acid (PABA), pangamic acid (calcium pangamate), superoxide dismutase (SOD), and lecithin — are not necessary to the human diet. Several products are sold as "vitamins," but are not. For example, the bioflavonoids and hesperidin are sometimes called vitamin P, and laetrile has been falsely promoted as vitamin B-17. Selenium taken as a food supplement is claimed to protect against some cancers. But the American Cancer Society warns that such claims do not apply to humans, and the medically unsupervised use of selenium can cause selenium poisoning.

More Facts about Vitamins

- Extra vitamins do not provide extra energy.
- Athletes and people who increase their exercise levels do not need vitamin supplements.
- Smokers cannot offset the effects of their habit by taking megadoses of vitamin C.
- "Stress formulas" containing extra niacin, biotin, selenium, and other substances do not protect against stress-related symptoms.
- Water-soluble vitamins, once considered safe, are dangerous when taken in large amounts.
- Natural vitamins are no more effective than synthetic vitamins. However, foods may contain other nutrients that do not come in supplements.

The bottom line is that megavitamins — better named megachemicals — will not produce megahealth. Many people mistakenly assume that vitamins and minerals must be safe and effective because they are regulated by the Food and Drug Administration. But Congress does not allow the FDA to review these products for safety and efficacy, leaving the consumer both unwary and unprotected. If you have been taking unprescribed vitamin and mineral supplements, especially in large doses, and decide to stop, reduce the dosage gradually rather than stop suddenly, so that your body can readjust.

Vegetarian Diets and Health Food

Vegetarian diets provide more fiber and less fat than the average American diet. Studies of vegetarians show they have a lower incidence of obesity, hypertension, and coronary heart disease than the general American population. Although these studies suggest a cause-effect relationship, they do not take into account smoking, alcohol intake, physical activity, and other factors that may affect the health of vegetarians.

Vegetarian diets — especially those of the strict "vegans" who do not eat eggs, dairy products, meat, poultry, or fish — may be deficient in protein, zinc, iron, calcium, and vitamins (especially B-12 and D). Male "vegans" need to consume protein-rich vegetables, such as dried beans and peas, garbanzo beans, navy beans, lentils, tofu, whole grains, corn, pasta, and moderate amounts of nuts and seeds. Lacto-ovo vegetarians will probably get enough protein because they eat cheese and other dairy products. All vegetarians should eat a wide variety of foods to obtain essential nutrients, and lacto-ovo vegetarians should avoid eggs, use low-fat dairy products, and use vegetable fats and oils to keep their blood cholesterol at safe levels. (See the section on cholesterol, pp. 14–18.)

How healthy is "health food"? Some diets rely heavily on vitamin and mineral supplements, protein powders, wheat germ, wheat germ oil, vitamin E, ascorbic acid, lecithin, royal jelly, bee pollen, gelatin, phosphates, kelp, and brewer's yeast, none of which you need. Macrobiotic diets that include a very narrow range of foods — tea, brown rice, beans, and nuts — and very little fat can cause malnutrition and mental stunting in infants. Some macrobiotic diets call for reduced fluids and emphasize grains and vegetables to a degree that could cause loss of important nutrients and fluids.

So-called Junk Food

Just as not all health food is good for you, not all "junk food" is bad. Many people confuse sugary snack foods, which are not nutritious, with "fast foods," which can be nutritious in moderation. Foods that are sugary, fatty, and salty (candy bars, pastries, cakes, cookies, soft drinks, prepackaged puddings, and potato chips) satisfy your taste buds but not your nutritional needs. The worst food product in America — and one of the most tempting — is the ubiquitous doughnut, laden with fat, sugar, and calories.

Fast foods served in carry-out restaurants often contain adequate protein, carbohydrate, and B vitamins. Some are rich in other nutrients as well. But fast foods by themselves seldom offer a well-balanced diet. They tend to contain too much fat, salt, sugar, and calories, and too little dietary fiber, vitamins A and C, and other nutrients. The Burger King Whopper with cheese, for example, contains 10 teaspoons of fat and 760 calories, and Wendy's Triple Cheeseburger contains 15 teaspoons of fat and 1,040 calories, according to the Center for Science in the Public Interest. Many fast foods, such as fried chicken and fish, would not be high in saturated fats if they were broiled, baked, or poached instead of deep-fried.

Still, you can east fast food and have a reasonably balanced diet. If you have a hamburger, french fries, and a milkshake for lunch, try to eat a high-fiber breakfast of fruit and cereal, and a light dinner of salad or vegetables, baked or broiled fish, and fruit for dessert.

The Best and Worst Fast Foods

The Best

- salad bars (low calorie and high fiber if you skip the salad dressings, croutons, and bacon bits)
- cheese- or broccoli-stuffed baked potatoes (high calcium, high fiber)
- pizza with tomato sauce, cheese, and green peppers (high calcium; vitamins A, C, and D)
- tacos (high fiber; high calcium; vitamins A, C, and D)
- hot dog with sauerkraut (low calorie, high fiber, vitamin C, iron)
- cheeseburger with lettuce and tomato (high calcium; vitamins A, C, and D)

The Worst

- deep-fried chicken and fish
- french fries and onion rings
- shakes
- desserts
- catsup, mayonnaise, salad dressings, and "special" sauces

Nutrition for Athletes

Former U.S. Olympic Committee physician Dr. Daniel Hanley has said that "dietary fads, special supplements, and gimmicks will not improve athletic performance, but a well-balanced diet can." Thus you do not need supplementary vitamins and minerals to boost energy levels, improve athletic performance, or undergo brief periods of intense exercise and profuse sweating. The best physical performance results from the same balance of foods recommended for the average American, that is, 50 to 60 percent of daily calories from complex carbohydrates, 30 to 35 percent from unsaturated fat, and 10 to 15 percent from protein.

Nor do you need salt tablets, which were taken almost indis-
criminately in earlier decades and frequently caused nausea, vomiting,
and gastric distress. During regular exercise, loss of sodium and of
chloride through sweating is so small that a normal diet can replace
these electrolytes within twenty-four hours. Salt lost through sweating
up to 8 liters can be replaced by the foods you eat after an athletic
event. The value of sugar/salt solutions such as Gatorade is
questionable. Athletes who drink these solutions to restore fluid
balance during competition may end up with extra fluid in their
stomachs because sugar and salt reduce gastric emptying and slow the
absorption of water. It helps to dilute Gatorade and other sports
drinks half and half with water before or during exercise. After
exercise, they can be drunk undiluted.

Plain water, on the other hand, is so indispensable a nutrient that
reducing your water level up to 3 percent of total body weight causes
impaired performance, up to 10 percent causes heat stroke, and over 10
percent causes death. Stated another way, you can live thirty to forty
days without food; you simply convert stored fat and protein into
energy. But you can live only five to eight days — and possibly fewer —
without water. Thus you should consume fluids before, during, and
after exercise, especially in warm weather. To prevent dehydration,
weigh yourself before and after exercising, and drink one pint of water
for every pound of body weight lost. In general, you should drink eight
8-ounce glasses of water or other liquid daily. Alcoholic beverages,
coffee, tea, and colas cause water loss through urination and are not
the best way to "rehydrate" yourself.

Bottled water is becoming increasingly popular, but nobody has been
able to document greater health benefits (for athletes or anybody else)
from drinking it than from drinking tap water. Some bottled waters,
moreover, contain significant amounts of sodium, a hazard to people
on salt-restricted diets. Read the labels to learn the salt content.

Marathoners and recruits in basic military training need to increase
caloric intake during prolonged and vigorous physical activity. Most
people, however, do not need consciously to eat more since exercise
naturally increases appetite. Some athletes engage in "carbohydrate
loading" several days before a contest. This technique should be practiced only under the supervision of a trainer or dietitian. In one version, you eat a low-carbohydrate diet for three days followed by a
high-carbohydrate diet of pasta, vegetables, and fruit for three days. A
safer version of "carbohydrate loading" is to decrease the duration and

intensity of exercise for a week as you increase the consumption of complex carbohydrates. For example:

	Eat	Exercise
Day 1	50 percent carbohydrates	60 minutes
Day 2	50 percent carbohydrates	40 minutes
Day 3	50 percent carbohydrates	40 minutes
Day 4	75 percent carbohydrates	30 minutes
Day 5	75 percent carbohydrates	30 minutes
Day 6	75 percent carbohydrates	Rest
Day 7	75 percent or more carbohydrates (to replenish fuel stores)	Event

NOTE: Avoid eating foods that are not part of your usual diet.

Such a diet may increase endurance during marathons and other athletic events lasting sixty minutes or longer. But "loading" offers no advantage in brief, high-intensity competitions. It should be used very selectively by high school and college athletes and rarely, if ever, by younger athletes, for whom the technique may be harmful.

The Ideal Precontest Meal

- Eat three to five hours before competition to allow time for food to digest and fill your liver and muscles with stored sugar (glycogen).
- Eat foods you enjoy and are accustomed to, and preferably that are high in complex carbohydrates* but low in simple sugars, protein, and fat.†
- Eat foods that are nongreasy, bland, and easy to digest.
- Drink at least three glasses of liquid.

* Found in fruits, vegetables, pasta, and whole grain bread and cereal.

† Protein stimulates gastric secretion and raises acid levels in your body during exercise, while high-fat meals are slow to digest and provide less energy.

The postcontest meal is often neglected, but it is equally important. If you are excited about winning or upset about losing, you may not feel like eating. The postcontest meal, once appetite returns, should consist mainly of complex carbohydrates and liquids served in a relaxed, congenial atmosphere, followed by extra carbohydrates and liquids for up to two weeks.

The Cholesterol Connection

Cholesterol, one of several kinds of fatty substances that circulate in the bloodstream, has been linked to heart disease and stroke. Yet cholesterol helps the body form cell membranes, produce bile that aids digestion, and manufacture sex hormones and other important hormones. You cannot see, smell, or taste cholesterol, but it is present in all foods of animal origin, especially egg yolks and organ meats like brain, kidney, and liver. In addition, your own body — particularly your liver and intestines — manufactures all the cholesterol you need. Therefore, if you eat a typical American diet, you burden your body with more cholesterol than it needs.

Since cholesterol is not soluble in the blood, the body wraps it in protein "packages" called lipoproteins that transport it through the bloodstream. Scientists have identified thirteen lipoproteins, including three major types: beneficial high-density lipoproteins (HDL), harmful low-density lipoproteins (LDL), and very-low-density lipoproteins (VLDL). The latter contain triglycerides, basic fats used for energy storage that may also be harmful at high levels.

Studies of populations throughout the world have shown that high levels of LDL and VLDL cause the gradual accumulation of fatty deposits in the cells lining blood vessels throughout the body. When these deposits narrow the arteries around the heart so much that the blood supply to the heart could suddenly be blocked, the risk of heart attack increases. In contrast, high blood levels of HDL seem to clear cholesterol from the blood. Women have higher HDL levels than men, which may be why they consistently suffer fewer heart attacks.

A safe *total* blood cholesterol level (including HDL, LDL, and VLDL) is 200 mg/dl (milligrams per deciliter of blood) if you are over age thirty, and 180 mg/dl if you are under thirty. The typical middle-aged American's cholesterol reading is 215 to 220 mg/dl. Higher levels raise the risk of coronary artery disease and heart attack. In a very strong statement on the relationship between high blood cholesterol and coronary heart disease, a panel of heart disease experts said that half the U.S. population is at some increased risk for coronary heart disease based on total blood cholesterol levels. These experts, who met in December 1984 at a National Institutes of Health conference on lowering blood cholesterol, called high blood cholesterol a *direct cause* of coronary heart disease, not just an associated risk factor. They cited studies proving that reducing blood cholesterol will also reduce the risk of heart attack.

For example, a ten-year study of 3,806 middle-aged men with cholesterol levels exceeding 265 mg/dl — the Coronary Primary Prevention
Trial (CPPT) — showed that every 1 percent reduction in cholesterol
lowers the risk of coronary heart disease by 2 percent.

The NIH panel concluded that *all* Americans — not just those at
high risk — should know their blood cholesterol level and eat less
cholesterol as well as less saturated fat, which is the greatest contributor to elevated blood cholesterol. These experts also recommended
exercise and weight loss (since obesity is known to increase cholesterol
levels) for people with blood cholesterol levels of 265 mg/dl and higher.
And they recommended treatment with cholesterol-lowering drugs if
these lifestyle changes do not lower cholesterol to a safe range.

These recommendations may seem far-reaching because they advise
dietary changes for many Americans who, along with their physicians,
may have considered their cholesterol levels "normal." Yet the American Heart Association has made the same recommendations for more
than a decade.

The average American consumes 300 to 500 milligrams of cholesterol
daily. This is lower than the 700-milligram level of a few years ago, but
still higher than the upper limit of 250 to 300 milligrams of dietary
cholesterol now recommended to reduce the overall risk of heart disease and heart attack (see table on p. 16).

Fat in the Pan

Food can contain little or *no* cholesterol and still raise your blood cholesterol because it is high in saturated fat. Most Americans eat 40 percent
of calories as fat, including saturated fat, monounsaturated fat, polyunsaturated fat, and cholesterol. "Saturated" and "polyunsaturated" refer
to the chemical structure of fat molecules. Saturated fats usually are solid
at room temperature and come from animal products (beef, pork, ham,
butter, cream, ice cream, whole milk, and cheese made from whole milk)
as well as from many vegetable shortenings, coconut, coconut oil, cocoa
butter, palm oil, prepared baked goods, nondairy milk and cream substitutes, mayonnaise, avocado, and granola. Polyunsaturated fats —
abundant in safflower and other vegetable oils — are soft or liquid at
room temperature. Polyunsaturates help lower blood cholesterol, but
only half as much as saturated fats raise it.

Although fat is needed for many body functions, too much fat in
your diet raises the risk of high blood cholesterol and heart disease.
Thus the National Heart, Lung, and Blood Institute, National Cancer

THE CHOLESTEROL CONTINUUM

	Milligrams of cholesterol per 3.5 oz.	
Fruits, grains, vegetables	0	Low
Margarine, all vegetable fat	0	
Peanut butter	0	
Milk, skim	6	
Milk, whole	14	
Ice cream, 10% fat	25	
Oysters, cooked	45	
Scallops, cooked	53	
Frankfurter, all meat	62	
Tuna, in water	63	
Clams, cooked	65	
Mayonnaise	70	
Chicken/turkey, light meat, without skin, cooked	80	
Lobster, cooked	85	
Pork	89	
Beef, lean, cooked	90	
Chicken/turkey, dark meat, without skin, cooked	95	
Crab, cooked	100	
Shrimp, cooked	150	
Butter	250	
Egg yolk	270	
Whole egg	270	
Beef liver, cooked	440	
Beef kidney, cooked	700	High

SOURCE: National Heart, Lung, and Blood Institute and American Dietary Association.
NOTE: Recent analyses show that the cholesterol levels of most shellfish are lower than previously believed.

Institute, and American Heart Association recommend that you cut total dietary fat intake to 30 percent of total calories.

To cut cholesterol and saturated fat from your diet:

- Use liquid vegetable oils and tub margarines with at least twice as much polyunsaturated as saturated fat. Monounsaturated fats such as olive oil also may help lower cholesterol.
- Eat no more than two egg yolks a week, and no more than 7 ounces a day of lean meat, fish, or poultry.
- Remove skin from poultry and trim excess fat from red meat before cooking.

HOW FAT HIDES IN YOUR DIET

Type of oil or fat	Percent polyunsaturated (good) fat	Percent saturated (bad) fat
Safflower oil	74	9
Sunflower oil	64	10
Corn oil	58	13
Average vegetable oil (soybean plus cottonseed)	40	13
Peanut oil	30	19
Chicken fat	26	29
Average vegetable shortening	20	32
Lard	12	40
Beef fat	4	48
Butter	4	61
Palm oil	2	81
Coconut oil	2	86

SOURCE: National Heart, Lung, and Blood Institute.

- Avoid fried foods. Broil, roast, bake, poach, steam, stew or microwave; use oil sparingly; drain or skim off fat.
- Eat several meatless lunches or dinners a week.
- Cut down on butter, cream, whole milk, ice cream, nondairy milk and cream substitutes, mayonnaise, and avocados.
- Use skim or low-fat milk, cheeses, and yogurt.
- Avoid liver, kidney, brains, sausage, bacon, processed luncheon meats, and food that has "hydrogenated" on the label.
- Avoid commercial pastries, cookies, and cakes made with lard, coconut oil, palm oil, or shortening.
- When eating out, choose broiled or ethnic (Chinese, Japanese, Italian, Greek) foods, ask for sauces and dressings on the side, use them sparingly, and order from the vegetable and salad sections of the menu.

Studies reported in the May 9, 1985, *New England Journal of Medicine* suggest that fish oil in the diet can dramatically decrease blood cholesterol and triglyceride levels. The oils contain large amounts of a class of polyunsaturated fats called omega-3 fatty acids. They are found in fish with fatty layers that live in cold, deep-sea, and, in some cases, fresh waters. These include salmon, mackerel, tuna, herring, and trout. The oils are present in both fresh and processed fish unless processing removes the oil. A second report in the same journal showed that deaths from coronary heart disease were more than 50 percent lower among a group of 852 middle-aged men in the Netherlands who consumed at least an ounce of fish a day than among those who did not eat cod, herring, or mackerel. The investigators — citing low death rates from coronary heart disease in Japan and Greenland, where fish consumption is high — concluded that one or two fish dishes a week may help prevent coronary heart disease. This point was repeated at a conference on the health effects of polyunsaturated fatty acids in seafoods, held in June 1985 in Washington, D.C. An expert on atherosclerosis, Dr. Scott M. Grundy, said he could see no ill effects, and many benefits, from substituting fish for meat several times a week.

FISH WITH OMEGA-3 FATTY ACIDS

Species	Grams per 4-oz. serving
Chinook salmon	3.6
Albacore tuna	2.6
Sockeye salmon	2.3
Mackerel	1.8–2.6
Herring	1.2–2.7
Rainbow trout	1.0
Whiting	0.9
King crab	0.6
Shrimp	0.5
Cod*	0.3

* Cod store fat in the liver rather than the flesh.
* SOURCE: *The Harvard Medical School Health Letter*, May 1986.

The Fiber Factor

Fiber, known as roughage or bulk, consists of plant food substances that travel through most of your digestive tract largely undigested. High-fiber foods include bran and other cereals, whole grain breads, most vegetables and fruits, popcorn, and brown rice.

Bran, the foremost dietary fiber, comes from the husks of grains. It holds up to 200 times its weight in water, assuming that you drink up to 2 quarts of liquids a day. This makes stools large and bulky and better able to move through your large intestine quickly. A diet adequate in fiber and liquids can shorten stool "transit" or travel time through the intestine from ninety to about forty hours. Thus dietary fiber prevents constipation. It also helps prevent diverticulitis — inflammation of weak spots in the wall of the large bowel that collect intestinal debris. Fiber appears to prevent or alleviate hemorrhoids and other intestinal diseases caused by straining at stool, and is a boon to the dieter because fiber-rich foods are relatively "filling."

Epidemiologic studies suggest that populations that consume about 20 to 35 grams of dietary fiber daily have a lower rate of cancer of the colon and rectum. Other studies show that certain high-fiber members of the mustard family — known as cruciferous vegetables — may help reduce the risk of cancers of the gastrointestinal and respiratory tracts. These include bok choy, broccoli, brussels sprouts, cabbage, cauliflower, collards, kale, kohlrabi, mustard greens, rutabaga, turnip greens, and turnips.

These findings that high-fiber diets protect against some cancers are still quite controversial. But even if fiber proves less protective against cancer than some studies suggest, fiber-rich foods are sufficiently beneficial, especially as an alternative to cholesterol and saturated fats, to warrant including them in your diet. Accordingly, the National Cancer Institute, based on recent research findings, recommends consuming 20 to 30 grams of dietary fiber daily, with an upper limit of 35 grams. Since the average American currently eats only 10 to 15 grams of fiber daily, this translates roughly to cutting fat intake from 40 to 30 percent of total calories and doubling fiber intake. (See Dietary Guidelines, pp. 3–4.)

Many people think salads are high in fiber, but the percentage of fiber in leafy vegetables is comparatively small. A simple way to increase fiber in your diet is to substitute whole wheat bread for standard white bread, and eat more breakfast cereals and other foods containing bran and fruit (see table on p. 20).

Increase fiber intake gradually over several weeks so your body can adjust, and drink more fluids to help fiber move easily through your digestive tract. High-fiber foods may cause gassiness and amounts in excess of 35 grams may prevent you from absorbing minerals such as iron, calcium, and zinc. If you are taking digoxin, a drug commonly used to treat heart disease, or a similar medication, or if you have an intestinal disorder that interferes with absorption of nutrients, consult your physician before increasing fiber intake.

About Additives

Food additives include colorings that enhance appeal, chemicals that improve taste, and preservatives that increase shelf life. The American Cancer Society reports that cancer-causing additives already are banned. But the Food and Drug Administration had not, as of this

SOME HIGH-FIBER FOODS

	Serving size	Grams of fiber
All-Bran-Extra Fiber	½ cup	13.0
All-Bran	⅓ cup	8.5
100% Bran	½ cup	8.4
Bran Chex	⅔ cup	4.6
Bran Flakes	¾ cup	4.0
Whole wheat spaghetti	1 cup	3.9
Whole wheat bread	2 slices	2.8
Popcorn, air-popped	1 cup	2.5
Kidney beans	½ cup	7.3
Peas	½ cup	3.6
Corn	½ cup	2.9
Parsnips	½ cup	2.7
Potato, with skin	1 medium	2.5
Carrots	½ cup	2.3
Broccoli	½ cup	2.2
Apple	1 medium	3.5
Orange	1 medium	2.6

SOURCE: Elaine Lanza, Ph.D., and Ritva R. Butrum, Ph.D., *American Journal of Dietetics*, 86 ((June 1986): 372.

writing, completed a review of 204 food dyes begun in 1960. Six cause cancer in laboratory animals, including the widely used Red No. 3 and Yellow Nos. 5 and 6. Industry spokesmen say you would have to eat 280,529 pounds of maraschino cherries a year to be affected by Red Dye No. 3. Dr. Sidney Wolfe of Public Citizen, Ralph Nader's public interest group, replies: "No scientist other than those from industry will say you can find safe levels of carcinogens."

Even though some fifteen thousand food additives can be found in the American food supply, additives are a very small percentage of your diet. Of the 1,500 pounds of food you eat in an average year, less than 1 percent consists of additives, and nine-tenths of that 1 percent consists of salt, sugar, corn syrup, dextrose, and sucrose. Dr. Michael F. Jacobson, who directs the Center for Science in the Public Interest and is known as "the Ralph Nader of foods," puts additives in perspective in *The Complete Eater's Digest and Nutrition Scoreboard*. "Most food additives are safe and some are positively beneficial," he writes. "However, a few are hazardous, and some of the safe ones may be used to cheat or deceive shoppers. . . . If a widely used additive proves to be hazardous, thousands or even millions of people may be harmed."

A Few Safe and Unsafe Additives

Safe
ascorbic acid
EDTA
carrageenan
sodium benzoate
Questionable
BHA
propyl gellate
sodium bisulfite
*Unsafe**
sodium nitrite (used to cure bacon, hot dogs, and luncheon meats)
BHT (butylated hydroxytoluene)
brominated vegetable oil (used in carbonated or noncarbonated fruit-flavored drinks)

* These additives still appear in foods because the Food and Drug Administration has not banned them.

Salt

Salt flavors and protects foods, and it helps your body maintain blood volume, regulate water balance, transmit nerve impulses, and perform other vital functions. However, many studies show that Americans eat too much salt. The Food and Nutrition Board of the National Academy of Sciences recommends limiting daily sodium intake to 1.1 to 3.3 grams (½ to 1½ teaspoonsful) of common table salt daily for adults. But most Americans consume from 4 to 10 grams of sodium (2 to 5 teaspoonsful) of table salt daily. Table salt and naturally occurring sodium contribute to only 10 to 25 percent of sodium consumption. The rest comes from processed foods. Indeed, food processors load their products with so much salt — usually without labeling — that you would get enough salt in your diet even if you never salted your food again.

Some physicians, noting that salt does not hurt everybody, contend that reducing its use for the general population would benefit only individuals who are salt-sensitive. But the American Cancer Society warns that salt-cured and pickled foods appear to be associated with an increased risk of cancers of the stomach and esophagus. Excess sodium in the diet is also believed to contribute to high blood pressure by causing the body to retain water, which increases blood volume. Thus people with high blood pressure are often advised to eat low-salt diets. In some cases, low-sodium diets plus weight loss reduce the need for long-term high blood pressure medication.

To cut back on salt, first learn which foods contain less sodium. Fresh vegetables, fruits, and meats are lower in sodium than processed and canned products. Plain frozen vegetables are generally low in sodium, as are frozen and canned fruits and fruit juices. Many foods have salt added during processing. These include most products that come in a box or can and that list sodium as one of the first three ingredients. A primary ingredient of canned soup, for example, is salt. Fast foods, snack foods, processed meats, frozen dinners, and other convenience foods also are very salty.

SODIUM CONTENT OF SOME COMMON FOODS

1 pretzel	101 mg
10 potato chips	200 mg
1 oz. bologna	350 mg
1 oz. American processed cheese food	406 mg
1 tbsp. MSG (Accent)	492 mg
1 dose of Alka-Seltzer	521 mg
1 frankfurter	540 mg
1 cup tomato juice	878 mg
1 dill pickle	928 mg
½ can soup	1,500 mg
1 three-piece Kentucky Fried Chicken dinner	2,285 mg

NOTE: Some brands of the same food contain substantially more salt than others, indicating that manufacturers could greatly reduce the sodium content of their products.

You can remove excess salt by soaking kosher and other salty meats in water before cooking, or by draining salty water from canned vegetables and heating them in plain tap water. This will save money if you are on a low-sodium diet. Salt substitutes, which usually contain potassium, are expensive and sometimes bitter. Moreover, they can be harmful to people with kidney disease and certain heart conditions, as well as to people using "potassium-sparing" diuretics. Check with your doctor before using a potassium-containing salt substitute.

Shaking the Salt Habit

- Taste food before salting it.
- Keep the salt shaker off the dinner table.
- Cook with pepper, lemon, herbs, spices, onion, garlic powders, and other flavorings instead of salt.
- Avoid processed and brine-soaked foods, cured foods, prepared sauces, gravies, and mixes.
- Substitute low-sodium snacks such as fruits and vegetables for potato chips and pretzels.
- Cut down on high-sodium seasonings such as mustard, catsup, chili sauce, horseradish, meat and vegetable extracts, meat sauces, meat tenderizers, soy sauce, Worcestershire sauce, celery salt, garlic salt, onion salt, baking soda, and baking powder.
- If food tastes bland, try chewing it more thoroughly instead of salting it.
- Remember that a taste for salty foods is acquired, and will diminish with time.

Sugar

Each year the average American consumes 127 pounds of sugar and corn sweeteners, according to the U.S. Department of Agriculture. Much of the sugar is consumed in soft drinks, candy, sweet baked goods, syrups, sweetened cereals, fruit-flavored yogurt, and processed foods such as catsup (which contains more calories than chocolate fudge topping), relish, and cream-style corn. Sugar or sucrose is not harmful per se. It is the *amount* of sugar Americans consume that causes tooth decay and overweight. A meal laden with sugar also might cause problems two to five hours later because sugar enters the bloodstream very rapidly. The body then releases insulin to clear the blood of sugar, resulting in low blood sugar and hunger pangs.

Some people believe that certain forms of sugar — such as honey — are more nutritious than others. But honey is nutritionally as poor as processed white sugar, brown sugar (table sugar coated with molasses), turbinado sugar (less processed than table sugar), or maple syrup. One form of sucrose — molasses — contains fairly high amounts of iron, plus lesser amounts of calcium, potassium, and the B-vitamin niacin. People also believe that table sugar is high in calories. If they realized that 1 teaspoonful contains only 16 calories, they might skip the artificial sweeteners, which do not satisfy hunger.

It is not clear whether the new noncaloric aspartame (Nutra-Sweet) is safe or not. A report in the July 19, 1985, *Journal of the American Medical Association* called it a safe sugar substitute for healthy humans. However, the manufacturer, G. D. Searle & Co., has received about one thousand reports of adverse reactions, such as headaches. Saccharin causes bladder cancer in rats, but there is no clear evidence that its moderate use causes cancer in humans. The FDA proposed banning saccharin from the market in 1977, but Congress has repeatedly prevented the prohibition from taking effect. Another chemical sweetener, cyclamate, was marketed from 1949 to 1969; the FDA banned it in 1970 after tests showed that a mixture of ten parts cyclamate and one part saccharin caused tumors in rats. The safest low-calorie sweeteners — allspice, cinnamon, ginger, nutmeg, and lemon juice — enhance sweet flavors.

Caffeine

Over half the U.S. population aged ten and older drinks coffee, according to the coffee industry. The average American consumes 3.2 cups of coffee daily, which usually causes no problem. But an estimated five million people drink more than 10 cups daily. Americans consume additional milligrams of caffeine in tea, colas, chocolate, cocoa, and pain relievers such as Anacin, Excedrin, and Vanquish.

Caffeine stimulates the central nervous system, which is why so many people like it. Excess caffeine (about 6 cups a day) can cause chronic headache, insomnia, anxiety, stomach upset, and — in susceptible people — heart rhythm disturbances. Scientists have explored whether caffeine may be related to birth defects, fibrocystic breast disease (breast lumps) in women, intestinal ulcers, high blood pressure, high blood cholesterol, heart disease, and cancer of the bladder and pancreas. But most studies so far have produced no conclusive evidence of harmful effects, especially if daily consumption is limited to 2 to 3 cups of brewed coffee or 3 to 4 cups of tea or instant coffee.

The Overweight American

Being safe at the plate depends not only on *what* you eat, but *how much*. About 34 million adult Americans — including more women than men — are clinically obese or overweight to a degree that may interfere with good health and long life. Two major causes of this epidemic are inactivity and overeating, hallmarks of an affluent society. There now is evidence that heredity is an important factor in causing obesity proneness in adults. Obesity also tends to be a problem because people usually need fewer calories as they grow older.

Obesity is an excess of body fat associated with *increased size* of fat cells, particularly around the waist, flank, and abdomen. Extremely obese individuals also have a *greater number* of fat cells. A practical definition of obesity is an increase in body weight of 20 percent or more above desirable body weight as suggested by life insurance height-weight tables. According to a panel of experts who met in January 1985 at the National Institutes of Health, obesity is an illness, not a state of mind as is loneliness. Moreover, it is "a killing disease" that affects more than physical appearance. Recent life insurance statistics show that men who are 20 percent above desirable body weight reduce their life expectancy by 20 percent. Women reduce theirs by 10 percent. Thus obesity is a more serious health problem for men.

The otherwise healthy person who is 60 percent above desirable body weight has three times the normal risk of death from heart disease, cancer, diabetes, stroke, and digestive diseases. Obese males have higher death rates from cancer of the colon, rectum, and prostate than the nonobese, regardless of smoking habits. People of either sex who are overweight frequently suffer from high blood pressure (a significant risk factor for heart disease) and premature, degenerative arthritis. Obese persons also are poor surgical risks and have greater than normal chances of suffering negative side effects from anesthesia.

In addition, people who become overweight *at younger ages* tend to die sooner than people of average weight. If you are age twenty to forty-four and obese, you stand five times the normal risk of hypertension (versus three times the risk if you are older) and twice the risk of high cholesterol (versus no additional risk if you are older). Many people who are as little as 5 to 10 pounds over desirable weight may incur health risks, the NIH panel warned. Even cosmetic overweight is of concern because it so often leads to obesity.

Some recent studies suggest that the location of fat deposits in your body may be a better predictor of mortality than overweight as determined by height-weight tables. Abdominal obesity in both men and women apparently raises the risk of coronary heart disease, stroke, and death, regardless of the degree of overall obesity. When the size of your waist, abdomen, and upper body is greater than the size of your hips, you are at risk. (See chapter 8, pp. 216–218, for ways to reduce potbellies.)

There is considerable confusion about what constitutes "desirable weight." For years Americans used the 1959 Metropolitan Life Insurance Company's height and weight table. In 1983, Metropolitan issued a new table that seemed to say Americans could weigh more without increased risk of death. But neither the 1959 nor 1983 table takes into account many factors that affect weight, such as cigarette smoking, age, and race. Despite these limitations, many nutrition experts prefer the 1959 Metropolitan weight tables. The federal government, in *Dietary Guidelines For Americans*, combines the 1959 Metropolitan ranges for small, medium, and large body frames into this simplified table:

DESIRABLE BODY WEIGHT RANGES — AGE TWENTY-SIX AND OVER
(All measurements are without clothing or shoes.)

Height	Men	Women
4'9"		90–118
4'10"		92–121
4'11"		95–124
5'0"		98–127
5'1"	105–134	101–130
5'2"	108–137	104–134
5'3"	111–141	107–138
5'4"	114–145	110–142
5'5"	117–149	114–146
5'6"	121–154	118–150
5'7"	125–159	122–154
5'8"	129–163	126–159
5'9"	133–167	130–164
5'10"	137–172	134–169
5'11"	141–177	
6'0"	145–182	
6'1"	149–187	
6'2"	153–192	
6'3"	157–197	

(Adapted from the 1959 Metropolitan Height and Desirable Weight Table.)

A second way to define overweight is to measure the proportion of fat in the body, a difficult task even with professional training. The best way is to calculate your body mass index (BMI; percentage of body fat) by dividing your weight in kilograms by the square of your height in meters. A professional football player might be 30 percent overweight, but not be obese because he is muscular. A small woman might be obese, even though her weight is in the normal range, because she has too much fat on her body. From the health standpoint, males should maintain body fat of 16 percent or less, and females 22 percent or less.

To determine your body mass index:

1. Convert your weight to kilograms by dividing the number of pounds you weigh without clothes by 2.2.
2. Convert your height to meters by dividing your height in inches without shoes by 39.4 and then squaring it.
3. Your body mass index is (1) divided by (2).

Dangerous Dieting

About 65 million Americans — most of them women — are on a weight-loss diet at any given time. They have more than thirty thousand methods of weight control to choose from. But 95 percent of people who lose weight by dieting regain it within the next year, mainly because most mass-market diets are bizarre, untested, and medically unsound, and produce no permanent change in eating habits. Such diets continue to "sell," however, because they promise the impossible: fast and easy ways to lose weight.

"Quick fix" diets include pills that claim to "conquer fat forever"; magic metabolizer diets; new European formulas that promise weight losses of 45 pounds in two months; and even a diet bread that miraculously curbs your appetite and hunger.

One of the most popular diets in recent years — and the most hazardous — is the liquid protein diet, a syrupy fruit-flavored mixture of amino acids and collagen consisting of 300 calories of formula daily. The diet caused fifty-eight deaths in 1977–78 alone. An investigation of seventeen of these cases revealed that otherwise healthy people had died unexpectedly of cardiac arrhythmias (irregular heartbeats that prevent the heart from pumping blood to the body) caused by loss of protein in the heart muscle. Fatter dieters survived, the Columbia University investigators concluded, because their heart muscles retained more protein. This study was reported in the May 1984 *American Journal of Clinical Nutrition*.

Another very low calorie formula, the Cambridge Diet, then became so popular that by November 1982, five million persons had used it — nearly nine times the number who tried the liquid protein diet. The Cambridge Diet contains 330 calories, mainly carbohydrates and protein. A report in the *Journal of the American Medical Association* recently warned that while the diet is not basically unsafe, its use without medical supervision may be hazardous. The Cambridge Diet was recently changed from 330 to 420 calories, probably to increase its safety. Very low calorie diets cause loss of lean body mass and are dangerous for pregnant women, teenagers, children, and diabetics.

Unsafe diets include Dr. Atkins's Diet Revolution (which the *Journal of the American Medical Association* says is "without scientific merit"), the Stillman Diet (which causes weight loss from water, not body fat), the Beverly Hills Diet (which can cause serious nutritional deficiencies), the Rice Diet and Fit for Life Diet (which also can cause serious nutritional deficiencies), Dr. Berger's Immune Power Diet (which the *Harvard Health Letter* calls "a collection of quack ideas about food allergies"), the Rotation Diet (which the American Dietetic Association says sets calorie levels too low), high-protein, low-carbohydrate diets (which cause you to lose water, not fat, and upset the body's chemical balance), and single-food diets. Other diets of questionable value are the Mayo Diet (which has no affiliation with the Mayo Clinic) and the Scarsdale Diet (which, like the Mayo Diet, is difficult to follow and offers dieters little in the way of reeducation toward a more healthful lifestyle that will keep weight off).

Some people diet by fasting. This practice does not trim pounds any better than a low-calorie diet and is a poor way to lose weight because it stresses and dehydrates the body. Generally, fasting as a means of weight loss should be done only under the strict supervision of a physician and is usually recommended only for grossly obese individuals. Dehydration is an unrecognized hazard of fasting and dieting. Certain diets low in fats and carbohydrate and high in protein can cause dehydration because your body needs water to metabolize protein. If you are using such diets — and there are far better ways to lose weight — drink enough water (2 to 3 quarts) to pass at least a quart of urine daily.

Skipping entire meals — a variation on fasting — does not help you lose weight. It usually makes you feel miserable and invites overeating at the next meal. Diet pills or appetite depressants decrease the urge to overeat. But their effects are temporary, and they may be habit-forming and harmful to some people. Prepackaged foods and supplements are expensive and nutritionally unbalanced. And franchised weight-loss programs rely on an external "authority figure" to keep you on the plan, so you never learn how to control food intake on your own.

The Pritikin Diet, on the other hand, emphasizes the value of eating fruits, vegetables, and other low-fat foods; avoiding fats, cholesterol, sodium, and refined sugars; and engaging in regular aerobic exercise. Although the diet has been criticized for being too stringent and no more effective than the more moderate American Heart Association diet in reducing cholesterol and arterial blockage, Nathan Pritikin ultimately proved the value of the diet he developed. His blood cholesterol level, which had been around 300 before he changed his diet, quickly dropped to around 100, and was 94 shortly before he took his life in February 1985 after learning he had incurable cancer. His autopsy revealed arteries that were amazingly clear of atherosclerosis or its effects, according to a report by his pathologist, Dr. Jeffrey D. Hubbard, in the July 4, 1985, *New England Journal of Medicine*.

Assessing a Diet

Fad diets

- make spectacular promises, such as "eat all you want"
- offer fast, easy, effortless weight loss
- promise weight losses of greater than 2 pounds a week
- focus on one or a few foods
- are based on pills, "secret formulas," "famous persons," "famous places," or other gimmicks

Healthy diets

- recommend reducing the number of calories
- are based on eating a variety of foods
- encourage slow, permanent weight loss of 1 to 2 pounds a week
- help you make positive changes in eating habits
- include a reasonable increase in physical activity

The One "Diet" That Works

The best diet is not low-fat, or low-carbohydrate, or low-protein, but a combination of low-calorie *and* low-fat. The type of calorie does not count, scientists long have hypothesized, only the *number*. Recent studies show, however, that when dietary fat is not immediately metabolized to fuel the body, it is stored as fat tissue, whereas carbohydrates are stored as glycogen first and then fat tissue. Thus it appears that calories derived from fat may make you fatter. Eating 500 fewer calories per day through portion control will take off 1 pound of fat per week and include all the nutrients you need. Add a moderate amount of exercise, and you will burn off even more calories (see chapter 2, pp. 59–60).

An active, healthy man in his thirties can consume 2,000 or more calories a day without gaining weight. But in his sixties, his caloric needs may be one-third to one-half that amount. Most active men can lose 1 pound of weight per week on an intake of 1,500 to 1,800 calories daily. Men lose weight twice as fast as women because they have more muscle mass, which burns calories faster than does fat tissue.

There is a theory that your body strives to maintain a natural weight or setpoint, no matter how much you eat. Your setpoint may be higher than your ideal weight. Thus many diets fail because your body produces hunger pangs and burns fewer calories whenever your weight drops below setpoint. But this is not a license to give up on weight control. Recent studies show that regular exercise, such as bicycling or aerobic dancing for thirty minutes each day, lowers your body weight setpoint by adjusting its metabolic rate. General Foods Corporation has developed a diet based on the setpoint theory. A kit, including the booklet *The Setpoint Diet*, is available for $2.75 by writing to The Setpoint Diet, P.O. Box 5500, Bradley, IL 60915. A book of that title has also been published.

Sporadic exercise does not help because it is likely to cause drops in blood sugar that stimulate hunger and overeating. But regular, moderate exercise makes your body burn calories faster and, more important, keeps your body in energy balance. For example, overeating 100 extra calories a day can make you gain 10 pounds a year; walking one mile daily burns them up. Thirty minutes of daily walking can work off 15 pounds of body weight per year, and thirty minutes of daily bicycle riding can work off 30, assuming your diet remains unchanged. This is far more than most crash diets promise — let alone deliver. (See the calorie expenditure table in chapter 2, p. 60.)

Dieters who do not exercise sabotage their bodies by wasting muscle mass during severe calorie restriction and by adding fat when they regain weight. If you need any further convincing about exercise and weight loss, consider the Marine recruit who consumes a rich, high-fat diet and is not only lean, but mean.

Perhaps the real reason diets fail is that the emphasis is on staying on "the diet." You starve yourself, lose weight, return to old eating habits, regain weight, and then diet again. Successful dieting depends on more than "the diet" itself. There is no quick, easy solution to overweight. Permanent weight loss is better achieved if you inventory your food intake, avoid situations that entice you to overeat, and change your eating and exercise habits gradually. If your motive for reducing comes from within, rather than from an outside authority, you will make permanent changes in the way you eat and live.

Changing Your Eating Habits

- Do not skip meals or go hungry. Just eat smaller portions.
- Do not eat the same foods over and over. Eat a nutritionally balanced diet.
- Eat slowly. It takes your brain about twenty minutes to signal your body that you have had enough. In that time you could eat thousands of calories before your brain knows it.
- Start your meal with liquids followed by high-bulk foods to fill your stomach.
- Gradually cut back on portions and on second helpings.
- Eat fewer fatty foods and fewer sweets, including hidden sugar in catsup and condiments.
- Try fruit for dessert.
- Fend off snack attacks with low-calorie foods such as air-popped popcorn. Do not keep high-risk foods like ice cream or candy in the house.
- Cut alcohol consumption. One drink of 86 proof alcohol contains 105 calories, and alcohol turns directly to fat, unlike solid food. Two cans of beer beyond your normal caloric needs could add 33 pounds a year.
- Increase physical activity.
- Join support groups like Weight Watchers, Overeaters Anonymous, or TOPS (Take Off Pounds Sensibly). These organizations encourage dieters to eat healthy food in realistic amounts, deal with underlying problems that cause overeating, and lose weight in a gradual, but permanent, way.

There is a myth that eating before bedtime causes you to gain weight because your body cannot burn up the calories and they are deposited as fat. Actually, over a twenty-four-hour period, your body uses the same number of calories whether they are consumed early or late in the day. Still, certain times, events, and states of mind make overeating more likely. Beware of

- holidays (which lead to the "immoderation mentality")
- fall/winter (which is a sedentary season and a time of less day-

light when some researchers believe carbohydrate craving may
increase)
- boredom (which tempts you to spice up your life with food)
- television time (which means snacktime)
- coffee breaks (which lead to doughnut breaks)
- restaurant meals (which undermine self-restraint)
- depression, anxiety, and work stress (which many people offset
  by eating)

Rather than saying, "If I eat one bite, it's all over," tell yourself you
can keep weight off. Set realistic goals, and forgive yourself when you
stray. The bottom line is that you are responsible for your weight, and
only you can keep it under control.

The Way You Eat

Many people *think* they are making healthful changes in their diet by
modest changes, such as eating more of one food or less of another.
But changes that impact positively on health must be far more extensive. Men have a particular problem because they have traditionally
leaned toward heavier foods and diets of steak, fries, bacon, eggs, and
apple pie. The food industry plays up these preferences with
"manhandler" brands and "manwiches" that are heavy on proteins
and fats, and light on fiber. Another complication is that men drink
more alcohol than women, which contains many calories and few, if
any, nutrients.

Many men have chosen to give control of their diets to their mothers
and wives, who have selected and prepared everything their sons and
husbands eat at home. But modern men are learning more about food
and nutrition and are taking charge.

Taking charge of the way you eat will be easier if you perceive that
eating is, or should be, a pleasure. Mealtime need not be an ordeal of
guilt about fats, sugar, salt, and calories. A life completely devoid of
steak, cake, fast foods, fats, salt, and even doughnuts would be bleak
indeed. As long as you eat a variety of foods, in moderate amounts, in
a peaceful, unhurried atmosphere, with attention to the way food is
prepared, served, and enjoyed, you will eat healthfully and well. Enjoying food — as opposed to loving to eat — is basic to mental and
physical health and will help make you safe at the plate.

Reliable Sources on Nutrition

- *Dietary Guidelines and Your Diet*, seven pamphlets by the U.S. Department of Agriculture, available for $4.50 from Superintendent of Documents, U.S. Government Printing Office, Washington, D.C. 20402-9325.
- *Some Facts and Myths about Vitamins* and *A Primer on Dietary Minerals* are available free from Consumer Information Center, P.O. Box 100, Pueblo, CO 81002. Also available for $4.50 from the center is *Nutritive Value of Foods* a listing of 730 common foods, their caloric values, and nutritional content.
- *Eater's Digest and Nutrition Scoreboard*, by Michael F. Jacobson (New York: Anchor Books, 1985).
- *Jane Brody's Good Food Book: Living the High-Carbohydrate Way* (New York: Norton, 1985).
- *The Setpoint Diet* (New York: Ballantine, 1985).
- *Fit or Fat?* by Covert Bailey (Boston: Houghton Mifflin, 1978).
- *The Living Heart Diet*, by Dr. Michael E. DeBakey (New York: Simon and Schuster, 1984).
- *Tufts University Diet and Nutrition Letter*, P.O. Box 10948, Des Moines, IA 50940 ($18/year, 12 issues).
- *Nutrition Action Healthletter*, published by the Center for Science in the Public Interest, 1501 16th Street, N.W., Washington, D.C. 20036 ($19.95/year, 10 issues).
- *Diet, Nutrition, & Cancer Prevention: The Good News*, published by the National Cancer Institute. For information on how to obtain a free copy, call 800-4-CANCER. (In Alaska call 800-638-6070. In Washington, D.C., area call 202-636-5700. In Hawaii call 808-524-1234 on Oahu. Neighbor islands call collect.)

Getting/Staying Fit

Why Work Out?

In 1840, Henry David Thoreau wrote, "They are fatally mistaken who think that while they strive with their minds, they can suffer their bodies to stagnate in luxurious sloth." If you are tired of being reminded of the bounty of the fit, you may prefer to read other chapters on health and lifestyle. If you are already established in a fitness program, you might want to skip to the sections on sports medicine, starting on page 47. But if you are thinking about starting a fitness program and have not gotten around to it, consider what you can gain from working out.

What Are Your Goals?
- Lose weight
- Flatten stomach
- Improve health
- Lower heart attack risk
- Tone up body
- Build endurance
- Build muscles
- Increase flexibility
- Generate energy
- Increase productivity
- Improve athletic performance
- Control stress
- Cut medical bills
- Live longer

Nearly everybody can benefit from exercise and is capable of doing it, even the handicapped. Inactive people can benefit from increased activity even more than active exercisers, according to reports from a workshop on physical activity and exercise sponsored by the Centers for Disease Control in September 1984. Workshop participants defined physical activity as muscular movement that results in energy expenditure. Exercise, or working out, was defined as physical activity that is planned, repetitive, and intended to produce physical fitness.

Some people consider age a barrier to exercise and fitness. Yet Leo Tolstoy learned to ride a bicycle at age sixty-seven. A contemporary gentleman took up skiing at age fifty-five and became chairman of the U.S. Ski Committee. Elderly marathon runners are commonplace in a sport once thought too strenuous for middle age and beyond. Men and women in their sixties and older are scaling mountain peaks, skiing cross-country, swimming the English Channel, and succeeding at other feats of endurance.

Should you talk to a doctor before starting an exercise program? Some experts say to go ahead and exercise sensibly and gradually if you are under sixty, feel well, and have no symptoms. The problem is that many Americans have no idea what constitutes a sensible, gradual approach. Thus groups like the President's Council on Physical Fitness and Sports, the American Heart Association, and the American Running and Fitness Association are more conservative. They recommend that you get medical advice if

- you are more than 15 pounds overweight
- you are over age thirty-five, and have not been physically active for many years
- you have heart trouble, heart murmur, or heart attack
- you have pains or pressure in the chest, neck, or arms during or after physical exertion
- you often feel faint or dizzy
- you experience extreme breathlessness after mild exertion
- you have uncontrolled high blood pressure or you don't know whether your blood pressure is normal
- you have bone or joint problems, such as arthritis
- you have a family history of premature coronary artery disease
- you have insulin-dependent diabetes or other conditions that might need attention in an exercise program

Your doctor may recommend a treadmill stress test. Dr. Kenneth H. Cooper, the aerobics expert and founder of the Institute for Aerobics Research in Dallas, cites two benefits of stress testing. It can detect whether you are currently suffering from, or are likely to suffer from, coronary heart disease, and it can help you design a safe and effective exercise program.

Which Sport?

In choosing a physical activity, your current age is less important than choosing an activity you can enjoy throughout your lifetime. If exercise becomes part of your lifestyle, you will enjoy it in the long run, whether measured in years or in miles. Many men and women who play the fitness game — and lose — have picked the wrong kind of activity: one that they do not enjoy or that does not suit their personality, physical capability, lifestyle, health, age, or income. They start to jog, but find it boring; swim, but do not have easy access to a pool; ski, but cannot afford to do it very often. Many people turn off on exercise because they do not consider themselves "jocks." But exercise is not the same as athletics, and it is available, at some level, for everybody.

Choose an exercise — or combination of exercises — you enjoy. If working out is a chore instead of a pleasure, or if you pick an activity that reminds you of a difficult coach or poor past performance, you may eventually quit. Recall, instead, an activity you enjoyed as a child. Was it bike riding, tennis, hiking, basketball, swimming, canoeing? That is the activity you will probably enjoy — and stick with — now. Some people who were not athletic as kids especially enjoy becoming "jocks" later in life and make their newly adopted sports not only paths to fitness but ways of life.

Choose exercises that suit your personality and physique. Do you like to exercise outdoors or indoors, at a health club or at home? Do you feel more like working out in the morning, afternoon, or evening? If you are very heavy, you probably should not choose running because you will be prone to knee and weight-supporting joint problems. If you are a loner or enjoy setting your own pace, pick an individual sport. If camaraderie is important, pick a team sport.

Choose exercises that are convenient. If you work late and then drive forty minutes to a fitness center or indoor pool, you are apt to skip exercise sessions. If the weather can seriously affect your ability to exercise, have a number of alternative activities available. Finding time to work out is often the hardest task of all. Exercise must become part of your regular routine. If you are getting started, it helps to have a partner exercise with you or a class that you commit yourself to attend.

Choose exercises with high fitness value. If your workout does not produce sweat, heavy breathing, a more rapid heartbeat, and — at the outset — sore muscles, you probably are not exercising long enough or hard enough. Sedentary individuals do not need a vigorous program to achieve these results. They should intensify their exercise program gradually.

You cannot benefit from electronic devices, springbars, and other gadgets that tense and relax your muscles but place no real demands on your heart, lungs, and other body structures. The American Medical Association's Committee on Exercise and Physical Fitness says these "effortless exercisers" may give you a false sense of fitness. Real physical fitness comes from regular overloads in both the duration and intensity of exercise, the AMA says, and is based on endurance, strength, and flexibility.

If you decide to join a fitness center, find one within fifteen minutes of home, or between home and work. You should use the facility at least three times a week to get full financial benefit. Be sure its hours fit your schedule. Ask someone who has used the fitness center for several months for the "inside story" on how well it is operated.

Checkpoints for Choosing a Fitness Center

- Is the facility clean?
- Is the equipment in good repair?
- Are the instructors certified by the American College of Sports Medicine, the YMCA, or the Institute for Aerobics Research?
- Does the exercise program include cardiovascular fitness, warm-ups, stretching and flexing, and cool-down?
- Is the facility overcrowded?
- Do contracts allow for trial periods and refunds if you become ill or disabled or move to another area?

  SOURCE: *Joining a Health Club,* available free from the Association of Physical Fitness Centers, 600 Jefferson Street, Suite 202, Rockville, MD 20852; telephone 301-424-7744.

How Often, How Long, How Hard?

How often should you exercise? Studies by heart experts advise working out at least three times a week to condition your body and gain the greatest health benefits. If you enjoy exercise and recover quickly from it, you will benefit even more from vigorous exercise *every day*. Such exercise should be varied (to avoid injury) and should include all the components of physical fitness: heart-lung endurance, muscle strength, muscle endurance, flexibility, and body composition.

How long should you exercise? Each workout should include at least twenty to thirty minutes of continuous exertion — not including warm-up, stretching and flexing, and cool-down — but you should build up gradually to that duration.

How hard should you exercise? Many people begin exercising with unrealistically high goals, but do not realize it because overdoing it does not feel bad — at first. Then overuse injuries disable their unconditioned bodies, and they have to quit. Exercise is a lifetime proposition. There is plenty of time to build up. So if you are out of shape, do not pump iron for an entire hour or run three miles the first few weeks or months. To avoid injury, build up gradually, under the guidance of a trained exercise professional or a good book on fitness.

Once you are exercising regularly, your workout should be intense enough to raise your pulse to a target heart rate (THR) appropriate to your age and fitness level. When blood is pumped at "target heart rate," your muscles can more efficiently use oxygen as fuel. To calculate THR, subtract your age (e.g., 40) from 220. This gives you a maximum heart rate (MHR) of 180. Multiply your maximum heart rate of 180 by 50, 60, 70, or 80 percent — depending upon your physical condition — to obtain your target heart rate (THR). A forty-year-old man might start exercising at 60 percent of MHR and build up gradually to 80 percent. For example:

$$220 - 40 = 180 \text{ MHR} \times .60 = 108 \text{ beats per minute THR}$$

Then build up to

$$220 - 40 = 180 \text{ MHR} \times .80 = 144 \text{ beats per minute THR}$$

Working out at 90 or 100 percent of MHR is dangerous, and it takes longer to recover with no added benefit for the average person. You will benefit even from exercising at "half speed," that is, at 50 to 70 percent of maximum heart rate. According to research at the Institute for Aerobics Research in Dallas, reported in the June 1986 *Running & FitNews*, swimmers should subtract their age from 205, which gives a lower target heart rate, because they pump more blood with each beat while working out in a prone position.

Check your progress by monitoring your pulse for ten seconds several times during a vigorous workout. To take a ten-second pulse reading, divide the beats per minute in your THR by 6. If your target heart rate is 108 beats, your ten-second pulse would be 18 beats.

TARGET HEART RATE ZONES

Age	Beats per minute	10-Second pulse
20–25	120–160	20–27
26–30	114–156	19–26
31–35	114–150	19–25
36–40	108–144	18–24
41–45	108–144	18–24
46–50	102–138	17–23
51–55	102–132	17–22
56–60	96–132	16–22
61–65	96–126	16–21
66–70	90–120	15–20

SOURCE: National Institutes of Health Fitness Center.

An easy way to tell if you are exercising too hard is the "talk test," which correlates well with heart rate. If you cannot converse comfortably while working out, or if "recovery" time after exercising exceeds ten minutes, slow down.

For runners the question "How hard should I exercise?" often translates to "How far should I run?" Dr. Kenneth H. Cooper, who founded The Aerobics Center in Dallas, used to think that no distance was too great. But he has since declared that anybody who runs more than fifteen miles per week (which translates to twenty to thirty minutes of running four times a week) is running for reasons other than cardiovascular fitness. Workouts are better measured in intensity and duration than in miles.

Whether you run, swim, or engage in some other aerobic activity, you are overexerting and need to back off if

- you feel pain
- you get nauseated, dizzy, or faint
- your heart rate does not return to normal within a few minutes after working out

To achieve the best physical and psychological results from exercise, your program should safely improve your cardiovascular efficiency, endurance, muscular strength, flexibility, and agility. The most important of these is cardiovascular efficiency, which is best achieved through aerobics.

Working Out Aerobically

Exercise that has aerobic value — that challenges your heart, lungs, and blood vessels to deliver large amounts of oxygen to muscles for a sustained length of time — has become increasingly popular in recent years. No other element of exercise has as high a fitness value or allows you to progress as readily to higher levels of fitness. Cross-country skiing, jogging, running, walking, bicycling, aerobic dancing, and swimming are excellent aerobic exercises that condition your entire body as well as your heart and lungs. You can also jump rope, climb stairs, run in place, walk on a treadmill, ride an exercise bicycle, row, dance, jump on a minitrampoline, or do any other activity, provided it steadily pushes your heart rate to its target zone for prolonged periods of time and works major muscle groups.

Your body does not know which exercise you are doing, as long as it is vigorous. Unfortunately, the physical pursuits that build strong hearts, lungs, and bodies normally do not include popular activities like fishing, camping, hunting, boating, bowling, bodybuilding with equipment, golf, softball, football, and volleyball. These sports do not build strong hearts and lungs because they make you "stop and go." Tennis, for example, is aerobic but tends to be a sporadic workout. Nor can cardiovascular fitness be achieved with high-risk, high-thrill sports, such as hang gliding, scuba diving, and parachuting; with mechanized activities, such as motorcycle racing and snowmobiling; or with quiet strolls and leisurely bike rides. To sports like these, the concept of the President's Council on Physical Fitness and Sports applies: "Get fit to play, don't play to get fit."

Jogging	148 points
Bicycling	142 points
Swimming, skating, handball, squash	140 points
Cross-country skiing	139 points
Downhill skiing and basketball	138 points
Tennis (singles)	128 points
Calisthenics	126 points
Walking*	102 points
Golf (with riding cart)	66 points
Softball	64 points
Bowling	51 points

* The exercise value of walking increases with the pace.
SOURCE: The President's Council on Physical Fitness and Sports.

The sports in the table on page 40 were rated by the President's Council on Physical Fitness and Sports according to such factors as stamina, muscular endurance, muscular strength, flexibility, and balance.

Aerobics is the process of consuming and distributing oxygen throughout the body. Thus aerobic exercise makes your heart pump more oxygen-carrying blood with each stroke to make your muscles and other body tissues work more efficiently. Once you get in shape, your heart does not pump as often because it is stronger and more efficient, thereby lowering your heart rate. In addition, an aerobic workout should make you breathe deeply from the diaphragm and use full lung capacity, not just the upper half.

Fast swimming and other "sprinting" activities that demand intense bursts of energy are "anaerobic" because your cardiovascular system cannot pump enough oxygen to give your muscles the energy they need. After a few minutes of such activity, your body reaches a state of oxygen debt and breaks down small amounts of sugar stored in muscle anaerobically (without oxygen) as an alternate source of energy. This causes lactic acid to accumulate in your muscles, making them ache, "burn," and feel unable to continue. Meanwhile, if you continue exercising, aerobic metabolism begins to produce a steady source of energy throughout your body.

The untrained body must wait as long as ten minutes for this "second wind" of aerobic metabolism, which explains why the first minutes of exercise can be so uncomfortable. The highly trained athlete switches to aerobic metabolism a minute or two after warming up. World class marathoners run at a pace at which their bodies can deliver enough oxygen to the muscles to support aerobic metabolism.

One of the most demanding aerobic exercises is cross-country skiing, which requires steady effort involving most of the muscles in the body. People who watched the 1984 Winter Olympics may recall commentaries that cross-country skiers were in the best shape of all the Olympic athletes. Unfortunately, cross-country skiing is available only in season, or not at all, in most of the United States. Indoor cross-country ski machines, which cost $400 to $800, afford most of the benefits of outdoor skiing, except for the scenery.

One popular aerobic exercise in this country has long been running. It certainly is among the most convenient. You just step outside. Running is also an inexpensive pursuit: good shoes are the only equipment you need. In terms of participation, however, swimming, bicycling, and walking are the most popular.

About 100 million people swim. The sport takes more time than jogging to achieve aerobic conditioning, but is a better conditioner because it uses the smaller muscles of the upper body as well as the large muscles of the lower body. Swimming is less apt to cause injury than many other sports and is an excellent way to work out while recuperating from knee and other injuries.

Another excellent aerobic exercise that has more than 70 million participants is bicycling. But the cyclist who pedals one minute and coasts the next takes two or three times as long to benefit aerobically as does a runner. Pedaling should be constant, even when going downhill. Indoor bicycling on a stationary exercise bicycle, however unscenic, is also an excellent aerobic workout that can be done at two o'clock in the morning or during a snowstorm. Indoor exercise bicycling is often recommended for patients recovering from a heart attack because they can start slowly and gradually build up.

Brisk walking is probably the best aerobic exercise for the beginner. Some 50 million people walk for exercise. People who cannot exercise strenuously — especially those who have joint problems, are obese, or are age sixty or older — can achieve their target heart rates by walking half an hour at least five times a week. As your fitness level increases, however, it becomes more difficult to attain target heart rate through walking. One way to escalate walking to more vigorous activity is to pump your arms, increase your speed and distance, and cover more ground in less time. Most people do not need to carry "heavy hands" weights. They should be used carefully because they can be dangerous for people with underlying cardiovascular problems, and they can trigger bursitis in the arms and shoulders. Race walking and Swedish walking are difficult to do and require special training to minimize injuries.

Jumping rope is an efficient but, for many people, unattainable aerobic exercise because it is difficult to jump nonstop for twenty minutes. According to research reported in the June 1986 *Running & FitNews*, however, you can get full aerobic benefit from jumping rope for one minute, jogging in place, arm waving, or some other less intense movement for a minute, then jumping rope for another minute and continuing to alternate until twenty-two minutes have passed.

While it is important to get aerobic exercise, it is no less important to get a balanced workout. Runners need to lift weights to build upper body strength; swimmers need to run or bicycle to build lower body strength and aerobic endurance. In other words, the ideal fitness program should include aerobic training three to five days a week, a daily twenty-minute workout to increase muscle endurance and strength, and stretching and flexibility exercises five to ten minutes a day. A balanced fitness program includes

- 5 to 10 minutes of warm-up/flexibility
- 20 to 30 minutes of cardiovascular training
- 5 to 15 minutes of strength/weight training
- 5 to 10 minutes of flexibility/cool-down

Weight Training

The old concept of weight lifting — which produced the muscle-bound, bulky look for specific sports calling for muscle mass — has been replaced by a newer, healthier way of exercising with weights. Weight training allows you to increase muscle strength and endurance and to tone your body. The most popular weight-training methods involve the use of free weights and exercise systems or stations. Weight training is a good supplement to an aerobic exercise and stretching program. Without weight training a runner, for example, would have very little upper body strength. In fact, the "running revolution" has produced such an imbalance in lower versus upper body strength that the President's Council on Physical Fitness and Sports is encouraging Americans to also develop their upper body muscles. Weight training can help strengthen and enlarge muscle tissue because the male sex hormone testosterone helps form muscle. But weight training will not result in undue enlargement of women's muscles. This "look" is sometimes seen on professional women weight lifters who may produce higher-than-usual levels of male hormones or take hormone supplements to develop big muscles.

Weight training is based on the principle of progressive overload or the contraction of muscles against gradually increased resistance. A good weight-training program should be balanced so that all the major muscle groups of the body are exercised, especially the chest, shoulders, back, legs, arms, and neck. To complete a balanced program, count on devoting about twenty to thirty minutes three times a week to weight training and developing grip strength.

The following is an example of a balanced weight-training program using Universal-type equipment and free weights:

Exercise	Primary muscles used
Bench press	pectorals, triceps, anterior deltoids
Leg press	quadriceps, hamstrings, gluteals
Shoulder press	deltoids, triceps, upper pectorals
Leg extension	quadriceps
Lateral pulldown	latissimus dorsi, biceps
Leg curl	hamstrings
Tricep pushdown	triceps
Bicep curl	biceps
Toe press	calves
Toe raise	shins

SOURCE: Janet Vizard and Tom Klein, National Institutes of Health Fitness Center.

Fewer repetitions (eight to twelve) with heavier weights tend to develop muscular strength. More repetitions (twelve to eighteen) with lighter weights tend to develop muscular endurance. Take a full day's rest between workouts to allow muscles to recuperate. Each session, as your body adapts, increase the weight or number of repetitions. Proper technique and weight selection will prevent injuries to your back, spine, and skeletal muscles. Thus weight training should be done — at least initially — under the supervision of a certified athletic trainer or instructor. (See p. 37.)

Warm-up/Cool-down

Watch a cat or dog stretch. They instinctively know how and when to tune up the muscles they are about to use. Proper warm-up, especially stretching stiff muscles, could prevent many common athletic injuries because the process of stretching stimulates blood circulation and warms the muscle. The untrained athlete needs to stretch muscles that have never been stretched before, while the trained athlete needs to elongate muscles constantly tightened by hard workouts. A seasoned runner who takes up swimming needs a new set of stretches to protect muscles and joints used primarily in swimming but not in running. Flexibility not only prevents injuries, it promotes better performance, and is so important that most professional football teams hire a flexibility or conditioning coach.

You should always start a workout with a brief warm-up — such as jogging in place or riding a stationary bicycle — followed by at least ten minutes of gentle stretching exercises. For running or walking, slowly stretch the hamstring muscle at the back of your upper leg, the quadriceps or thigh muscle, the Achilles tendons at your heel, the calf muscles, the inner thighs and lower back. Stretching should always be slow and gradual, and should never cause pain. Bouncing or jerking can cause injury. Bob Anderson's *Stretching: For Everyday Fitness and for Running, Tennis, Racquetball, Cycling, Swimming, Golf, and Other Sports* includes stretches for more than two dozen sports and for early morning stiffness, lower back tension, and even for television watching.

After stretching, slowly move the muscles and joints you will be exercising. Increase the pace gradually for at least five minutes. Warming up your muscles increases their blood supply and makes them more pliable and less prone to injury. Your cardiovascular system also needs warming up so your body can use oxygen efficiently as you exercise. Many runners first walk fast, then jog slowly and gradually increase the pace. Skiers take an easy downhill "run," and tennis players rally for ten minutes or so. Stretch within an hour of exercising or engaging in a sport, and stretch *afterward* as well to keep muscles from tightening up or becoming sore.

A ten-minute complete cool-down is important after a vigorous workout. During exercise, blood flows to muscles in your extremities and tends, under the pull of gravity, to pool in the legs after a workout. If you stop exercising suddenly without gradually slowing down in the same way that you warmed up, the blood flow slows down while your heart is still beating fast, causing lack of blood to the heart and head. This could lead to fainting from lack of oxygen-carrying blood in the brain or even, in rare instances, to a heart attack.

"Cooling down" used to mean subjecting a heated body to a cold shower. No more. It is now considered a dangerous way to cool down after vigorous exercise, according to an Atlanta Braves team physician, Dr. John D. Cantwell. He reported in the July 20, 1984, *Journal of the American Medical Association* that cold showers constrict the blood vessels and make them unable to deliver enough oxygen-carrying blood to the muscle around the heart (myocardium). Meanwhile, blood pools in the legs and cannot meet the brain's or heart's oxygen needs, which could lead to fainting or heart attack. A warm shower is just as bad because it dilates the blood vessels and could further reduce the already-low blood pressure that occurs for ten to fifteen minutes after exercise. So hold the shower until after you have cooled down by moving swiftly at first and then gradually slowing the pace. A swimmer, for example, could tread water and a runner could walk briskly for *at least* five minutes and keep moving (i.e., not stand or sit still) for five minutes more.

The Overuse Syndrome

Your body knows — or soon learns — when exercise is harmful, but often it learns too late. Deep knee bends, for example, can injure knee joints, and sit-ups with the legs flat on the floor can injure the back. Exercise requiring great muscle tension and little motion — such as weight lifting — can cause blood pressure to rise without a corresponding increase in the amount of blood pumped by the heart.

Even "safe" sports can cause injury. Just as there is no completely safe sport, there is no athlete — novice or professional — who is immune to getting hurt. The ways to prevent sports injuries are the same for amateurs and pros, and most are simple, commonsense precautions.

The number one cause of sports injuries is the overuse syndrome. It is the pitfall of the weekend athlete who runs two miles on Saturday, runs three miles on Sunday, and escalates to six the following Saturday. The marathoner who continues to run, against doctor's advice, after an injury is no less prone to the overuse syndrome.

A common pitfall of the athlete, especially the male athlete, is to ignore pain and "run on the other leg." Many athletes do not feel pain until the contest is over, and by then they are injured. Morning-after stiffness is another warning sign that you should slow down.

To avoid the overuse syndrome, you might begin with "interval training" or walking most of your target running distance at first, then alternating walking/running until you are running most of the way. After that, you might "interval train" by running at specific speeds every second or third day and alternating short, easy runs with long, hard ones. Even experienced athletes should never train hard for more than three days a week, and never for two days in a row, because muscles need twenty-four to forty-eight hours to recuperate from a hard workout. Some athletes alternate activities, such as swimming one day and running or cycling the next, because each sport uses different muscle groups.

You also should adapt to endurance exercise gradually, according to your age and physical condition. In a running or bicycling program, this means increasing your distance on flat terrain no more than 10 percent a week if you are unaccustomed to working out, then decreasing the distance as you begin to run or cycle on hills, and gradually building up again. Using this approach, even an older, out-of-shape person can eventually attain the fitness level of someone much younger.

If you have a cold, flu, or respiratory infection, stop for a few days and resume exercising at a lower level of intensity to avoid overuse injuries. You will soon regain lost ground. If, for any reason, you get into condition and then stop working out, resume at a lower level. Many accomplished athletes injure themselves by trying to pick up exactly where they left off. In general, avoid working out on hard surfaces, overexerting, and racing against fellow athletes or the clock.

Common Sports Injuries

The litany of athletic injuries includes torn muscles, torn ligaments (that connect bone to bone), inflamed tendons, shin splints, hamstring pulls, heel pain, sprains, dislocated shoulders, stress fractures, concussions, bone bruises, muscle cramps, abrasions, and lacerations. Three of the most common problems are tennis elbow, knee injuries, and Achilles tendonitis.

Tennis elbow is caused by movements that strain and inflame the tendons, ligaments, and soft tissues of the elbow. These include hitting the ball with a wrist, rather than upper-arm, movement; gripping the racket improperly; and using a racket that is too heavy or has too large a handle. Golf, baseball, skiing, swimming, bowling, gardening, carpentry, handshaking, and even washing dishes can cause tennis elbow. In fact, any activity involving wrist curls and rotations, as well as gripping, can stress the elbow and inflame its tissues.

Weekend athletes are especially prone to tennis elbow since they lack the muscle strength, endurance, and flexibility needed to protect the forearm while smashing a tennis ball. Weight training helps prevent tennis elbow by strengthening the upper and forearm muscles. Isometric exercise also helps.

Good playing form also fends off tennis elbow. Your backhand stroke, in particular, should come from the shoulder muscles, not the forearm, and your elbow and wrist should be firm at impact. It also helps to use lesser tension on your racket strings. The best treatment for tennis elbow is rest and, once the pain subsides, proper preventive exercise to strengthen the forearm muscles. If pain persists, see a physician. The saying "Once a tennis elbow, always a tennis elbow" applies mainly to people who neglect the problem.

Knee injuries. The knee is the most famous joint in sports. Although it is one of the strongest joints in the body, it is the most commonly injured. Skiers are especially prone to knee injuries. In a tug-of-war between a ski and a tight knee ligament (the connective tissue that holds the upper and lower leg bones together), the ligament is nearly always the loser. Skiers' knee injuries can be prevented by strengthening the calf, hamstring (back of thigh), and especially the quadricep (front of thigh) muscles; warming up and stretching these muscles before skiing; testing bindings to be sure they release under appropriate pressure; and year-round conditioning to improve flexibility, endurance, agility, and balance. Another common mishap is *"runner's knee,"* so named because up to four times a runner's weight lands on his knees while running, compared to only half his weight while walking. Weekend athletes and marathoners are equally vulnerable to soreness around the kneecap, which grows worse when running uphill or climbing stairs.

Achilles tendonitis — the runner's version of tennis elbow — is the curse of all athletes who run and jump. This injury to the tendon that connects the heel bone to the calf muscle is caused by tight calf muscles. The best protection against Achilles tendonitis is to stretch the calf muscle and tendon gradually about six times before and after running (see p. 44). It also helps to wear proper footgear. A flexible shoe with a built-in heel lift will help control tendon problems. Overexertion is an invitation to tendonitis, as are sudden switches to shoes with lower heels or to different running surfaces.

Pulled muscles differ from muscle soreness. The former cause a sudden, localized, and persistent pain. Muscle pulls are usually caused by continuous use without adequate rest or by stretching a tight muscle during sudden, powerful movement. This injury commonly occurs to the calf muscles of tennis players, hamstring muscles of sprinters, back muscles of rowers and weight lifters, shoulder muscles of white water paddlers, and the biceps and triceps of pitchers and javelin throwers. Heat before mild activity and cold and compression afterward are the best self-treatment for mild muscle pulls that cause only minor loss of function and strength. More seriously pulled muscles — that swell and will not function properly — need *r*est, *i*ce (fifteen to twenty minutes three to four times a day), *c*ompression, and *e*levation — the RICE treatment described in *The Sportsmedicine Book* by Dr. Gabe Mirkin and Marshall Hoffman. If pain and swelling persist after forty-eight hours, apply heat for twenty to thirty minutes three times daily. Muscle injuries that cause severe pain and disability should be seen by a physician, as should any muscle pull that does not heal in seven to ten days. Jacuzzis and hot tubs are good for massaging slightly aching muscles after a workout, but will make more seriously inflamed muscles worse because hot water increases blood flow. Similarly, although massage and such liniments as Ben-Gay increase blood flow to stiff, sore muscles and feel good, the best treatment for pulled muscles is RICE.

Shin splints are caused by prolonged irritation rather than sudden injury to the shin muscles in the front of the leg. They are an overuse injury, often caused by overextending the stride in walking or by running repeatedly on hard surfaces, especially if you are an unconditioned or highly trained runner whose calf muscles are much stronger than your shin muscles. Shin splints also are the bane of tennis and basketball players. The treatment for shin splints is rest and the passage of time. They are best prevented by avoiding hard surfaces such as dry clay and concrete, especially during early training, wearing well-fitted shoes that absorb shock well (see p. 50–51), and doing strengthening and stretching exercises. Strengthen shin muscles by running up stairs (be sure to build up gradually) or by doing ankle lifts with low weights. Stretch calf muscles with wall push-ups. Keep your heels on the ground and repeat at least five times for ten seconds each. If the pain does not subside after three weeks, or if shin splints persist despite your efforts to prevent them, see a doctor.

Heel spur is a small extra piece of bone formed by continuous wear and tear to the lining of the heel bone. It often causes pain and stiffness in the bottom of the heel, especially when getting out of bed in the morning, or at the beginning of a run. The pain usually subsides after walking or running for a few minutes, but can grow worse with the continued abuse of running and jumping, especially in shoes with poor rear-foot shock absorption. The best treatment is protection: wear shoes with a custom insert that takes direct pressure off the painful area. In *How to Doctor Your Feet Without a Doctor*, podiatrists Drs. Myles J. Schneider and Mark D. Sussman tell how to make your own heel cushion pad, with sponge rubber, or a quarter-inch of felt with a hole cut in the pad under the specific spot where you feel pain. If a homemade pad does not feel comfortable, have a podiatrist make one for you. Be sure to wear a pad under *both* feet so you will not create a leg-length imbalance. It sometimes helps to apply ice to the bottom of the heel for thirty minutes when you first feel pain, they advise, or to use aspirin to help reduce inflammation (two aspirin every four hours for two to three days, then two every six days for up to another week, assuming that you do not have ulcers or other sensitivities to aspirin). Daily exercises to stretch the heels may help: sit on the floor with your legs stretched out straight, grasp your toes, and pull gently and gradually for thirty seconds, repeating several times. If this irritates your heels, stop or ease up.

Some sports medicine physicians feel that steroid injections with cortisone, which can stop the inflammation and pain of heel spurs, also may weaken tendons and other tissues and stop nature's warning signal that you should be taking it easy. Other physicians routinely give cortisone injections for sports injuries. You may want to discuss this treatment beforehand, since steroids are powerful drugs with powerful side effects.

Blisters, arch pain, and other foot ailments are best prevented by avoiding overuse and by wearing properly fitted shoes that protect feet from shock and friction that might otherwise be intolerable. Many new athletes buy inexpensive tennis or cross-country shoes and end up with muscle, tendon, and bone damage. Or they use the wrong kind of shoes. Running shoes are built to protect feet that are moving forward at a steady pace. Court shoes support side-to-side lateral motion, and tend not to protect a runner's feet and Achilles tendons. So do not wear court shoes to run or jogging shoes to play tennis.

Well-fitted shoes with flexible soles and a built-in heel lift reduce shock to the feet and knees, and support the arches of anybody who jogs, jumps, or walks. To get a proper fit, shop when you have an hour or more to try on different brands. Discuss your footwear needs with the store's shoe consultant: your training program, foot specifications, and gait peculiarities. Your old running shoes often reveal unusual patterns of wear, so take them along. Shop for shoes at the end of the day when your feet have swollen to full size, and take along the socks you will wear with your new shoes.

Unfortunately, most running shoes are made only in C and D widths. If your foot is narrow, you will have to search for a store that carries a brand that comes in variable widths. If your shoe is too wide, you will develop blisters, corns, calluses, and other foot problems. The shoe should be long enough to allow a thumb's width between the tip of your big toe and the end of the shoe when you are standing. Walk and, if possible, run in the shoe before buying. According to Dr. Gabe Mirkin in *The Sportsmedicine Book*, a good sports shoe should have

- a flexible sole that bends easily at the ball of the foot
- a "cookie" or soft arch support built into the shoe
- a flared heel that stabilizes your gait

- a firm heel counter: the rims of the shoe that are right above the heel
- a firm saddle: the part that extends down from each side of the shoe laces

These last four features prevent your foot from excessive pronation or rolling inward (flat feet).

If your feet or any other part of you is injured, you are better off with a sports medicine center or physician who specializes in sports medicine, preferably one who is familiar with your sport. He or she will be less likely to misinterpret apparently abnormal diagnostic tests as illness. Unfortunately, finding a sports medicine doctor sometimes can be like searching for the legendary unicorn. This is because few physicians treat athletic injuries on a full-time basis and therefore do not list themselves as sports medicine specialists. Dr. Gabe Mirkin recommends finding a physician who also is an athlete, or getting a referral from the trainer for a local college or professional team, a local medical school or medical society, or other athletes. *The Sportsmedicine Book* lists orthopedists and podiatrists who specialize in sports medicine. In addition, the American Running and Fitness Association gives medical referrals to physicians, podiatrists, trainers, physical therapists, nutritionists, and sports medicine clinics.

Thermal Injuries

Heat stroke is a life-threatening emergency caused when the body cannot cool itself because its main cooling device, sweating, shuts down, causing the body to overheat up to 110°F. The brain, quite literally, is cooked. Blood circulation diminishes and the kidneys close down because of inadequate blood supply. The warning signs of heat stroke are confusion, chills, headache, dizziness, nausea, dry skin, euphoria, or feelings of impending doom.

Heat stroke is sometimes preceded by *heat exhaustion,* a less serious condition characterized by clammy skin, sweating, weakness, dizziness, and nausea. *Heat stress* is a mild disorder caused by inadequate blood supply to the brain. It can cause fainting, cramps, and a prickly-heat skin rash.

Heat injuries are more likely to level experienced runners than novices because the former so often push themselves beyond their limits. Others who are prone to heat injuries tend to be out of shape, unaccustomed to exertion during heat, hung over, sleep deprived, overweight, and very young or very old. People suffering from heart, lung, and kidney disease, diabetes, or hypertension, and those who have had a previous heat injury, are also more vulnerable to heat stroke or exhaustion. The high-risk category includes people taking diuretics, sedatives, tranquilizers, and heart and blood pressure medications that alter their ability to sweat.

Heat exhaustion or heat stroke is a medical emergency. The victim should stop physical activity immediately and move to a shady location. Somebody should pour cool liquids over the victim's body, rub the skin with ice, raise the feet above the head, refrain from forcing liquids, and call for medical help immediately, a situation that attests to the value of having a workout partner.

To prevent heat injury:

- Don't overexert if you are in a high-risk group.
- Acclimatize yourself by working out in the heat at least fifteen minutes daily for about three weeks. (Lying out in the sun does not acclimatize you to heat.)
- Beware of dangerous weather when the outdoor combined temperature-humidity index rises above 80°F.
- Drink a cup or two of liquid every twenty to thirty minutes during prolonged, intense activity.
- Avoid alcohol before and after workouts in hot weather to prevent dehydration.
- Wear light-colored, lightweight, loose cotton clothing — including a hat — that allows air to circulate and evaporate.
- Avoid extra salt, which increases thirst.

Hypothermia is the opposite of heat stroke. It is an exposure sickness in which body temperature drops below 95°F. This can happen even when the outdoor temperature is well above freezing. Symptoms include violent shivering, dizziness, loss of strength and motor control, loss of mental clarity, hallucinations, drops in pulse and blood pressure, and heart stoppage, followed sometimes by death. Typical victims include hikers, skiers, climbers, canoeists, swimmers, marathoners who run in cold, wet weather, and cyclists exposed to rain and wind. The most susceptible are unfit, underweight, underclothed, uninformed weekend sportsmen who discount the dangers of prolonged exposure to rain, wind, and cold. The extent of hypothermia is not known since many victims appear to die from drownings, falls, and other accidents that would not otherwise have occurred.

Rapid rewarming is the most essential life-saving measure for hypothermia victims. They should be wrapped in blankets or a sleeping bag or undressed and pressed between two warm bare bodies inside blankets or a sleeping bag. A hot beverage, such as tea, also helps. Do not give alcohol: it worsens the situation by causing an increased volume of cold blood to rush to the heart. At home a hypothermia victim can be revived in a hot shower or bath at 100–116°F. Keep the arms and legs above water and heat the torso first. You can also use hot-water bottles and heating pads. Never try to revive an unconscious hypothermia victim by shaking him. Handle him gently and see a physician as soon as possible. Even after apparent revival, a person with hypothermia is still in danger for several more days.

Frostbite, a freezing of tissue water in the skin, threatens skiers and other winter sportsmen, even in areas where temperatures seldom dip below freezing. A frostbitten nose may appear pale or whitish, and frostbitten fingers or feet may feel numb. Sometimes a slight purplish discoloration and numbness are the only signs of frostbite. Lungs do not become frostbitten, however. The upper respiratory tract can warm even the coldest air to body temperature by the time it reaches the lower lungs. For example, residents of Fairbanks, Alaska, have no trouble breathing air at −70°F, assuming they are in good health.

Ski instructors in Canada recommend nose-watching. At the first sign of whiteness, they advise removing your glove and holding your palm, without rubbing, against your nose for a minute or so. Toe wiggling and arm flapping are also recommended when extremities begin to feel numb, especially while riding chairlifts or standing still. Joggers and cyclists who wear shorts and a T-shirt (instead of layered clothing) in freezing weather risk hypothermia and frostbite, as well as penis freeze.

To prevent hypothermia and frostbite:

- Dress in layers and wear underclothing like polypropylene that will wick perspiration away from your skin and insulate by trapping a layer of air near the skin. Cover with a water-repellent parka made of Gore-Tex or other material that "breathes."
- Keep dry. Do not overdress or wear tight shoes or clothing that will cause sweating. Waterproof clothing causes perspiration to accumulate, producing wet clothes that stick to the body and do not retain body heat.

- Eat balanced, regular meals and avoid drugs and alcohol. The latter does not "warm" you. Rather, it causes blood vessels to dilate and hastens heat loss.
- Beware of wind chill. Even winds of 20 mph — enough to move small branches or blow snow around — increase hypothermia and frostbite danger if the outside temperature is 15°F or lower. Motorcyclists, snowmobilers, bicyclists, and even runners can lose considerable body heat merely through their exposed faces.
- To avoid the sweat/freeze syndrome, start running or cycling *into* the wind, and return downwind.
- Move around to keep blood circulating. When trying to survive in cold water, however, assume the fetal position and keep still to minimize heat loss and the cooling effect of water flowing over your body.
- Avoid dehydration; you may not sweat in cold weather, but you still lose fluids, even through breathing.
- Avoid fatigue. It will make you more susceptible to cold injury.
- Do not smoke: it constricts blood vessels, limits blood supply to the extremities, and adds to the risk of frostbite.

The Heart Attack Hazard

Many people die while sleeping, making love, driving a car, and even defecating, but they do not make news as readily as people who die while working out. Most exercise-related deaths are caused by overexertion in people with existing heart conditions. These include heart defects present at birth or that occur in people over forty years old, and coronary artery disease (buildup of fat deposits in the arteries that supply blood to the heart).

Many individuals who die during exercise experience — and ignore — warning signs of a heart attack, such as chest discomfort or pain; pain in the jaw, arm, neck, throat, or shoulders; dizziness or lightheadedness; fainting; mild to severe fatigue; and/or extreme breathlessness, often as a result of exercise.

The late runner/author Jim Fixx, who died of a heart attack at age fifty-two, apparently ignored arm pain and tightness in his chest and throat (both symptoms of angina, a sign of coronary heart disease) while running during the months before his fatal heart attack on July 20, 1984. Fixx's father had suffered his first heart attack at age thirty-five — the same age Fixx began running — and had died of coronary artery disease at age forty-three. Still, Fixx refused to take a treadmill stress test during many visits to Dr. Kenneth Cooper's Institute for Aerobics Research in Dallas, including a trip made about six months before Fixx's death. An autopsy showed severe narrowing of three major vessels of the coronary arteries that supplied blood to his heart.

In his recent book, *Running Without Risk: How to Reduce the Risk of Heart Attack and Sudden Death During Aerobic Exercise,* Dr. Cooper discusses many issues concerning Fixx's death, including whether jogging prolonged his friend's life (it did) and whether Fixx's heart disease could have been diagnosed with a treadmill stress test (it could have). Cooper also presents a plan for avoiding sudden death during exercise.

A fourteen-month study of exercise-related deaths in the Seattle area, reported in the October 4, 1984, *New England Journal of Medicine,* suggests that the risks of dying of sudden cardiac arrest are indeed higher during strenuous exercise, but the magnitude of risk is greatly reduced if men are regular exercisers. For example, men in the study who exercised vigorously at least two hours and twenty minutes weekly were five times more likely to die of heart attack *while exercising* than at other times. But men who almost never worked out were fifty-six times more likely to die of heart attack while exercising. Men who exercised regularly — even for only twenty minutes a week — had fewer heart attacks at any time than the more sedentary. In other words, the temporarily increased risk of sudden death during vigorous exercise is outweighed by the overall reduced risk of coronary heart disease from regular exercise. An accompanying editorial noted that this study resolves some apparent contradictions in which deaths occur even though exercise benefits people with coronary heart disease.

The bottom line is that exercise is more helpful than harmful, providing you have a complete medical evaluation if you are in a risk group (see p. 35), learn how to exercise safely, and know and heed the symptoms of heart trouble.

Other Pitfalls

Road Accidents

Athletes, particularly runners and cyclists, are as likely to be crushed by a car as by a heart attack. Dangers are greatest at night for runners and cyclists who wear dark clothing and run or ride with the traffic.

Safe Road Work

- Remember that automobiles are larger, heavier, and harder than you are.

- Always assume that the driver does not see you, and that some drivers may feel they have a legal right to hit runners, especially after sundown.
- Avoid running on roads at night.
- If you *must* run after dark, wear light-colored clothing and a fluorescent vest and arm bands, or wear fluorescent tape on the moving parts of the body where it is most visible. Carry a small flashlight to alert oncoming cars.
- Run against, rather than with, traffic. Watch for vehicles crossing over into the wrong lane.
- Run on the shoulder or away from the edge of the road so that vehicles nearest you need not alter their paths.
- Carry identification, especially when running alone.

Dehydration

Dehydration is a hazard of vigorous workouts, especially in warm weather. During a marathon, runners can lose as much as 8 liters of sweat. Resulting dehydration can be prevented by drinking eight glasses a day of cool water before and during prolonged exercise. Drinking small amounts of water during workouts does not cause leg or other cramps. *Do not wait until you are thirsty.* Thirst is not a reliable guide to the body's need for water in extreme heat. The body absorbs cool water more quickly than fluids containing other ingredients, including electrolytes.

"Athletes' drinks" containing potassium, sodium, and chloride are not necessary, except possibly during a marathon or for athletes undergoing heavy training in the heat. To speed the absorption of water, even marathoners should dilute these drinks until they can barely be tasted. Do not take extra salt or salt tablets; they increase thirst and dehydration (see chapter 1, p. 12).

Improper Clothing and Technique

Athletes, as noted earlier, should wear loose, comfortable clothing (except when skiing, biking, or engaging in other sports where clothes could get caught). Above all, they should avoid vinyl or rubberized sweatsuits, which, because they prevent evaporation of perspiration and its cooling effect, increase body temperature and the chances of collapse from heat exhaustion or death from heat stroke. Some people mistakenly believe that rubber sweatsuits enhance weight loss. But you lose only water weight, which is easily regained.

Improper technique also can cause injury. For example, a jogger's foot should strike the ground on the heel and then rock forward to the toe. Landing directly on the ball or toe of the foot will cause leg problems such as shin splints. Bouncing is hard on your feet and legs. Cultivate smoothness in your running style by looking toward the horizon as you run. If you watch a branch or other object ahead of you and it does not move up and down against more distant objects, you are gliding and not wasting energy.

Gravity Inversion Boots

Originally designed to relieve spinal disk pressure by suspending you head down from three to twenty minutes at a time, gravity inversion boots are also used to relieve back pain and muscular tension or just to "hang out." These devices create intraocular pressures that threaten vision and marked rises in blood pressure and pulse rate. They are particularly dangerous for people with high blood pressure, cardiovascular disease, glaucoma, and related conditions. There are far better ways to prevent or relieve lower back pain. They involve strengthening the abdominal muscles and lying flat on the floor with your legs up (see chapter 8, pp. 216–218).

Anabolic Steroids

Anabolic steroids (the male hormone testosterone and its synthetic derivatives), human growth hormone, stimulants such as amphetamines and cocaine, and other drugs purportedly improve athletic performance and heal muscle and other tissues injured during prolonged exercise. Blood doping, or infusing athletes with red blood cells, purportedly improves endurance by increasing the amount of oxygen in the blood. Although these practices are common in Europe, they are officially banned by the U.S. Olympic Committee on the grounds of safety and ethics. Until the risks and benefits of such drugs and treatments are established, they hardly seem worth the competitive edge. Amphetamines are also hazardous because they keep athletes from knowing when to slow down and lead to overuse injuries.

Sex

Athletes throughout history have wondered whether sex affects athletic performance adversely — and whether heavy training affects sexual performance. (The latter can cause sufficient fatigue to affect sexual *interest* at times.) The AMA's Committee on the Medical Aspects of

Sports says sex on the night before an event does no harm as long as (1) you are used to it, (2) you believe it will do no harm, and (3) you get enough sleep. As Casey Stengel of the New York Yankees once said, "It isn't sex that wrecks these guys, it's staying up all night looking for it."

Après Workout: The Sauna?

Many health clubs and fitness centers offer saunas, steam baths, and Jacuzzis. What can a healthy adult hope to gain from exposure to heat of about 180°F at 15 percent humidity (in a sauna), 120°F at 98 percent humidity (in a steam room), or 104°F (in a hot tub)?

These facilities are more a source of pleasure than of health. Sitting in the dry heat of a sauna or the moist heat of a steam room may soothe your body and help you relax mind and muscles. A shower or dip in the pool afterward can be invigorating. But physiologically, saunas, steam rooms, and hot tubs are of little benefit aside from inducing sweating, cleaning the pores, and increasing blood circulation at the skin level. They do nothing to promote physical fitness, cause weight loss, clear up acne, or cure arthritis, hangovers, or the common cold — as various claims contend. Saunas and steam rooms do nothing for injured muscles; they do not relieve fatigue and they do not dissolve fat.

The main purpose of saunas and steam rooms is to make you sweat. Therein lies the danger: weight loss that results from sweating is only temporary because it is caused by water loss. If you lose two pounds or more by sweating, you are in danger of dehydration and should replace the fluid loss immediately.

The danger of heat stroke also lurks in saunas. During the first two to four minutes your skin heats up. Then your internal organs and body begin to warm while your skin temperature rises more slowly. This phase feels very pleasant. But as you reach your limit of heat tolerance, a kind of fever develops, breathing becomes difficult, and your heart races. You will probably become uncomfortable enough to leave before you become dehydrated, dizzy, and faint, or before you collapse from heat stroke. Other traumas of saunas include burns in facilities lacking proper heat controls, fungus infections, athlete's foot, and "sauna taker's disease," an allergic reaction to mold inhaled after pouring water from a sauna bucket over the heating element.

Although people with heart disease, hypertension, and diabetes should check with their doctors before using a sauna, most people can enjoy one with little hazard, assuming that they

- drink extra water before and after a sauna
- limit exposure to five or ten minutes at first, working up to twenty minutes maximum
- avoid saunas immediately after exercise, eating, smoking, or drinking
- remove watches, rings, and other jewelry; they overheat in the sauna and can cause burns
- do not exercise while in the sauna

The Rewards

Weight Control

A primary benefit of exercise is less flab and flatter stomachs. It not only burns calories, it makes you more aware of your body and more motivated to stay on a diet. Even men and women in their twenties may have trouble seeing their shoes. Since overweight and obesity trigger so many other health problems, weight control may be the most significant, as well as most visible, benefit of working out. Although Americans now eat 10 percent fewer calories than their ancestors, they exercise considerably less. Hence the cure for overweight and obesity must include good nutrition and exercise.

Eating less without exercising more causes you to lose mainly lean body mass, while exercise causes you to lose mainly body fat — which is what you want to lose. If you diet *and* exercise, you will also lose primarily body fat.

Since you must burn off about 3,500 calories to lose one pound of body weight, exercise would appear to be a poor way to lose weight. This is true over the short term. For example, to burn off 600 extra calories consumed in a day, you would have to spend an hour playing squash or handball, or bicycling at a speed of 13 mph. Running 10 mph for an hour would burn off 900 calories. Most physical activities — such as swimming, volleyball, walking 3.5 mph, golf, lawn mowing, or rope skipping — burn off only 300 calories per hour. But over a year, expending only 300 additional calories per day through physical activity will result in a weight loss of about 20 pounds, assuming your food intake remains the same.

On the next page the table shows the average number of calories expended per hour by a 150-pound person. A lighter person burns somewhat fewer calories, a heavier person somewhat more.

To burn the greatest number of calories in the least amount of time,

Activity	Calories per hour
Lying down or sleeping	80
Sitting	100
Driving an automobile	120
Standing	140
Housework	180
Walking, 2½ mph	210
Bicycling, 5½ mph	210
Gardening	220
Golf; lawn mowing, power mower	250
Bowling	270
Walking, 3¾ mph	300
Swimming, ¼ mph	300
Square dancing; volleyball; roller skating	350
Wood chopping or sawing	400
Tennis	420
Skiing, downhill or cross-country, 10 mph	600
Squash and handball	600
Bicycling, 13 mph	660
Running, 10 mph (a six-minute mile)	900

SOURCE: Dr. Robert E. Johnson, Professor Emeritus of Physiology, University of Illinois, and colleagues, *Physiological Measurements of Metabolic Functions in Man* (New York: McGraw-Hill, 1963).

exercise should be aerobic. But exercising harder or faster for any given activity will only slightly increase calories spent. A better way to burn up calories is to exercise a longer time or cover a greater distance. It is possible, however, to burn calories faster when your body has a higher basal (resting) metabolism rate. Exercise can increase your metabolism rate by 10 percent. In addition, muscle tissue burns more calories than fat tissue.

There even is evidence that an exercise-elevated metabolism rate allows you to burn calories at an accelerated rate after exercise is over. Some studies show that aerobic exercise can increase your metabolic rate 25 percent above basal level for fifteen hours after exercise ceases, and 10 percent for up to forty-eight hours thereafter. More recent research, however, disputes this finding.

Cardiovascular Fitness

There is strong evidence that regular endurance-type (aerobic) exercise improves the efficiency of your heart and lungs by lowering heart rate at rest and during exercise. In addition, exercise accompanied by weight loss reduces most of the risk factors associated with heart attack, including high blood pressure, high blood cholesterol, excess low-density lipoproteins (LDL), stress, and diabetes (since people of normal weight are less likely to develop this disease). The same factors that motivate people to start exercising on a regular basis may also make them less likely to smoke, another risk factor for heart disease.

Exercise significantly increases levels of beneficial high-density lipoproteins (HDL), which have been associated with decreased risk of blocked arteries and heart attack in men, although apparently not in premenopausal women. Recent reports suggest that exercise may also increase the body's ability to dissolve blood clots, which lead to heart attacks, strokes, and pulmonary embolism. This effect is more pronounced in women than in men because female sex hormones keep HDL levels high until menopause.

Regular physical activity can cut the risk of heart attack *in half*, even for people who smoke, are overweight, are under stress, or have high blood pressure. Many heart attack patients are in better physical condition than they were *before* their heart attacks.

Stress Management

Regular, vigorous exercise lasting at least thirty minutes is said to release beta endorphins, natural opiumlike brain chemicals that calm the nervous system and alleviate pain and anxiety. In this sense, exercise acts as a natural tranquilizer. It makes you feel "mellow" rather than react to stress in ways that contribute to coronary heart disease and many other illnesses. Exercise also helps relieve the kind of anxiety that makes you overeat.

Many studies show that depressed patients improve with exercise, especially with vigorous, continuing, aerobic-type exercise. This is not surprising, considering that physical confinement has long been used as a punishment and that depressed people tend to "punish" themselves through self-imposed inactivity. Exercise is especially valuable for older people suffering from anxiety and depression. It relaxes them and elevates their mood far better than the tranquilizers so commonly overprescribed for this age group.

Longer Life

It now appears that exercise can even extend life expectancy by 25 percent or more. According to a study of nearly 17,000 Harvard alumni, reported in the March 6, 1986, *New England Journal of Medicine*, the exercise need not be strenuous, as long as it expends 2,000 calories a week. This is equivalent to running an 8.5-minute mile or bicycling at 10 mph for four and a half hours a week. No additional benefit occurred above 3,500 calories a week. The study, headed by Dr. Ralph S. Paffenbarger, Jr., of Stanford University, proved that exercise per se is protective, not just that the healthiest people exercise. Moreover, the study showed that physical activity can partly counteract the deadly effects of smoking, high blood pressure, and hereditary tendencies toward early death.

In addition to extending life, exercise improves its quality. Regular, moderate exercise can counteract age-related loss of physical strength and, according to experiments in animals, helps preserve the tissue of the aging heart. Active people lose far less lung power as they age than do the sedentary. (See chapter 10, p. 265.)

Productivity

People who achieve physical fitness often report they feel more self-sufficient, competent, emotionally stable, and productive. Although scientific proof is still lacking, some people attest that aerobic exercise enhances alertness, concentration, and creative thinking. Runners have been known to compose lectures, gain new insights, and set new priorities while clocking the miles.

Dr. George Sheehan — the cardiologist who took up running again at age forty-four to stay in shape after a tennis injury and who has written nearly half a dozen books on running — links fitness to a full, successful life. He once told an audience at the National Institutes of Health that running for an hour a day clears his mind of mundane details and "becomes a source of power, energy, and creativity for the other twenty-three hours."

Miscellaneous Benefits

Exercised bones do not lose calcium as quickly as sedentary bones, and therefore are stronger and less likely to succumb to such diseases as osteoporosis, which causes loss of bone tissue and fractures (see chapter 8, p. 229). Exercised joints are more flexible and less likely to break or lose their range of motion. Doctors often recommend exercise for arthritics to help them maintain mobility and muscular strength. For arthritics and nonarthritics, working out ensures fewer backaches and helps prevent weight gain that overburdens and damages joints. Exercise generally decreases insulin requirements of diabetics and is of particular value to people with adult-onset (Type II) diabetes in maintaining normal weight and controlling their disease.

At any age, exercise helps you work better, sleep better, eat better, digest better, and have more energy for all activities, including, it appears, lovemaking. In *The Sportsmedicine Book,* Dr. Gabe Mirkin quotes Dr. William Masters, the sex researcher, as saying that a physically fit person "invariably functions more effectively sexually than a person in poor shape."

Making Fitness Part of Your Lifestyle

Two generations ago, men routinely used to chop wood, pitch hay, lift buckets, push wagons, and swing axes. Today well-oiled machines do all this, while your body rusts out. Yet even modern work — whether pushing paper or minding machines — demands safety, speed, and productivity that physical fitness helps ensure. If you have been out of shape for years, it will take time to recover (fortunately, not as long as it took to get out of shape).

The average American's participation in exercise is even worse than his voting record. Only 20 percent of adult Americans (most of them men) get enough exercise to maintain cardiovascular fitness. Even people who have compelling reasons to exercise do not. As many as 50 percent of men who have had heart attacks drop out of physician-recommended exercise programs within a few months.

Thus you must overcome the inertia of living in a society that prefers cars, elevators, and moving sidewalks to walking. Stop thinking of exercise as a painful duty to your health, or as a detestable "exercise program," and think of *moving more* with natural activity you enjoy. Give up the split lifestyle of straining on weekends and slouching all week. Get off the bus two stops early, and look for the farthest parking spot from your office door instead of the nearest. Take a fifteen-minute walk at lunchtime. Use stairs instead of elevators. Stair climbing uses more energy per minute than almost any other form of exercise. Stop parking in front of stores and driving two blocks between errands. Convert chores into exercise. When mowing the lawn, raking leaves, shoveling snow, or planting the garden, move vigorously. You will finish sooner and feel better.

Turn walking into exercise by lifting your knees higher than normal, adding a spring to your step, tensing your calf muscles, taking longer strides, and walking faster than usual. Do strengthening and stretching exercises for ten minutes of every hour that you watch television. Install a stationary bicycle next to the television set.

Keep moving, even in a desk job, by standing up every half hour or so, reaching one arm at a time toward the ceiling, rotating your head in a clockwise, then counterclockwise, direction. Shrug your shoulders, touch your toes, do side bends. When trapped at your desk, stretch your legs and extend and flex each foot several hundred times to increase blood circulation. Practice good posture all day long by sitting up straight in your chair and walking tall, with your gut sucked in.

Even when you are traveling, you can keep moving by avoiding taxis and subways, by carrying your own bags, by hiking around the concourse during layovers at airports, and by walking the length of a train. Carry a jump rope with you when you travel and a compact tape player with exercise tapes for impromptu exercise sessions. Tune in to a television exercise class. Stay at a hotel with exercise facilities. Call 800-555-1212 for the toll-free number of the reservation center for the hotel chain you are using and request a free directory that lists their fitness facilities.

Extraordinary efforts are not necessary. Marathoning is fine if you enjoy it. But the ordinary person needs only to find natural activity that makes his lungs and heart work harder. A little creativity can convert your usual activities into a self-tailored physical fitness program that will keep your body running smoothly.

If you choose to remain inactive, you might not notice as "negative adaptation" to inactivity progresses in your body. Then your car breaks down, or you shovel snow, or decide to play basketball one weekend. You behave as if you are fit, but you are not. The consequences — depending upon your age and physical condition — can range from sore muscles to a heart attack.

Positive adaptation is your other choice, but it takes time. There is a principle of behavior known as "shaping," meaning that true change comes only from gradual movements toward a desired goal: a leaner body, a healthier body, a more energetic body, and more. Each step must build upon the previous, in the same way that you build muscles or running distances. The day-to-day steps you take by asking more of your body add up to miles toward better health.

Further Reading

- Dr. Kenneth H. Cooper's book, *The Aerobics Program for Total Well-Being* (New York: M. Evans, 1982), assigns points to the leading aerobic exercises and provides workout schedules for gradually building fitness in each activity.
- *The Sportsmedicine Book* (Boston: Little, Brown, 1978), by Dr. Gabe Mirkin and Marshall Hoffman, is an excellent reference source on avoiding and treating sports injuries.
- *Stretching*, by Bob Anderson, is published by Shelter Publications, Inc., P.O. Box 279, Bolinas, CA 94924.
- The President's Council on Physical Fitness and Sports has published guidelines for a basic sixteen-week jogging program for inactive adults in *Introduction to Running: One Step at a Time*, available for $2.75 from the Superintendent of Documents, U.S. Government Printing Office, Washington, D.C. 20401-9325.
- *Walking for Exercise and Pleasure*, available for $1 from the U.S. Government Printing Office, Washington, D.C. 20401-9325, provides information on what to wear, warm-up and conditioning, and how fast to walk.
- *Running & FitNews* is a newsletter providing sports medicine and nutrition information, published by the American Running and Fitness Association, 2001 S Street, N.W., Suite 540, Washington, D.C. 20009 ($25/year).

Good Sex,
Healthy Sex

What Is This Thing Called Sex Appeal?

Sex appeal, for some folks, is a great mind in a great body, or even a mediocre mind in a great body. But in the song "Don't the Girls All Get Prettier at Closing Time?" country and western singer Mickey Gilley suggests that sexual attraction blooms as opportunities for meeting and interacting wither and die. Hence:

> Ain't it funny, ain't it strange,
> The way a man's opinions change,
> When he starts to face that lonely night?

Psychologist Chris L. Kleinke describes another facet of sex appeal in *First Impressions: The Psychology of Encountering Others*. While physical appearance is important, he says, after the first meeting the look in your eyes, your actions, general approachability, smile, and especially your willingness to talk determine how close you are to a "10." Most people are uncomfortable with long silences and appreciate a verbal individual's ability to revive a flagging conversation. Attraction often is strong among people who are alike because they reinforce the way they judge themselves. Yet opposites also attract — often to passionate extremes.

Early experiences, especially those involving the opposite-sex parent, influence what kind of person attracts — or repels — a man or woman. Did a woman's father have a well-muscled body and hairy chest? What was her first boyfriend like? All have left their imprint. If a girl's father admired her femininity and beauty, she will grow up believing she is attractive. The same applies to men and their mothers.

The bottom line on sex appeal is how good you feel about yourself. People with self-esteem can trigger in others a state of intense attraction one writer calls "limerance": preoccupation with the desired person, ecstasy in his or her presence, and agony over the possibility of rejection. In other words, people who *have* sex appeal are those who *think* they have sex appeal!

What Affects Sexuality?

Sexuality — in contrast to sex appeal — courses through every human being, regardless of sex, age, race, religion, or how much that person tries to suppress it. Traditionally, sexuality meant sexual intercourse and all the actions that precede and follow it. But the sex act is only one facet of sexuality, which encompasses sex appeal, liveliness, sensuality, and, especially, the need for physical contact. This need starts with life itself, when the unborn infant spends nine months continuously embraced by his mother's womb. The contact is abruptly broken at birth and, in our culture, writes zoologist-philosopher Desmond Morris in *Intimate Behavior,* is never again fully satisfied. Morris considers this overwhelming need for — and lack of — physical intimacy central to human existence.

Intimate behavior, Morris notes, can take many forms: handshaking, hugging, backpatting, comforting, or the lavish body contact that takes place between lovers. When the need for human intimacy is unsatisfied, he says, our contact-hungry world provides touch substitutes: doctors, pets, hairdressers, barbers, cigarettes, cups of coffee, and even our own bodies. (How often during the day do you touch your face, cross your knees, or clasp your hands together?)

Anthropologist Ashley Montagu maintains, in *Touching: The Human Significance of the Skin,* that not only is physical contact pleasurable, it is a basic biological drive necessary for survival. Animals, especially primates, instinctively huddle together and lick their young. Dogs, cats, horses, and dolphins enjoy being stroked, and studies show that petting by a human hand causes sudden and significant decreases in the heart rates of agitated animals. Many farmers swear that cows give a finer grade of milk when they are hand-milked. Even rats, given extra handling in the laboratory, become better able to learn and retain learning than unhandled rats.

Distinguished physicians, including the late Sir William Osler, have observed that physical contact relieves pain and stress and promotes more rapid healing. (The child's request to "kiss it and make it well" may not be so childish after all.) Psychologist James J. Lynch, in *The Broken Heart: The Medical Consequences of Loneliness*, tells of a man who lay dying in a hospital bed for fourteen days with no visitors. He was in a coma, paralyzed, and able to breathe only with a respirator. But when a nurse held his hand, his heart rate, which had been rapid and irregular, slowed down and stabilized.

Touching in our society, however, either tends to be sexual or does not occur at all. How often do you see male friends hugging one another? In *The New Male*, Dr. Herb Goldberg states that men's early social conditioning makes them repress sensuality and touching. They tend to take responsibility for successful lovemaking and see themselves as sex stereotypes rather than as individuals with free choices. This perception that sex means strictly intercourse, Goldberg says, destroys men's potential for joyful, authentic, spontaneous sexual responsiveness. He concludes that "one can only speculate and create visions of what might someday be if the male freed himself of these powerful and destructive role bindings."

Sexuality in the narrower sense of sex drive changes as personal problems, family demands, work, social pressures, physical health, emotions, partners, life stage, and levels of experience change. Sex drive sometimes becomes suppressed, especially during periods of high creativity and functioning at full potential. Such self-developed people do not fear or forsake sexual activity; they just put it on the back burner for a while. Men whose jobs give them a strong sense of identity often engage more successfully in relationships, including sexual ones. Some men, however, substitute career success for sex, throwing their energies into work rather than love relationships.

A healthy lifestyle enhances sex drive at any age. Regular exercise tunes your body to respond better sexually and helps energize it for the rigors of lovemaking. But heavy indulgence in food or alcohol just before making love may have an inhibiting effect. Similarly, during temporary illness or times of stress and fatigue, you may not feel like making love. Yet many people with chronic illnesses, such as heart disease, maintain an interest in sex. Indeed, there is evidence that making love aids recovery from a heart attack, once it is safe to resume moderate physical activity.

Power struggles between partners can dampen sex drives. Some couples repress erotic feelings for fear of becoming "a slave" to one another. Partners may become frigid or impotent to gain power in relationships; lack of cooperation during lovemaking is a way of controlling the other by ignoring his or her wishes. For some women, their only weapon against a mate who dominates in all other areas is withholding sex. Partners who share power — whether in one- or two-career marriages — have the best sex lives, according to psychologists David Olson and Herbert Laube, who studied ninety-five couples in their thirties at the University of Minnesota in Minneapolis.

Anger — particularly "armed truce" anger that is unstated, unacknowledged, and unresolved — can also kill sexual desire. Carried far enough and long enough, anger leads to impotence, premature ejaculation, and absence of orgasm. Many people communicate anger destructively with threats, name-calling, sarcasm, interruptions, shouting matches, and dramatic exits and door-slamming. But constructively expressed anger — in which each partner states how "I feel" and willingly listens to the other — can produce greater closeness and be a sexual turn-on.

Aphrodisiacs

For centuries men and women have searched for the perfect aphrodisiac. They have tried to excite themselves sexually through sight, hearing, touch, taste, and smell. They have swallowed or injected foods and chemicals ranging from harmless to deadly. In the harmless category are foods that resemble genitalia. Throughout history, lovers have dined on asparagus, onions, tomatoes, oysters, spices, herbs, ginseng, and eryngo root (which resembles testicles). Animal plants, including ambergris (formed in the intestines of sperm whales), reindeer horn, elephant trunk, and monkey blood, have long been used as aphrodisiacs. Even ordinary food can have aphrodisiac properties, as the joys of a well-cooked meal stimulate desire for more joys.

Opium and other narcotics are sometimes considered aphrodisiacs because their users tend to have sexual fantasies. Narcotics, however, create the illusion — not the reality — of heightened sexual drive. Alcohol and marijuana depress inhibitions and, in small doses, may *seem* to have aphrodisiac qualities. In large doses, however, these drugs depress everything, including sex drive.

Spanish fly, made from the powdered Mediterranean cantharis beetle, is one of the most dangerous "aphrodisiacs." When swallowed, this substance irritates the mucous membranes of the intestines and urinary tract, affecting the penis and vagina in ways some people consider sexually stimulating. Spanish fly can also cause inflammation of the skin and kidneys, vomiting of blood, and even death.

Another dangerous "aphrodisiac" is amyl nitrate, which some people inhale to heighten the intensity of orgasm. This drug causes the heart to race and blood pressure to drop to dangerously low levels, even in healthy people, and it can inhibit the immune system.

The hormone HCG (human chorionic gonadotrophin), used to treat male infertility, has improved some men's sexual performance, but has not done so consistently. Yohimbine hydrochloride, originally obtained from the bark of an African evergreen but now made synthetically, reportedly works as an aphrodisiac. Dr. Julian Davidson, a Stanford University physiologist, wrote in the August 24, 1984, *Science* that the drug doubled the mounting behavior and increased the sexual activity of *male rats*, but has since concluded that "there is no such thing as an aphrodisiac." Dr. Davidson is now testing the drug on men as a treatment for impotence and plans to report his results in 1987. (For more information about impotence, see pp. 72–77.)

Healthy people need no chemical aids to "turn on." Most so-called aphrodisiacs merely relax inhibitions and let the powers of suggestion and illusion run free. Perhaps this is why so many sex therapists advise emptying the mind of everything except sensual pleasure.

Laughter, according to psychiatrist Dr. Avodah K. Offit, may be the aphrodisiac everybody ignores. Offit says laughter can stimulate and even prolong sexual pleasure. Sex drives are strongest when they involve some strong emotion. The best orgasms occur at the peak of such feelings, he says, and when they are repressed, they take with them the opportunity for the deepest response to sex. The aphrodisiac that works best is tenderness, elation, grief, love, or some other strong feeling — and that is no illusion.

Sex after Sixty

Age affects sexuality, but not as adversely as many people believe. Sexuality is one of the last bodily functions affected by the aging process. The prevailing view is that a man's sexual decline begins in the late teens, when physical sexuality peaks. Herb Goldberg, in *The New Male*, calls this often-repeated notion about men "primarily an artifact of conditioning rather than a biological phenomenon." This so-called decline, he says, occurs because men in their late teens begin to deny feelings, drown out impulses, and live up to expectations that they become husbands/fathers/providers and continually prove their sexual expertise and masculinity.

The main age-related sex change is a slowing of sexual response. It may take older men — how much older depends on the individual — a few minutes longer to attain an erection than it takes adolescents, whose erections occur at the slightest provocation. The angle of erection and the frequency of awakening with erections may decline. Erections may be less firm and less large than before, and the sensation that ejaculation is about to occur may be of shorter duration. Finally, erections may take half a day rather than half an hour to repeat and may fade more quickly following orgasm.

But healthy older men still produce sex hormones at levels that taper off so gradually they hardly differ from levels found in younger men. Studies of human sexual response by the famous sex therapists Dr. William H. Masters and Virginia E. Johnson have established that most older men do not lose their capacity for erection and ejaculation. And the National Institute on Aging, in a long-range study of over one thousand volunteers, found that among men aged seventy to eighty-nine, sex hormone levels were higher in those who maintained active sex lives. In other words, men over sixty, seventy, or even eighty are able — as long as they are willing — to enjoy sex. Indeed, older men tend to remain more sexually active than older women, mainly because by age seventy, women vastly outnumber men their age and are without partners. For either sex, masturbation is one alternative and healthy way to remain "sexually active."

Many men maintain that their sex lives become more satisfying as they grow older, and that they do not miss the "good old days" of intense and uncontrollable need for a quick orgasm. Because older men take longer to climax, their sexual encounters may vastly improve over earlier years when they reached orgasm before their partners.

In addition, older lovers often enjoy deepening emotional ties and harmony with their mates. Sexuality evolves into sensuality, and that transforms the entire body — and not just the genitals — into a source of pleasure. Sensuality, in turn, leads to intimacy — deep caring for and trust of another person — which is the emotional side of sensuality.

Sex in mid-life is potentially the best sex you will ever have. If you are sexually active in middle age, you will remain sexually active as you continue to grow older. Use it or lose it, the saying goes. Even if you take a sexual sabbatical — should you fall ill, lose your mate, or spend a year in Antarctica — there is no reason why you cannot become sexually active once again, even at age eighty.

Sex reassures people, at any age, that their bodies are still functional, according to Dr. Robert N. Butler and Myrna I. Lewis, authors of *Sex*

After Sixty and _Love and Sex After Forty_. Humans have an emotional need for sex that endures regardless of age or, in most cases, physical condition.

Impotence

If lovemaking's sole objective were to give sensual pleasure, impotence would not be a problem, for every man can enjoy the sensuous dimensions of touch, whether given or received, whether through massage, fondling, stroking, or back scratching. But for centuries impotence — defined as problems having or maintaining an erection during at least one out of four sexual encounters — has been, in author Leo Tolstoy's words, "the tragedy of the bedroom."

Men in Tolstoy's time had little idea what caused their problem. They had been told for centuries that impotence was a "divine curse," witchcraft, or the result of sexual excess and gonorrhea. Even in the 1960s, Masters and Johnson encountered clients who believed impotence was caused by masturbating after age thirty, homosexuality, and irregular church attendance. Several men were told by clergy that their problem with impotence was a form of penance for adultery or for agreeing to a partner's abortion.

For years the prevailing view has been that impotence is primarily a psychological problem. At a meeting at the National Institutes of Health in November 1986, Dr. Masters said that three myths about sex underlie many of the perhaps 20 million cases of impotence that exist, and handicap males with "thou shoulds" and expectations. The first is that males should have a greater capacity for and interest in sex than females. The second is that males are sex experts, "a role that males have graciously accepted," Dr. Masters noted. The third is that the male "does for the female," that is, is responsible for her orgasm. This is physiologically impossible, Dr. Masters said. Impotence begins with belief in these myths, followed by "spectatoring" or watching one's own performance, and culminating in panic and persistent impotence.

At a Conference on the Scientific Basis of Sexual Dysfunction in June 1986, Dr. Joseph LoPiccolo, psychologist at Texas A&M University, suggested some other reasons for psychogenic impotence. It tends to occur in men who

- were raised in a conservative, fundamentalist religion with negative sexual attitudes
- have difficulty being playful and relaxed in any situation

- consider the female genitals unsanitary, smelly, or otherwise unattractive
- are transvestites who prefer to cross-dress during sexual activity
- fear that their partners might become pregnant
- suffer from widower's syndrome: active pursuit by another woman shortly following the death of a wife
- are concerned about body image, especially as they grow older, or who find their wives no longer sexually stimulating
- feel physically repelled, rather than attracted, by their partners
- have partners who lack sexual skills
- feel at a power disadvantage with their wives and use erectile failure as a way to resolve the conflict
- cannot merge their feelings of love and respect with their sexual feelings toward their partners (the "Madonna/prostitute syndrome")
- have sex with women who can reach orgasm only through penile-vaginal intercourse
- overreact to normal aging changes, such as taking longer to get an erection
- attempt to have sex in an inappropriate setting

As an example of the last, Dr. LoPiccolo cited the case of a man who was having an affair with a married woman in her house. Every time they had sex she wept and threatened suicide because of her guilt about having committed adultery. She also frequently reminded her lover that if her husband — a police officer who occasionally came home unexpectedly during the day — found them together, he would shoot the lover dead with his service revolver. Dr. LoPiccolo noted that despite these reality issues, this man was puzzled as to why he could not have an erection!

Dr. Herb Goldberg, in *The Hazards of Being Male*, calls impotence the tip of an iceberg of frustration, anger, and unhappiness in a man who has stayed in a "good" marriage out of guilt, remained in a job he hates in order to be "responsible," and fathered children to prove his potency and please his wife and society. For such men, Goldberg contends, seeking medical causes of impotence is far less threatening than exploring "the psychological and emotional lies of compulsive masculinity. . . . Were I to write slogans for a men's movement," Goldberg concludes, "one bumper sticker would read, 'Your penis is years ahead of your brain.' "

Only recently have organic causes of impotence been explored. More than one hundred diseases can cause impotence: primarily, decreased functioning of the testes, thyroid dysfunction, diabetes, chronic alcoholism, liver or kidney disease, neurologic disorders, decreased blood flow to the penis caused by hardening of the arteries, defects in trapping blood in the penis, and injuries to the pelvis or spinal cord. Sixteen of the top two hundred prescribed drugs can cause impotence. They include antihypertensives for high blood pressure, diuretics for heart disease, the widely prescribed ulcer drug cimetidine (Tagamet), and major tranquilizers.

Dr. Masters reports that in recent years 18 to 20 percent of his impotent patients have had preexisting physical problems. Other experts estimate that a far higher percentage of cases are organic in origin. For example, a report in the April 1, 1983, *Journal of the American Medical Association* noted that 80 percent of the impotence experienced by a group of 188 men had physical causes. Only 14 percent were caused by emotional problems. The survey covered 1,180 middle-aged males, of whom 401 reported problems with impotence and 188 agreed to be evaluated. The investigators, Dr. Michael F. Slag and colleagues from the Veterans Administration Medical Center and University of Minnesota in Minneapolis, noted that only 6 of the 401 impotent men had previously had their problem medically diagnosed by a physician. The remaining men had been reluctant to call it to the attention of their own physicians, although the 188 who were evaluated were eager to discuss it with the investigators.

The line of distinction between psychogenic and organic impotence can be difficult to draw. "We believe that impotence is either organic or psychogenic, but there are all manner of variations," Dr. Masters notes. Often, physical and psychological factors operate together. For example, a man might fail to have an erection after drinking too much (more than 4 ounces a day, according to some studies). But the failure so upsets him that the next time he attempts to have intercourse, he again has erection problems because of fear of failure. The bottom line is that regardless of cause, impotence is a symptom of some underlying disorder and a source of severe emotional pain.

An estimated 10 to 20 million men are afflicted with, but undiagnosed and untreated for, impotence. Sleep researchers long ago noticed that erections in physically healthy males occur throughout the night during rapid eye movement (REM) sleep, indicating that impotence is probably psychogenic. The nocturnal penile tumescence (NPT) test, in which a strain gauge is attached to the penis during sleep, is about 80 percent accurate. Psychological states of depression and anxiety sometimes distort test results. The NPT costs about $1,500 plus a trip to a sleep lab. Self-testing at home by wrapping a strip of postage stamps around the shaft of the penis is not an accurate test, according to Dr. Paul Schiavi of Mount Sinai School of Medicine in New York City. The stamps may tear along the perforations even if nocturnal erections are not rigid enough for intercourse, or the stamps may not tear because the man did not experience states of sleep in which erections occur. There are a number of other diagnostic tests for impotence that must be performed by a physician.

If men could take a pill for impotence, probably very few would choose to "live with" their problem. Yet a wide range of successful surgical and other treatments now are available. According to one impotence expert, "We can reach close to a 100 percent cure rate if the man wants it."

Erection problems caused by low testosterone or other hormone imbalances often can be treated by administering hormones or drugs. For drug-induced impotence, a physician may recommend a change of brand or dosage. Diabetes-caused impotence can sometimes be relieved by controlling the disease itself, and alcohol-related impotence can be remedied by not drinking. Impotence caused by poor blood circulation has been treated by transplanting a healthy artery from the abdomen to the penis. This surgery is called revascularization.

Many physicians recommend a bendable or inflatable penile implant for men with organically caused impotence. Penile implants have helped hundreds of thousands of men since the 1970s. One less expensive and more popular type is a semirigid pair of silicone rods surgically implanted in the penis to create a constant but somewhat flexible erection that is easily concealed under clothing. The second device consists of a pump with a fluid-storage reservoir implanted in the scrotum. This device inflates two balloonlike cylinders implanted in the penis. The inflatable implant is more prone to mechanical failure and costs two to four times as much as the semirigid type, which cost $800 to $900 in 1986, plus the surgeon's fee and the cost of an overnight hospital stay. Men who could ejaculate before having an implant usually can experience orgasm, ejaculate, and father children afterward. Several new types of inflatable implants are now available.

Relatively painless injections of relaxant drugs into the penis have a growing success rate in treating impotence. These include vasodilators that increase blood flow to the penis and a smooth-muscle relaxant that induces erections by allowing more blood to enter the penis than can leave it. One muscle relaxant, papaverine hydrochloride, is injected with a very small needle into the base of the penis. Papaverine appears to have success rates of up to 40 percent. Although the long-range effects of these injections are unknown, short-range side effects — including priapism (permanent erections) and scarring that leads to Peyronies disease (a bending of the penis) — often can be controlled by careful control of dosages. The injections, which were tested in more than 500 men at the University of California at San Francisco, produced erections lasting from several minutes to six hours. In a program at Boston University, about 150 patients aged forty-five to seventy-five, many of whom have diabetes, self-administer the injections at home. Dr. Robert J. Krane reported recently that they took five to twenty minutes to develop erections that last one to one and a half hours. Dr. Krane notes that "some fifteen different drugs might work against impotence, and we've tried only two so far."

Sex therapy has a high success rate when impotence has emotional roots. Physicians and other therapists experienced in treating sex problems help patients explore their personal histories; build self-esteem; overcome fear, anxiety, and misinformation about sexual performance; improve relationships with their partners; "live down" distressing sexual experiences; and unlearn myths and propaganda that prevent them from feeling sexual pleasure. Some patients benefit in five to ten visits; others need many months of therapy. The Masters and Johnson approach to sex therapy is based on treating the couple, rather than the individual, and is described — along with other approaches to sex therapy and with choosing a sex therapist — in *Masters and Johnson on Sex and Human Loving.* Injections are sometimes successfully used as an adjunct to sex therapy on the premise that if impotence has a combination of causes, it might respond to a combination of treatments.

Masters and Johnson warn that men are very suggestible where impotence is concerned. It is hard to convince some men that one nonerection (a better word than failure) does not mean impotence. Fatigue, stress, financial worries, arguments, tensions between your partner and yourself, or one drink too many can all cause situational impotence. Instead of panicking, take time to recover. Work out, have a massage, relax in solitude, and set aside time with your partner for nonsexual touching and sex without intercourse. Consider the possibility that, for whatever reason, you may not *feel* like having sex right now. As Masters and Johnson have said, "No man can will an erection."

Many men fall into a three-way trap of anticipating impotence, panicking when it occurs, then telling nobody, not even their doctors. If your doctor does not seem comfortable with or knowledgeable about your problem, or attributes it to old age, visit a urologist or a specialty clinic that deals with men's sex problems.

Other men discover they can be sexual and satisfy themselves and their partners without an erection. If the cause of their impotence is organic, they may decide against surgery or medical treatment. Sexuality is more than good bedmanship, they discover, and includes spiritual as well as physical union with one's partner.

Sources of Further Information about Impotence

- A new book, *It's Up to You*, by Warwick Williams (Baltimore: Williams & Wilkins, 1985), is a self-help guide for men with erection problems and their partners.
- A free booklet, *Impotence — Help in the USA*, is available from the Impotence Information Center, Department USA, P.O. Box 9, Minneapolis, MN 55440.

Premature Ejaculation

Dr. Herb Goldberg, in *The New Male*, suggests that premature ejaculation, like impotence, may be a reaction against always having to prove one's masculinity through performance. Masters and Johnson also have found that premature ejaculation rarely has organic causes. Although they consider that impotence and premature ejaculation are separate problems, their early studies showed that impotence sometimes occurs when premature ejaculation continues, uncontrolled, for many years. While most premature ejaculators do not become impotent, enough do, they said, to cause concern.

Masters and Johnson found that the typical premature ejaculator is married and well into his thirties or forties. His impotence, if it occurs, develops after years of emotional tension caused by his wife's (and his) increasing frustration at the situation. He tries to count backward from one hundred, think about a problem at work, or plan a fishing trip. This conscious dulling of his sexual senses, Masters and Johnson warn, "is his first unintentional step toward . . . impotence." Repeated failures to control ejaculation eventually cause him to avoid sex altogether. He resorts to feeling tired, being sick, or having no time for sex.

Eventually, performance fears multiply until the day when he tries to have intercourse and cannot have an erection. His view of himself as a sexually adequate male goes downhill from there. Masters and Johnson estimate that 15 to 20 percent of American men have at least some difficulty controlling rapid ejaculation, yet less than one-tenth seek help for this problem.

Help is available. One particularly effective remedy made famous by Masters and Johnson is the "squeeze technique." For example, when genital touching begins, the woman periodically applies pressure to the penis in this way: she places her thumb against the underside of the head of the penis, and her index and middle fingers opposite the thumb on either side of the coronal ridge (the rim of tissue that separates the head of the penis from the shaft). Strong pressure is needed for about four seconds (the man can tell her how strong) to curb his urge to ejaculate. After about thirty seconds, the couple may resume sex play. During the early phases of treatment for premature ejaculation, the squeeze technique is recommended every time the man feels increased sexual tension. Gradually, as he gains better control, he needs it less often.

The squeeze technique can be practiced solo, but it will control ejaculation only during masturbation. To control ejaculatory urges during intercourse, it is necessary to practice the squeeze technique with a partner. A more detailed description of the technique appears in *Masters and Johnson on Sex and Human Loving*.

Phallic Fallacies

Masters and Johnson performed another service for humanity when they laid to rest two phallic fallacies:

- The larger the penis, the greater the sexual prowess of the male.
- The bigger the man, the bigger the penis, whether flaccid or erect.

The average penis, according to Masters and Johnson, measures 9.5 cm, or just under 4 inches, when nonerect. Their studies showed that smaller penises double or more than double in length when erect. But since longer penises, when erect, increase by about half of their flaccid size, the average erection is about equal. They found that penis size has nothing to do with a man's ability to achieve erections, orgasm, or ejaculatory control. The sex researchers also reported that one extremely large penis — 5½ inches long when flaccid — belonged to a man who was 5 feet 7 inches tall and weighed 152 pounds. Yet a penis measuring about 2½ inches when flaccid belonged to a 5-foot 11-inch man who weighed 178 pounds. Masters and Johnson concluded that even though the smaller penis, when erect, is somewhat smaller than the larger penis in an erect state, the sexually stimulated vagina involuntarily accommodates the penis, regardless of its length or circumference. Masters and Johnson note that a man's view of his own penis tends to make it look shorter because of the viewing angle — and tends to make other males' genitals look like a *Playgirl* centerfold.

Infertility

A woman physician, writing about her own problem with infertility, called it "a blow to my self-esteem, a violation of my privacy, an assault on my sexuality . . . [and] above all, a wound to my body, psyche and to my soul." Men are less articulate about how the inability to conceive a child affects them. "But just because men keep quiet," a male infertility expert says, "their feelings have no less impact." About one out of five couples is classified as infertile — medically defined as failing to conceive after one year of trying. Growing numbers of such couples are seeking treatment for their infertility. They will no longer settle for the traditional advice to "adopt a baby," "take a second honeymoon," or "accept it, it's God's will."

When a couple consults a physician about difficulty conceiving a child, he or she first tries to determine the cause. In the past, the assumption often has been that infertility is a woman's problem. But a matching set of disorders can affect male fertility as well. In general, about a third of infertility problems are related to the male, a third to the female, and the remainder either to a combination of the two or to unknown causes. In women, infertility often results from pelvic inflammatory disease (PID), endometriosis, hormone imbalances, or the aftereffects of a sexually transmitted disease. *Neisseria gonorrhoeae* and *Chlamydia trachomatis*, in particular, can cause upper genital tract infections that scar the tubes leading to the ovaries. Female infertility may stem from failure to shed a healthy egg, a blockage of its transport from the ovary to the womb, or a nonreceptive environment in the womb itself. Female infertility also is associated with the type of contraceptive previously used and the number of years childbearing has been delayed.

One major identifiable cause of male infertility is a varicose vein called a varicocele that forms in the scrotum. It is not clearly understood how this causes abnormal sperm, decreased sperm mobility, and low sperm counts. According to one theory, increased blood flow in the testicles may raise the temperature of the scrotum and thereby impair sperm production.

Hormone imbalances, thyroid malfunction, and impotence occasionally cause male infertility. Industrial chemicals are also implicated in some cases of male infertility — how many cases is unknown. Age alone does not appear to impair male fertility, contrary to some beliefs. Although fewer sperm have vigorous mobility as a man grows older, this in effect means only that the probability of fertilizing an egg decreases and that it might take a few more attempts or more time to achieve fertilization. Male infertility becomes a problem when a high percentage of sperm are weak and malformed or their movement is severely impaired. In many cases, methods exist to treat these conditions and improve the quantity and quality of sperm production as well.

For males, infertility treatment usually begins with a sperm test, in which semen is analyzed for sperm number and activity. "Low sperm count" is a relative matter, since many men with marginal semen quantity and quality have impregnated their wives. The average male produces over 20 million sperm per milliliter of semen (3 to 5 milliliters is the volume of a normal ejaculate), according to the American Fertility Society. Another test often recommended is a postcoital analysis to determine whether the vaginal mucus is "hostile" to the sperm. Sometimes this problem is easy to correct. A fertility expert may also recommend a laboratory analysis of the sperm's ability to penetrate a hamster egg and/or a hormonal analysis. For women, there are tests to determine whether ovulation is occurring normally, whether there are blockages or abnormalities of the fallopian tubes and uterus, and whether the uterine lining is properly prepared to receive a fertilized egg.

Once the cause of infertility is determined, many cases prove to be treatable. When male infertility is involved, surgical removal of a varicocele can correct testicular hyperthermia and improve semen quality in about half of all cases.

A cooling device resembling an athletic supporter was recently approved by the Food and Drug Administration for treatment of testicular hyperthermia. A small pump hangs from the belt and circulates water through the device, keeping the scrotum about three degrees cooler than body temperature. It must be worn regularly during the day for about four months and is not particularly comfortable, says the inventor, Andrew Sealfon. Many infertility experts, however, consider this device's general efficacy to be still unproven.

A new and promising treatment for infertility involves LHRH (luteinizing hormone-releasing hormone). This hormone is produced by the brain and acts on the pituitary gland, which regulates the reproductive organs. In small doses, LHRH can reverse certain types of female infertility. It also appears to help some men whose infertility is caused by a particular hormone deficiency. Hormone therapy using relatively inexpensive drugs to induce ovulation in women has become an accepted way to treat infertility associated with a diminished ability to shed eggs. Since these drugs may cause multiple embryos to develop, there is an increased risk of maternal and infant mortality associated with this treatment.

For women incapable of transporting fertilized eggs to the uterus, test-tube ("in vitro") fertilization (IVF), followed by surgical implantation of the early embryo in the uterus, is the most publicized and sophisticated treatment for infertility. This procedure costs $3,000 to $5,000 for each attempt at fertilization and succeeds about 10 to 20 percent of the time.

Artificial insemination is an alternative for some childless couples. Doctors tend to view the procedure as ethically equivalent to a blood donation, but some orthodox religious authorities consider artificial insemination by an anonymous donor as adultery. Accordingly, some couples view this prospect unfavorably. In cases of artificial insemination by the husband, such objections rarely arise.

For many couples, the desire to have children is so strong that they persist with treatment despite the fact that an "infertility workup" can be devastating. Couples undergoing treatment may feel stripped of their privacy, frustrated by expensive and often unsuccessful procedures, and forced to turn lovemaking into a clinical act performed on set schedules and under set circumstances. One researcher found that half the men undergoing infertility tests experienced temporary impotence or ejaculation problems. Couples involved in prolonged fertility workups sometimes experience marital stress not only because of the stresses of the procedures themselves, but also because of the strain of seesawing hopes and disappointments while seeking possible treatments for infertility. Other infertile couples are unclear about whether they truly want a child or whether they just want to *be able* to have a child. Thus psychological counseling and support should be a part of infertility treatment.

RESOLVE, a self-help group for couples with fertility problems, publishes a newsletter on issues of concern to would-be parents, including adoption information. Write to RESOLVE at P.O. Box 474, Belmont, MA 02178; telephone 617-484-2424.

Contraception: Condoms

Most people know very little about available methods of contraception, how they work, how effective they are, or how to use them correctly. The most widely used birth control methods today include the pill, IUDs (intrauterine devices), diaphragms, chemical spermicides, periodic abstinence (the "rhythm" method), douches, condoms, coitus interruptus (withdrawal), "tube-tying" (for women), and vasectomy (for men). While women have about a dozen contraceptives to choose from today, only three contraception options currently are available to males — withdrawal, condoms, and vasectomy — and the first two date back to antiquity.

In the past, condoms lacked respectability, in part because of complaints that they dull sexual sensitivity and in part because of associations with prevention of sexually transmitted disease. Today, the latter is a selling point. Latex condoms, used properly, are most effective in preventing AIDS, gonorrhea, chlamydia, hepatitis B, and nongonococcal urethritis (NGU); and somewhat less protective against herpes, syphilis, and genital warts. Major women's magazines recently began to accept advertising for condoms. The message is "sex these days can be a risky business, and you need all the protection you can get." Women buy nearly half of the estimated 800 million condoms sold annually, unlike the old days when only men bought them and quietly carried them off in plain brown bags. Today's condoms come in various sizes, colors, and thicknesses. (Ultrathins are more likely to break, however.) Several brands are lubricated with nonoxynol 9 — used in most contraceptive foams, tablets, and jellies — a spermicide that may provide added protection against AIDS and herpes viruses.

In the United States, misuse remains a major cause of condom failure. The most common misuse is inserting the penis into the vagina before putting on the condom. If putting on the condom were considered part of sex play, it would eliminate the hazard of accidental ejaculation into the vagina and would not interrupt intercourse. Other misuses include failing to unroll the condom the full length of the penis, allowing ejaculate to escape out the open end. Loss of the condom in the vagina after ejaculation can be avoided by withdrawing the penis before it becomes relaxed and holding the condom in place during withdrawal.

How to Use a Condom

1. Unroll the condom onto the full length of the erect penis before intercourse begins.
2. Leave a pocket at the tip of the plain-ended condom to catch the semen.
3. If the condom has a reservoir tip, hold the tip between your fingers to eject air before putting it on.
4. If a dry condom is used, use a water-based lubricant generously on the tip and the outside to prevent tearing.
5. After ejaculation, remove penis and condom while the penis is still erect.
6. Do not reuse a condom. Dispose of it immediately.
7. Store condoms in a cool, dry place and do not use those that are sticky, brittle, or otherwise damaged.

Condoms have great potential for helping control unwanted pregnancies among teenagers who do not have access to other birth control methods. Latex condoms also can prevent many sexually transmitted diseases if worn prior to genital contact. Note, however, that syphilis, herpes, and AIDS infections can be transmitted to and from other parts of the body. In addition, the condom lets partners share responsibility for contraception, does not require a doctor's prescription, is almost 100 percent effective when used with spermicidal vaginal foam, helps control premature ejaculation by reducing sensation, offsets aesthetic objections to intercourse during menstruation, and offers visible proof that contraception is being practiced.

Withdrawal is the most common method of contraception used throughout the world, but it is far from foolproof. The relatively high failure rate has been attributed largely to not withdrawing adequately, ejaculating too close to the woman's genitals, or repeating intercourse when the urethra still contains sperm from recent ejaculation. (In the latter case, urinating helps flush out the sperm.) Withdrawal, on the other hand, can give the man a sense of mastery and control if he knows when ejaculation is imminent; it also lets him share responsibility for contraception.

Chemical approaches to contraception for men are still in the experimental stage. They tend to be ineffective and have undesirable side effects. Most male "pills" studied so far dampen sexual desire. This disadvantage could be offset by administering testosterone to ensure a healthy sex drive, but male contraceptives studied to date also tend to shrink testicles, enlarge breasts, and raise blood cholesterol. A safe and effective chemical male contraceptive probably will not be available for years.

One male contraceptive under study, gossypol, inhibits sperm production without inhibiting sex drive, but it causes permanent sterility in as many as 20 to 40 percent of men who take it, and, in a small number of cases, can cause irreversible muscle weakness and paralysis. Some researchers are trying to make modified synthetic copies of gossypol or are using smaller doses to reduce the toxic effects. Other scientists are studying natural or chemical sperm inhibitors that can be injected, inhaled, or implanted under the skin, where they will not be inactivated in the digestive tract. Still other researchers are trying to develop ways to prevent sperm from maturing or transporting themselves.

Contraception: Vasectomy

About 10 million American men have had vasectomies, and about 500,000 more have the operation each year. Vasectomy is the surgical cutting of the two tubes — the vasa deferentia — that carry sperm from the epididymes (sperm storage ducts) to the urethra. A surgeon either ties, clips, or cauterizes the ends of each vas.

In early vasectomies, both ends of each severed vas were tied off. Today surgeons prefer the "open-ended" vasectomy, in which the end of the vas nearest the testes is left open. This relieves the buildup of pressure from sperm, which continue to be produced at a normal rate in the testicles. Although most sperm are absorbed in the body, some collect in the epididymis ducts that lead out from each testis and in each severed vas on the testes side. The resulting pressure and damage to the epididymis may make later reversal of a vasectomy more difficult, although it has no other known health consequences.

Many men are concerned about whether vasectomy will hurt. The operation normally takes less than thirty minutes and is performed under local anesthetic in a hospital operating room or doctor's office. The only pain occurs when the local anesthetic is injected. During the operation itself, a man might feel a tugging sensation when the vas is pulled out of its sheath in the spermatic cord. Afterward, he might feel some aching in the testicles at first, but this should disappear entirely within two or three days, depending upon the skill and experience of the surgeon. Some men experience skin discoloration, bruising, swelling, and discomfort, but these usually disappear a week or two after the operation. Aspirin and ice packs every half hour for several hours usually relieve this discomfort.

After a vasectomy, it takes about six weeks or fifteen ejaculations to clear the old sperm out. Two zero sperm counts, usually performed four months after the operation, virtually eliminate the chances of impregnation. Although vasectomy is one of the most reliable birth control methods available today, a report in the July 14, 1984, *British Medical Journal* noted that six men out of fourteen thousand impregnated their wives between sixteen months and three years after their vasectomies.

Vasectomy interferes with male reproductive function, not with virility. Testosterone and other male sex hormones continue to be produced at normal levels in the testicles of men with vasectomies. (Feminization results from castration, or removal of the testicles.) Postoperative lack of interest in sex passes in a week or less, and sex feels as good as before, if not better. The first few orgasms may cause some unaccustomed sensations, but these too pass quickly.

Concern about the safety of vasectomy arose during the 1970s when studies in monkeys suggested that the procedure might accelerate hardening of the arteries. A recent study of nearly five thousand men whose vasectomies had occurred an average of fifteen years ago showed that vasectomy does not lead to coronary heart disease, even many years later. The study showed that even men with high levels of sperm antibodies in their bloodstreams — a common aftereffect of vasectomy — did not have a higher risk of damage to the inner arterial walls, as some scientists had suggested.

More recently, a comprehensive study of vasectomy confirmed that men with vasectomies are just as healthy as other men, if not more so (they may have been healthier to begin with). Scientists surveyed more than twenty thousand men for nearly one hundred diseases and health conditions. The only problem more common in men with vasectomy was local inflammation near the site of the operation, a known complication that happens infrequently and usually disappears within the first year after vasectomy.

Unfortunately, the technology for reversing a vasectomy is far less advanced than the operation itself. Reversal appears to work in about 70 percent of cases. But *anatomical success*, in which sperm reappear, is far more common than *functional success,* in which impregnation occurs.

Functional failure occurs because changes in the testicles and epididymides keep sperm counts far lower than prevasectomy levels. Semen quality after vasectomy reversal can be only as good as it was before vasectomy. Sometimes nerve endings are temporarily or permanently damaged during vasectomy, hampering the powerful contractions needed to move sperm to the urethra during ejaculation. In general, the longer the time since the vasectomy, the lower the chances of successful reversal. Reversibility also depends to some extent on the type of vasectomy. Some surgeons claim that open-ended vasectomy, in which the testicular side of the vas is left open, is nearly 100 percent reversible.

The vas anastomosis (vasectomy reversal) procedure takes from three to four hours and requires a highly skilled and experienced surgeon. Very few specialize in this microsurgery, which requires reattaching a vessel whose inner diameter is narrower than a human hair. The operation costs between $3,500 and $4,500. Most health insurance plans pay for the procedure.

Requests for vasectomy reversal are relatively rare. Surveys show that between 1 and 6 percent of men with vasectomies consider reversal, usually because they've remarried a younger woman with no children who wants to become pregnant. Perhaps for many men who associate fertility with manliness, knowing that vasectomy *can* be reversed may be more important than actually reversing it.

Safe Sex

A person who has a sex life can never be entirely free of risk of sexually transmitted disease (STD). The safest policy is sex with only one partner, who, like you, is monogamous. If you are between partners, this places a premium on finding someone with whom you can develop a trusting relationship and with whom you feel it is worth taking the ever-present risk. Although it is awkward to ask directly about a prospective partner's sexual history on the first date, you can, early on, learn whether that person dates many people or has had a long relationship with just one partner. When asking about exposure to a sexually transmitted disease, you can say, "I'm really concerned about STDs. I read about them so much these days." Then await the response. The number and gender of sex partners (and of their partners) are important because the risk of sexually transmitted disease rises with the number and, in the case of males, with the bisexuality of partners. Indeed, this is one area where a double standard applies. It is unimportant — in the disease-transmitting sense — for a man to know whether a woman has had sex with another woman, but it is vitally important for a woman to know whether a man has had sex with another man. If you feel reluctant to ask such questions, remember that the answers will affect your health and — in an age of AIDS — perhaps even your life (see AIDS, pp. 93–97).

The bottom line is to be sexually responsible. This means:

- Know the major warning signs of sexually transmitted disease: genital discharge, painful urination, sores and other skin changes, genital itching, and (mainly important in females) abdominal pain. Sometimes these symptoms are hidden.
- Avoid partners who have sores, rashes, or discharges in the genital area and who have had sex with many partners.
- *Ask questions* if you are not sure about a partner's sexual history; that is, look under the bed before getting in it.
- Use latex condoms or other barrier contraceptives if you or your partner has other sexual contacts or if you do not know your partner well. Use nonoxynol 9 spermicide for added protection.
- Consult a physician, STD clinic, family planning clinic, or hospital clinic immediately if you suspect you have a sexually transmitted disease. Do not try to diagnose or treat yourself.
- During treatment for an STD, avoid sexual contact even with a steady partner who is also being treated for the same infection. Otherwise, a "Ping-Pong" infection can result.
- Have regular checkups for STDs if you are sexually active in nonmonogamous relationships, even if you have no symptoms.
- Notify your sex partner(s) immediately — or have a physician or STD case specialist do so — if you suspect a sexually transmitted disease.

NOTE: Washing and urinating immediately after sex are good hygiene, but have not been shown to reduce the risk of STD.

Remember that even when worn throughout sexual foreplay and during and after sexual intercourse, latex condoms protect only the genital area, not other parts of the body. They are most effective against AIDS, gonorrhea, chlamydia, hepatitis B, and nongonococcal urethritis (NGU); they provide limited protection against herpes, syphilis, and genital warts. Condoms will not protect against crabs, scabies, or other diseases not restricted to the genital area. Spermicidal creams or foams containing nonoxynol 9 (available without prescription in drugstores) may provide some protection when used in combination with a condom. Diaphragms provide only limited protection against STDs, and oral contraceptives do not prevent them at all. Do not rely on cheap condoms that are likely to break, especially if you thrust forcefully or take a long time to climax. Buy either latex or natural lambskin condoms. (See pp. 82–83 for more information on condoms.)

The notification rule of sexual etiquette may be the hardest to observe. "Decent people don't get sexually transmitted diseases," the saying goes. The fact is that today *anybody* who has sex can become infected. Infection raises concerns about the fidelity of a sex partner. Some STDs can be contracted months or years earlier without producing symptoms. The temptation is great to avoid telling a sweetheart, fiancée, or spouse. Women in particular — who are least likely to have symptoms and most likely to unknowingly spread the disease — need to be told they have been exposed and to be encouraged to see a doctor. A partner who is not informed might have developed serious illness by the time symptoms appear.

A partner who has contracted an STD needs all the support you can give. Offering to take your partner to a physician or clinic, especially for the first visit, is supportive in both the emotional and the practical sense. It conveys that you care about your partner and helps that person share feelings of reluctance to seek treatment, fears of the unknown, and perhaps even anger. It also helps ensure that your partner has actually sought treatment and that you are minimizing the chances of serious illness in your partner, reinfection if your partner is not treated, and perhaps the spread of disease to others.

STD records are kept confidential by law; information about an infection will be given only to sex partners involved, and neither they nor anybody else will be given the name of the person who initially reported an STD infection. In most states, even minors can receive treatment without notifying their parents.

The VD National Hotline (toll-free) is 800-227-8922 (in California call 800-982-5883; in Alaska and Hawaii call the health department). The AIDS Hotline is 800-342-AIDS.

Sexually Transmitted Diseases

When penicillin and other antibiotics became widely available in the 1950s, it seemed as if sexually transmitted diseases might at last disappear. By the late 1970s, however, STD rates soared as divorce rates and sexual activity increased. Since then, a "new generation" of sexually transmitted diseases has appeared. While the public eye is on herpes and AIDS (Acquired Immune Deficiency Syndrome), many less publicized sexually transmitted diseases are threatening the health of millions, particularly young people in their teens and twenties.

Nobody knows how many cases of sexually transmitted disease occur, but the number is far greater than official statistics indicate. Of about twenty known sexually transmitted diseases, the U.S. Centers for Disease Control (CDC) tracks *reported* cases of only five: gonorrhea, syphilis, chancroid, lymphogranuloma venereum, and granuloma inguinale. However, the states report a far broader range of diseases to the CDC.

LEADING SEXUALLY TRANSMITTED DISEASES

	Estimated number of new cases annually (as of October 1986)
Gonorrhea	1,800,000
Syphilis	90,000
Genital herpes	500,000
AIDS (cumulative cases as of April 6, 1987)	33,700
Nongonococcal urethritis (nonchlamydial)	1,200,000
Chlamydial infections	4,600,000
Genital warts	1,000,000
Trichomoniasis	3,000,000
Lymphogranuloma venereum	226
Chancroid	2,067
Granuloma inguinale	44

SOURCE: Centers for Disease Control.

Gonorrhea

Gonorrhea, known as "the clap" (from the French *clapoir,* meaning brothel), is caused by bacteria that thrive in warm, moist mucous membranes that line the body openings. Gonorrhea is transmitted during heterosexual or homosexual contact, including sexual intercourse and oral sex (gonorrhea of the pharynx has been reported in both sexes). Gonorrhea is not acquired through casual exposure to towels, toilet seats, or the like.

In men, the first symptoms of gonorrhea are hard to miss: a thick, puslike discharge from the penis, also known as "the drip," "the whites," or "morning drop." The urethra becomes sensitive and inflamed, and urination causes burning or pain. While symptoms usually occur within a week after infection, some men have no symptoms at all.

More men than women develop gonorrhea, yet it is a greater health risk to women. Ninety percent of gonorrhea complications — including pelvic inflammatory disease, which can cause ectopic pregnancy (in which the embryo begins to grow outside the uterus) — affect women. Nearly 85 percent of women — compared with fewer than 20 percent of men — notice no symptoms until gonorrhea has progressed to a dangerous stage.

If the early symptoms of gonorrhea are untreated or unnoticed, they will disappear. The bacteria then move deeper into the genital and urinary tracts where, in the male, the most common complication is epididymitis — inflammation of the ducts that convey sperm out of the testicles. Some cases of gonorrhea may spontaneously disappear without treatment; however, this is usually unlikely. Gonococci can invade other body organs and cause permanent, even fatal, damage if left untreated. However, painful symptoms usually send the infected male to a doctor long before this happens.

Gonorrhea is relatively easy to treat with penicillin if detected early. Since painful urination and puslike discharge are not conclusive proof of gonorrhea, a physician usually orders a Gram stain test in which suspected gonococci can be identified in fifteen to twenty minutes. No blood test exists for gonorrhea. Although research scientists are working on a vaccine to prevent the disease, none is expected in the near future.

Meanwhile, the gonorrhea epidemic continues, in part because people treated for gonorrhea can get it again. Penicillin- and tetracycline-resistant strains of gonorrhea have become an increasing problem. While treatment with other antibiotics is possible, the new strains of gonorrhea make it even more difficult to stop its spread. The best way to prevent gonorrhea is to wear a condom in combination with a spermicide containing nonoxynol 9 during sexual intercourse, and be aware that this protects only the genitals.

Syphilis

Syphilis is caused by spirochete bacteria that enter the body during sexual contact through mucous membranes — including the sex organs, mouth, and anus. It is impossible to contract syphilis from a drinking glass, door knob, public toilet, or other casual contact because the bacteria can live only in human body tissues.

The symptoms of syphilis, like those of gonorrhea, may be hidden or absent, particularly in women. The first symptom — a sore called a chancre — may appear on the genitals from ten to ninety days after infection (the average is twenty-one days) or may not appear at all. Since the chancre does not hurt or itch, it may be overlooked or mistaken for something else. Within one to five weeks, the chancre heals spontaneously. Meanwhile, *untreated syphilis* continues to spread quietly throughout the body. Within six months, a rash or sores usually appear. These second-stage symptoms may be ignored because they, too, are mild or mistaken for other disorders. Symptoms disappear during the third or latent stage of syphilis, which lasts from five to more than twenty years. The late stage of untreated syphilis may cause no symptoms or may cause severe, even fatal, damage to the nervous system and other body organs.

A person with untreated syphilis generally can pass the disease to sex partners during the first year after infection, although certain second-stage symptoms may extend this period. Untreated persons well into the third or latent stage of syphilis are not infectious and may be symptom-free for years or a lifetime.

Syphilis can be detected by microscopic examination of fluids from the chancre or by blood tests descended from the famous Wassermann test. Like gonorrhea, syphilis can be cured with penicillin or other drugs if treated early. Even when detected late, syphilis can be cured, although already-damaged tissues cannot be restored. Home treatment of syphilis does not work. Salves and ointments do little more than disguise chancres and rashes.

There is no vaccine against syphilis: a person who is cured can contract it again. A condom worn throughout sex play and intercourse is the best protection against the disease, especially when used with a spermicide or lubricant containing nonoxynol 9.

Herpes

People worry too little about gonorrhea and syphilis and too much about herpes, probably because the media in recent years have focused on the disease's rising incidence and incurability. Yet herpes is a benign, self-limiting infection that causes only minor physical discomfort in most healthy individuals. Although the virus that causes herpes, once it enters the body, never leaves and can cause recurrences, the worst effect is that herpes infection can be passed to a baby during childbirth, usually by a mother who has no symptoms.

Symptoms of an active herpes infection include small, painful, blisterlike sores. They appear in the area of contact: on the genitals, anus, buttocks, thighs, lower back, or mouth. The sores begin as red bumps, may turn into blisters, and then into shallow ulcers with flat edges. They may be as small as a pin head or as large as a quarter. They appear singly or in clusters and often are slow to heal. In women, these sores may go unnoticed if they occur in the upper vagina and cervix. Symptoms appear from two to twelve days after exposure, and generally disappear within three weeks. Early in the course of infection, the virus migrates to nerve cell centers near the lower spinal cord, where the virus remains dormant. Weeks or years later, it may reactivate and return to the site of the original sore via the same nerve. Recurrences are usually milder and briefer than the first outbreak. About one-third of individuals who develop genital herpes infections have an average of three recurrences a year. But most individuals, especially those who maintain a healthy lifestyle, have no recurrences.

Herpes can be transmitted by sexual intercourse or by touching actively infected sores. Initially, it appeared that the virus could not be transmitted while the infection was inactive and causing no symptoms. But recent reports indicate that people with herpes can transmit the disease even when they have no visible sores or other symptoms. Oral sex is another means of transmission. This was discovered after scientists began finding type 1 herpes virus (which causes cold sores and fever blisters) on the genitals and type 2 virus (the genital variety) in cold sores around the mouth.

A new pill for genital herpes, acyclovir (marketed as Zovirax), became available in early 1985. For many people, it reduces the duration and severity of outbreaks and helps prevent recurrences, but it does not eliminate the virus from the body. The drug is intended for people who have frequent outbreaks. An ointment form of acyclovir has been available since 1982 for relief of an initial outbreak of herpes symptoms. The ointment does not prevent herpes from recurring and is not very effective after the first bout. National Institutes of Health scientists reported in May 1985 that they had developed a vaccine that prevents recurrent herpes virus infections in mice. A safe and effective vaccine for general human use, they say, will take many years to develop.

The main weapon against herpes is prevention, a difficult matter since the disease can be transmitted by people who do not know they have it, and even when symptoms are absent. Once lesions appear, sexual activity should stop until they are healing—this takes about seven to ten days—and scabs have fallen off. Condoms help prevent herpes but are not 100 percent effective. There is some evidence that using condoms in combination with spermicidal preparations containing nonoxynol 9 may help prevent spread of the disease.

Often, the worst damage herpes causes is emotional. Many people with the disease consider themselves—and often are considered—sexual lepers. The announcement "I have herpes" can so harm relationships that herpes support groups have been formed throughout the United States. The American Social Health Association keeps a list of local herpes support groups. The address is 260 Sheridan Avenue, Palo Alto, CA 94306. Call toll-free 800-227-8922 (in California, 800-982-5883). The association also operates the Herpes Resource Center, Box 100, Palo Alto, CA 94302; telephone 415-328-7710.

AIDS

Acquired Immune Deficiency Syndrome (AIDS), like herpes, has received enormous media coverage in recent years but, unlike herpes, is a deadly disease. As of April 6, 1987, about 33,700 cases of AIDS had been reported to the Centers for Disease Control (CDC) since 1981. More than 19,500, or 58 percent, of these individuals had died. The number of cases could rise to 270,000 through 1991, according to the Public Health Service.

AIDS is caused by the human immunodeficiency virus (HIV), also called the HTLV-3/LAV virus, that destroys white blood cells that help the immune system resist infection. This makes AIDS patients susceptible to a variety of rare and deadly illnesses, including *Pneumocystis carinii* pneumonia (dry cough and shortness of breath followed by weight loss), Kaposi's sarcoma (a rare form of cancer), and severe brain and nerve destruction.

Some HIV infections cause persistent fatigue, fever, loss of appetite and weight, diarrhea, night sweats, and swollen lymph nodes in the neck, armpits, or groin. These symptoms, known as the AIDS-related complex (ARC), may last a long time, may disappear, or may progress to full-blown AIDS.

In addition to reported cases, an estimated 1.5 million people in the U.S. currently are infected with the AIDS virus. Even though they may never develop symptoms of disease, all of them, scientists believe, can transmit it. From 20 to 30 percent — and perhaps more — of these infected individuals may eventually develop AIDS and associated ill-nesses. AIDS can take five years or longer to develop after infection with the virus.

There is a saying these days that when you sleep with somebody, you are not just sleeping with them, but with everybody they — and their partners — have slept with in the past. How far back in the past has not been determined. Sexual contact accounts for about 70 percent of all AIDS cases reported in the United States, the CDC reports. This transmission occurs through contact with body fluids — particularly the semen or blood — of infected persons. The AIDS virus can be transmitted by infected males to their male or female sex partners. Less commonly, female-to-male transmission occurs, often via prostitutes. Female-to-female sexual transmission has not been reported to the CDC as of this writing, and appears to be a less efficient mode of transmission. Female-to-infant transmission has occurred during preg-nancy and childbirth. Some recipients of blood transfusions also have been infected, but blood and blood products now are tested for anti-bodies to the AIDS virus and are considered safe. Antibodies are spe-cific substances produced in the blood in reaction to a microorganism such as the AIDS virus.

AIDS does not spread through casual contact with bodily secretions of AIDS patients or medical instruments that have been sterilized after being used to examine AIDS patients. Nor does AIDS spread by talk-ing, sneezing, coughing, or by insect bites, or tears, or by using an infected person's towel, glass, or swimming pool. Infected food han-dlers, likewise, do not transmit AIDS in food. Children do not acquire the disease by sharing the same classroom, or even the same house-hold, with a youngster or adult with AIDS. Even the research scien-tists, lab technicians, nurses, doctors, health care workers, and ambulance drivers exposed to AIDS patients have not become infected with the virus, except in a few cases when they have accidentally stuck themselves with needles used to take blood samples from AIDS pa-tients. As of this writing, none of these individuals had developed AIDS.

Ninety-five percent of AIDS cases have occurred in certain high-risk groups. Homosexual/bisexual men — including more than 2.5 million who are exclusively homosexual plus an estimated 5 to 10 million who have some homosexual contact — will remain at highest risk of AIDS. Also at high risk are past or present intravenous drug abusers, persons with clinical or laboratory evidence of infection, persons from Haiti and

Central Africa, male or female prostitutes and their sex partners, sex partners of persons who already are infected or who are in high-risk groups, persons with hemophilia who received clotting factor products before March 1985, persons who had transfusions with blood or blood products before March 1985, and newborn infants of high-risk or infected mothers. AIDS already has spread to the heterosexual community in the United States and, to an alarming degree, in Central Africa. The number of cases in the United States is expected to increase from 1,100 in 1986 to nearly 7,000 by 1991.

In the winter of 1987, the Public Health Service (PHS) published guidelines, *Facts About AIDS*, for preventing the spread of this disease. The PHS advises everybody to avoid having sex with persons who have AIDS, who have had a positive AIDS antibody test, or who are members of high-risk groups mentioned above. The PHS also advises against having sex with multiple partners or with people who have had multiple partners, and against using intravenous drugs and sharing needles or syringes.

The PHS suggests additional precautions for members of the general public who have sex with someone they think is infected. Although the PHS guidelines do not specifically say so, it seems prudent that persons who are sexually active and not in mutually faithful monogamous relationships also take the following steps to reduce the risk of AIDS:

- Avoid contact with body fluids, including blood, semen, urine, feces, saliva, and women's genital secretions (including menstrual blood).
- Use latex condoms for all sexual encounters. (Note: Studies suggest that natural membrane condoms are less effective than latex in preventing AIDS, and that use of a spermicide containing nonoxynol 9 may provide added protection against AIDS and herpes simplex infections.)
- Avoid practices that may injure body tissues — for example, anal intercourse.
- Avoid oral-genital contact.
- Avoid open-mouthed, intimate kissing.

In addition to the above, the PHS advises homosexual and bisexual men and others in high-risk groups to see a physician about taking the AIDS antibody test; to protect partners from contact with body fluids; and not to donate blood, plasma, body organs, other body tissue, or semen. The Public Health Service further advises that persons who have AIDS or who have tested positive for AIDS antibodies:

- Seek regular medical evaluation and follow-up.
- Either avoid sexual contact, or inform a prospective partner that they have AIDS or AIDS antibodies and protect him or her against contact with their body fluids during sex.
- Never share syringes, needles, toothbrushes, razors, or other instruments that could become contaminated with blood.
- Tell medical/dental personnel about having AIDS or AIDS antibodies.
- See a physician for periodic medical evaluations. In addition, women with a positive antibody test or AIDS are advised to avoid pregnancy.

The gay community has circulated even more explicit guides for gay men, whose rates of sexually transmitted disease have been decreasing, probably because many have adopted safer sex practices. These include using latex condoms for oral and anal sex, avoiding "fisting" and other practices that might tear the rectal wall, and avoiding flossing (which occasionally causes the gums to bleed) prior to oral sex or wet kissing. "Safe sex" guides can be ordered by calling the National Gay and Lesbian Crisis Line (800-221-7044, 3:00 P.M.–9:00 P.M., Monday to Friday) or the AIDS Hotline operated by the Public Health Service (800-342-AIDS).

A commercial blood test that detects the presence of antibodies to AIDS virus in the blood became available in March 1985. But the test may not detect AIDS virus that was acquired during the past six months. Therefore, a person with a negative AIDS antibody test should be retested six months after the last risky exposure to be reasonably sure test results are not false negative. The antibody test is used mainly to protect blood supplies and screen individuals in high-risk groups. Experts emphasize that the presence of antibodies means only that a person has been infected with the AIDS virus and is capable of transmitting the infection, not that he or she has symptoms or is necessarily going to develop AIDS. It may be advisable for people at risk of acquiring the AIDS virus to take the test. However, as Surgeon General Dr. C. Everett Koop noted in October 1986, *compulsory* AIDS blood tests are counterproductive in combating the spread of this disease.

Meanwhile, research scientists are searching for a vaccine to prevent AIDS and for drugs to cure it. Treatment with one experimental drug, AZT (azidothymidine), appears to halt the spread of AIDS virus in the body, but does not eliminate virus already infecting cells. Until scientists develop proven ways to prevent and treat AIDS, lifestyle changes — predicated on the question, "Is it worth the risk?" — are the best hope for halting its spread.

Hepatitis B

Hepatitis B is a liver infection thought to be spread by fecal contamination or by contaminated blood or blood products. It is now known to be caused by viruses increasingly transmitted by sexual contact. Hepatitis B occurs more frequently among homosexual and heterosexual men with many partners and among heterosexual men and women who practice oral-anal sex or anal intercourse.

Symptoms often resemble a case of flu or grippe. In severe cases, jaundice, dark urine, light-colored stools, and fatigue develop. Hepatitis B can lead to chronic liver inflammation that lasts for decades and to liver cancer. In addition, about 10 percent of people who contract hepatitis B become carriers of the virus thereafter. Even though they may be symptom-free, they can pass the disease on to others.

Hepatitis B can be prevented by avoiding the blood, semen, saliva, and feces of infected persons. The hepatitis B virus vaccine can prevent the disease in 85 to 95 percent of those vaccinated. While the vaccine is not intended for the general population, it is recommended for people whose jobs or lifestyles expose them to hepatitis B. A new genetically engineered vaccine appears as safe as the current vaccine made from human blood, and may be more effective and less expensive. This hepatitis B vaccine is strongly recommended for gay men who do not already have natural immunity from exposure to the hepatitis B virus. A blood test can identify those who are already immune.

Nongonococcal Urethritis and Other Sexually Transmitted Diseases

Currently the most common and least publicized sexually transmitted disease in American men is *nongonococcal urethritis* (NGU), or inflammation of the urethra. NGU usually — though not always — is caused by chlamydia, an organism that resembles both a virus and a bacterium.

In men, NGU symptoms resemble those of early gonorrhea: mild burning or tingling during urination and a slight clear or milky discharge. Because NGU symptoms tend to be mild, men sometimes postpone getting medical treatment. Chlamydial infections, like many other sexually transmitted diseases, are even more difficult to detect in women. To diagnose NGU correctly, a physician must rule out gonorrhea or other urological problems with appropriate tests.

Once diagnosed, NGU can be successfully treated with tetracycline or other antibiotics. Untreated infections can lead to prostate infections or to epididymitis, an inflammation of the sperm ducts inside the testicles. NGU frequently coexists with gonorrhea, but symptoms take longer to occur. Thus the CDC recommends that individuals treated for gonorrhea also be treated for chlamydia. Condoms and other barrier methods of birth control may help prevent the spread of chlamydial infections, as will notification and treatment of sex partners.

Trichomoniasis, or "trich," is infecting an increasing number of men. Caused by the protozoan *Trichomonas vaginalis,* it typically causes painful urination, clear discharge, and slight itching of the penis. Infected women may experience an odorous vaginal discharge and lesions. "Trich" is rarely transmitted by contact with recently contaminated objects, such as towels, shower curtains, and bathing suits. The main mode of transmission is direct sexual contact. A woman who is treated may have already transmitted the infection to her symptom-free partner, who may pass it back to her or to other partners. To successfully treat "trich," both sexual partners must take the drug metronidazol by mouth. It is important to complete the weeklong treatment. Some people stop taking medication in midcourse because symptoms have disappeared. This allows some *trichomonas* to survive and become more resistant to future treatment.

The list of common sexually transmitted diseases includes *genital warts,* soft pink growths that appear one to three months after sexual contact. Genital warts occur singly or in cauliflowerlike clusters in the genital and anal regions or in the throat. They are caused by the human papillomavirus (HPV) that is related to the one that causes common skin warts. Like common warts, genital warts usually are burned, frozen, or cut off. Two-thirds of people exposed to infected individuals develop genital warts. A condom worn during sexual intercourse may provide some protection against this disease.

One of the less common diseases that can be transmitted sexually is LGV, or *lymphogranuloma venereum.* Like NGU, it is caused by certain forms of chlamydiae. The disease is common in the tropics and semitropics. LGV causes a small lesion, usually on the genitals or rectum.

If left untreated, lesions will heal. But from one to four weeks later, nearby lymph nodes may become enlarged and filled with pus, and the genital organs may swell. LGV is harder to detect in women than men. The disease is transmissible through sexual contact as long as fluid is escaping from open lesions. LGV can be treated with antibiotics.

Chancroid and *granuloma inguinale* are uncommon in the United States. Chancroid usually starts as a single painful ulcer on the genitals surrounded by a reddish halo. Sometimes multiple ulcers appear. Granuloma inguinale — also named Donovanosis after the man who discovered the bacterium that causes it — is characterized by spreading sores on the genitals, thighs, or lower stomach. Both diseases are far more common in men than women, although prostitutes often transmit the disease in areas where chancroid is common. If detected and treated early with antibiotics, the infections are insignificant. But reexposure can cause a new infection.

Several other severe intestinal infections — including amebiasis, shigellosis, and giardiasis — can also be transmitted through sexual contact, as well as through unsanitary food handling. These diarrheal diseases have increased markedly in the homosexual community, where they are called "the gay bowel syndrome." This is a misnomer since these infections also affect heterosexual men and women who practice oral-anal sex or anal intercourse.

Crab lice are probably the most contagious, and least serious, sexually transmitted disease. The chances of contracting "crabs" from one sexual exposure to an infected partner are extremely high. Moreover, "crabs" can easily be acquired by sharing clothing or sleeping in the same bed with other infected persons. Crabs usually invade the pubic hair. Infestations can be detected with the aid of a magnifying glass. Even if the lice are not present, their nits (eggs) are usually cemented to pubic hairs. They resemble dandruff, but do not brush off as easily.

Crabs can be eliminated with a 1 percent gamma benzene hexachloride (Kwell) shampoo, available with a physician's prescription. Another prescription shampoo is Nix, and an over-the-counter shampoo is Rid. Infested clothing and bedding should be either machine-washed, dry-cleaned, ironed, or machine-dried on a hot cycle. Although crabs can be treated at home, sexually active individuals with this infection probably should be examined by a physician for other sexually transmitted diseases. All sex partners should also be treated to prevent the spread of crabs.

One-Night Stands

The dictionary defines a one-night stand as a performance by a traveling musician. To most people, however, a sexual one-night stand usually occurs with no intention of repeating the experience or of getting to know the partner better.

The question is how one-night stands affect physical and emotional health. Before the era of concern about STDs, and AIDS in particular, casual sex was popular, especially among women who felt free to have sexual adventures once forbidden them. For some people, one-night stands can be satisfying, certainly in the physical sense. They satisfy the primal urge for newness and sometimes help you explore your sexuality. Many people feel that "I got married in my early twenties, and I've never had any sexual experience." Casual sex can also — at certain times in your life — be a search for a suitable partner, or a search for yourself.

But when casual sex substitutes for a loving and close relationship, when it becomes "sport sex," or when it is sought to gratify neurotic urges, it can be harmful. Many "swingers," for example, fear intimate and lasting relationships. They have been hurt emotionally in the past and fear risking another loss. They seek alliances that end automatically without pain or hassle.

Some people seek self-esteem through sexual conquest. They wish to avoid the realities of thinning hair, thickening waistlines, advancing age, and receding beauty. Some seek escape from domestic strife and responsibility. Others are rebelling against authority, personified by their spouse.

Habitual one-night stands for such reasons can lead to anxiety, remorse, rejection, disillusionment, frustration, and emptiness, not to mention AIDS and other sexually transmitted diseases. Yet many people have experienced one-night stands, either unintentionally or deliberately, with no ill effects. As a steady diet, however, sex without love can starve the body and spirit.

The Pleasure Bond

The problem is as old as human history. William Masters and Virginia Johnson, with Robert Levin, wrote about it in *The Pleasure Bond: A New Look at Sexuality and Commitment*. A current book with a similar theme, *How to Make Love to the Same Person for the Rest of Your Life (and Still Love It)*, was written by Dagmar O'Connor, who trained under Masters and

Johnson and directs the Sexual Therapy Program at St. Luke's–Roosevelt Hospital in New York. The problem is how to keep alive the physical attraction and sexual excitement that initially bring two people together, and how to keep repeated sex with the same person from becoming a stale and unrewarding routine.

Both books explore why the initially intense feelings seem to decline for so many couples and why passion seems so predicated on newness. Much of the decline stems from too many "shoulds" surrounding sexual pleasure. These include the myths that touching should always lead to sexual excitement, that sexual excitement should always lead to sexual intercourse, that sexual intercourse should always lead to orgasm, that sex is a physical skill that should be practiced like dancing or tennis, and that the man should have all the answers in bed. Males, according to myth, are sexual athletes, while females have limited enthusiasm for sex, especially after marriage. Meanwhile, both partners tend to adapt their behavior to such expectations.

A primary passion-killer is failure to communicate about sex (or anything else). Amazingly few people who sleep together speak freely about what turns them on (and off), let alone about differences in sexual desire, contraception, and the possibility of sexually transmitted diseases, according to William Masters, Virginia Johnson, and Robert Kolodny in their book *Masters and Johnson on Sex and Human Loving*. By daring to express yourself on such topics, you dare to be yourself and to let your partner be herself.

The Pleasure Bond focuses on couples who are satisfied with their relationships and can successfully negotiate differences in sexual desire. Negotiation is simpler, Masters and Johnson concluded, if both partners share the same basic beliefs about sex and base their relationship on genuine equality. This means that each partner accepts the other as the final authority on his or her sexual feelings. Equality also means that the male gives up responsibility for always being the expert and for being the perpetually potent instrument of *her* sexual pleasure.

Equality helps assure "mutuality," which Masters and Johnson define as an effort by each partner to discover what is best for both. Instead of proving who is right and who is wrong, each has concern for the other. Each accepts the other as a vulnerable human being with unique needs, expectations, and capabilities. Each approaches problems — sexual and otherwise — in a neutral, nonblaming way, and each shares responsibility for the failure or success of their efforts. In their studies of successful couples, Masters and Johnson have discovered that efforts to change are more important than actually making changes. Often the differences that divide two people are not over *making love*, but over *feeling loved*. If one partner sees the other trying to change, he or she feels valued, needed, and desired.

The knowledge that differences can be resolved builds loyalty and trust and heightens sexual pleasure in bed. Masters and Johnson have found that unresolved differences have the opposite effect: "Suppressed resentment or unhappiness tends to short-circuit sexual feelings, and desire goes dead."

The pleasure bond, Masters and Johnson conclude, is forged through a sustained sexual relationship that allows both partners to express their individuality. While it is important for a man to know — through sexual relationships with other women — that he is like other men, and for a woman to know that she is like other women, there is a greater need to be appreciated as a unique individual. The message of sexual infidelity is (1) "You do not meet my most basic physical and emotional needs" and (2) "You are not a unique, irreplaceable source of satisfaction and pleasure." The message of sexual fidelity is "You are worth the effort it takes to maintain our bond."

People united in the pleasure bond are committed. What is commitment, besides something many people say they do not want? Commitment is a pledge to do something. Someone promises and keeps the promise. Trust is requested, given, and repaid. Commitment can exist for practical or emotional reasons. In the latter case, a person promises because he or she cares about the other. Marriage does not necessarily produce commitment. A woman may be committed to being a loyal wife and mother, yet never entrust her husband with her deepest feelings.

Men and women who say "I don't want a commitment" probably mean they do not want to be burdened with expectations, unwritten assumptions, and dependencies. But these burdens have nothing to do with commitment, which is simply an expression of trust, and the straightest path to sex that is both healthy and good.

At Ease:
Sleep and Rest

How Much Sleep?

You will probably spend 220,000 hours, or twenty to twenty-five years, or one-third of your life sleeping if you live an average life expectancy. The average person needs seven to eight hours of sleep daily. That is the amount of sleep two-thirds of a population sample of about nine million Americans over age eighteen reported in a 1985 survey by the National Center for Health Statistics (NCHS).

But many people thrive on fewer than six or more than nine hours of sleep. About two people in ten (including slightly more men) sleep fewer than six hours daily, and about one in ten (including slightly more women) sleep more than nine hours, according to the NCHS. Albert Einstein needed up to twelve hours of sleep nightly. Thomas Edison needed about five. Even these hours Edison begrudged spending in sleep, and he expressed the hope that the electric light would change the human need to slumber all night, as indeed it did. A modern medical journal describes a seventy-year-old woman who reported feeling fine after having slept only an hour each day since childhood. During a week of medical observation, she averaged sixty-seven minutes of sleep daily, without apparent ill effect.

Sleep needs, like shirt sizes, are highly individual, as anybody knows who has tried to make his natural sleep pattern conform to someone else's. The amount of sleep you need is determined by your genes, metabolism, general physical health, lifestyle, and other factors that change from time to time. Sleep needs also decrease with age. According to Lynne Lamberg in *The American Medical Association Guide to Better Sleep*, you are born needing 16 to 18 hours of sleep daily. By age two, this declines to about 12 hours daily. From ages six to fourteen, most children need 8½ to 9 hours daily, and from age fifteen onward, 7½ to 8. After age sixty sleep becomes fragmented and people tend to sleep fewer than 7½ to 8 hours, not because they *need* less sleep, but because they awaken frequently during the night. Even so, they do not lose great amounts of sleep, because these awakenings are brief. Many older people make up for lost sleep by napping during the day.

Even if you have been awake for days, you probably need only one long night's sleep to recover. You do not have to "pay back" for lost sleep on an hour-for-hour basis. One seventeen-year-old who stayed awake eleven days for a science fair research project needed only fifteen hours of sleep to recover. You may also find that you sleep an extra hour or so on weekends to make up for sleep "lost" during the week. But this "making up" sometimes has disadvantages. If, for example, you make up for lost sleep by sleeping when you usually are awake and active, you are apt to suffer the "blahs" and awaken feeling tired and grouchy rather than rejuvenated. This happens because sleep is a biological rhythm, and your body is sensitive not only to its *amount* but its *timing*.

Despite the growth of sleep research studies, scientists still do not know why sleep is necessary. Sleep appears to rest and energize your body and, some researchers hypothesize, to restore your immune system. During sleep you secrete growth hormone, which some scientists report helps renew worn-out tissues, form red blood cells, aid bone synthesis, and, during adolescence, promote growth. Sleep's greatest gift may be that it restores you mentally, even though your mind does not truly rest when you sleep.

What, then, are the consequences of insufficient sleep, besides sleepiness? "Take hope and sleep from man," said the philosopher Immanuel Kant, "and he is the most wretched creature on earth." Sleep studies show that occasional sleep loss — whether caused by staying up too late or by insomnia — by itself does not endanger your health, although it may affect your mood. Consistent lack of sleep makes you drowsy, irritable, fatigued, inefficient, anxious, and unable to concentrate. It also raises the risk of accidents and athletic injuries. One study in 1979 showed that otherwise healthy people who habitually slept substantially less — or more — than average were far more likely to die within six years than controls who slept normal hours. As a 1982 report called *Stress and Human Health*, by the National Academy of Sciences, noted, "There are many potential explanations for this finding, but they all imply a complex relationship between sleep habits and general health." At the 1986 meeting of the Association of Professional Sleep Societies, psychologist David Dinges reported that 50 to 60 percent of adults may be chronically sleep-deprived. These people can function on as little as half of their usual amount of sleep as long as they remain motivated, he said. Below that amount of sleep, however, their ability to drive a car or operate other machinery deteriorates dangerously.

Sometimes you get more sleep than you think. Sleep lab experiments show that even insomniacs doze off for thirty- to sixty-minute stretches, even though they insist they slept only a few minutes. Just lying awake without moving can be almost as restful as sleeping, which is nice to know after suffering through a sleepless night.

Ultimately, only you can determine whether you are getting enough sleep. If you awaken feeling refreshed, alert, and cheerful, you are sleeping enough, whether for six hours or ten. But if you fall asleep during the day when you do not want to, have accidents or near-accidents while driving, and hate getting up in the morning, you probably need more sleep.

Some people tend to regard sleep as a waste of time and try to subsist on less sleep than they need. Most American adults are "chronically sleep-deprived," says Dr. William Dement, director of the Sleep Disorders Center at Stanford University. Another sleep researcher once theorized that if you sleep so efficiently that you need two hours less sleep each day, you could prolong your active (working) life by three years without changing your life span. The researcher tried to train laboratory animals, and then humans, to sleep less. But as soon as his experiments ended, his subjects reverted to their former sleep patterns. However, Lynne Lamberg's *American Medical Association Guide to Better Sleep* cites recent studies in humans showing that people *can* learn to sleep one to two fewer hours. This suggests that sleep, to some extent, is a learned behavior.

Normal Sleep

Sleep occurs in approximately ninety-minute cycles consisting of REM or rapid eye movement ("active") sleep and non-REM ("quiet") sleep. Slumber begins with non-REM sleep as brain waves become slow and regular, body temperature drops, and the five senses shut down. Paradoxically, you change body positions more often during the quiet phase of sleep. After about eighty minutes of non-REM sleep, you are ready for the REM phase. Your eyes dart behind closed lids, your heartbeat rises, your breathing and brain waves quicken and become irregular. Your toes and fingers twitch, but your body otherwise remains paralyzed. You dream, often vividly, for about ten minutes.

Another cycle of deep non-REM sleep begins. Thereafter, the REM or dreaming part of the cycle increases from ten to almost forty minutes by the final ninety-minute sleep cycle, while the non-REM periods of sleep grow shorter. Thus your first few hours of sleep are the soundest. An adult who sleeps 7½ hours will experience four to five cycles of non-REM/REM sleep and will spend a total of 1½ to 2 hours in REM sleep.

At one time scientists thought that REM sleep was essential to psychological health. They now report that REM sleep may serve a different function: learning. Recent studies in animals and humans show that lack of REM sleep impairs your ability to remember.

Sleep Rhythm Disturbances

Sleep research is a relatively new field. In 1975 there were only five sleep clinics in the United States; today there are about 150 members of the Association of Sleep Disorders Centers. Scientists at these centers have already identified some 120 disorders that disturb the sleep of one in five Americans. One of the greatest advances of sleep research has been to identify sleep rhythm disturbances as a problem of *timing* of sleep, rather than as a problem of sleeping per se. Perhaps you are convinced that you are an insomniac because your bedmate thinks you are not getting enough sleep. (She needs nine hours while you thrive on six.) Or you retire at 10:00 P.M. and your partner informs you the next morning that you tossed and turned until 2:00 A.M. The problem may be not insomnia, but different sleep needs and patterns.

Sleep patterns are governed by an internal biological clock — known as circadian rhythm (from the Latin *circa* [about] and *dies* [a day]). This biological rhythm governs your body temperature (making it drop at night and rise during the day), heart rate, blood pressure, hormone secretions, and other body functions. The circadian rhythm concept explains why some people function better in the morning and others better in the evening. The morning types experience rapid rises in body temperature soon after awakening and sleep-inducing drops in body temperature around 7:30 P.M. Evening people, by contrast, experience more gradual rises in body temperature throughout the day until it starts to drop at about 8:30 P.M.

Most people operate on a twenty-five-hour circadian cycle. Some, however, have a twenty-five- to twenty-seven-hour cycle, which causes a form of permanent "jet lag." Unable to fall asleep at their desired bedtime of 10:00 P.M., they lie awake until 2:00 or 3:00 A.M. Once they fall asleep, they can — if schedules permit — slumber a normal seven to eight hours and awaken refreshed. Their friends and family sometimes think they are lazy. Actually they are victims of the "delayed-sleep-phase syndrome." They fall asleep and awaken later than they wish because their timing is off.

Many victims of the "delayed-sleep-phase syndrome" try to change their natural rhythms with sedatives, psychotherapy, hypnosis, and biofeedback — usually to no avail. One treatment that seems to work is chronotherapy, or putting such individuals on a twenty-seven-hour day. They stay up, and then wake up, two to three hours later each day until they work clockwise around the clock to a normal bedtime and early morning awakening. Once chronotherapy puts these delayed sleepers in phase with the rest of the world, they tend to sleep normally again.

Shift work causes another kind of time-related sleep problem. About 27 percent of men and 16 percent of women rotate work schedules, according to the National Center for Health Statistics. People who work shifts can adapt to daytime sleeping after about ten days. But if work schedules rotate more often and in a counterclockwise direction, they can disrupt not only sleep, but other biological rhythms and work performance. You might have no trouble with short, stimulating tasks but nod off during boring or repetitive routines. If your job is driving a sixteen-wheeler or controlling air traffic at a busy airport, this could be disastrous. At best, you might tend, as many shift workers do, to overindulge in coffee and other stimulants to stay awake, and alcohol or sleeping pills to fall asleep.

A temporary type of "delayed-sleep-phase syndrome" afflicts people who are the life of the party on Saturday night, sleep late Sunday morning, and are insomniacs on Sunday night. When Monday morning work time rolls around, they are like zombies. Some researchers suggest that altered weekend sleep schedules may be a primary cause of "blue Mondays."

Insomnia

Insomnia, broadly defined, is inability to get the sleep you need to function efficiently when you are awake. Somnologists (sleep experts) define an insomniac as somebody who *complains* about trouble falling asleep or staying asleep, early morning awakenings, or any combination thereof.

A panel of sleep experts who met at the National Institutes of Health in November 1983 defined insomnia in terms of its severity: transient, short-term, and long-term. *Transient insomnia* afflicts normal sleepers who experience acute stress for several days that affects their sleep adversely. Travelers with jet lag or people undergoing brief hospitalizations often experience transient insomnia.

Short-term insomnia may last up to three weeks and is typically related to an extremely stressful situation, such as death or loss of a loved one, loss of a job, unpaid bills, or health worries.

Long-term, or chronic, insomnia lasts for months or even years and is seldom related to any specific event or stressor. It afflicts people who abuse alcohol or drugs; who have underlying psychiatric and medical problems, sleep rhythm disturbances, or sleep disorders such as myoclonus (leg twitching); or who have "conditioned insomnia," that is, who have learned to expect to sleep badly.

An estimated one-third of the U.S. population suffers from some degree of insomnia. More women than men are insomniacs. After age forty, women with long-term insomnia outnumber men almost eight to one.

Insomniacs may or may not experience actual sleep disturbance, defined as wakefulness that can be measured by an electroencephalogram (EEG). Researchers have discovered that insomniacs may doze off for thirty minutes or more. Some sleep half the night or longer without realizing it. Yet this does not mean that insomnia is "all in the head." Insomniacs may sense a severe defect in the quality of their sleep that cannot be traced by an EEG, yet still produces the agonies of sleep lack.

Insomnia is not a disorder but a symptom with as many psychological as physical causes. Insomnia may be caused by depression, anxiety, grief, or adverse reactions to stress. Some researchers hypothesize that these troubled states of mind cause changes in brain chemistry that affect sleep.

Physical causes of long-term insomnia include duodenal ulcer, angina (chest pain), heartburn, liver and kidney problems, arthritis, migraine headache, pregnancy, itching, asthma, and sleep apnea (breath stoppage during sleep; see pp. 114–115). Insomnia — especially nighttime awakenings — also increases as you grow older and sleep less efficiently than during your youth.

Environmental noise and room temperature can cause insomnia, as can behaviors that reinforce sleeplessness: too much time in bed, irregular sleeping schedules, napping, drug use, and heavy drinking. Alcohol may lull you to sleep, but withdrawal a few hours later will probably wake you up again. People who smoke often lie awake at night. An unpronounceable cause of insomnia is agrypniaphobia: fear of not being able to sleep.

Sleep Hygiene

If, as W. C. Fields once advised, "the best cure for insomnia is to get a lot of sleep," the worst may well be sleeping pills. Prescription and over-the-counter sleep drugs are among the most frequently taken drugs in America. They relieve occasional sleeplessness, but lose their effect after about three weeks, requiring increasingly higher doses. Sleeping pills such as flurazepam stay in the body longer than the few hours needed to aid sleep and may decrease daytime alertness and visual-motor coordination needed for driving. With continuing use, sleeping pills may become habit-forming.

Barbiturates are the most dangerous of the sleep medications because they can be lethal in high doses and cause drug dependence. They also suppress REM or "dreaming" sleep, which rebounds, or "takes over again," when you stop the drug. This, in turn, reduces time spent in deep, non-REM sleep and causes disturbing dreams and daytime fatigue.

Benzodiazepines, considered safer and more effective than barbiturates, are the sleep medications most physicians prescribe today. Still, the panel of experts that met at the National Institutes of Health in November 1983 recommended taking benzodiazepines such as flurazepam in the lowest possible doses for the shortest possible periods of time, with even lower doses for elderly people whose bodies tend to overreact to many drugs.

For short-term insomnia, the NIH panel recommended good sleep hygiene and, if that fails, a short-acting benzodiazepine for three weeks maximum, and preferably less. The panel advised using sleep drugs no more than three nights in a row and skipping nightly doses after one or two good nights of sleep. But you should:

- never mix sleeping pills with alcohol — the combination can be deadly;
- never use sleeping pills if you have kidney or liver problems, or are taking other medications.

In *The American Medical Association Guide to Better Sleep*, Lynne Lamberg reports that many sleep specialists recommend two aspirins at bedtime for occasional insomnia, or 1 to 2 grams of tryptophan, available in health food stores as a "dietary supplement."

How else can you help yourself get a good night's sleep? First, do not panic. Some people sleep more efficiently than others, and occasional sleep loss does not endanger your health. Many people overestimate how much sleep they need and underestimate how much they get during a restless night. Second, cultivate habits that will help you sleep. If insomnia lasts three weeks or longer, seek medical attention.

Good Sleep Hygiene

1. Exercise in the late afternoon at least three days a week. Regular exercise tends to deepen sleep. But exercising in the evening may cause overexertion and muscle fatigue and make it harder to sleep.
2. Work, eat, and sleep on schedule.
3. Do not oversleep in the morning, especially on weekends.
4. Do not nap if you sleep poorly at night.
5. Do not eat heavy meals or spicy foods near bedtime.
6. Avoid caffeinated coffee, tea, colas, and painkillers containing caffeine two to four hours before bedtime. (One "insomniac" was drinking thirty cups of coffee a day!)
7. Avoid smoking and nightcaps. The former may keep you awake, and the latter may lull you to sleep, but it will be light, unsettled sleep.
8. Keep your bedroom as cool as possible.
9. Bathe in warm water. A hot bath or shower will wake you up.
10. Reserve the bedroom for sleep and sex: no television, arguing with your bedmate, or brooding about business and personal problems within its walls.
11. Relax an hour or so before going to bed. Wind down with a dull book, watch television (but not in bed), or drink a glass of warm milk. The latter contains an amino acid, tryptophan, that has been reported to have sleep-inducing properties.

12. Go to bed only when you feel sleepy.
13. If you cannot fall asleep within ten to fifteen minutes, get up, go to another room, and read or do something boring. If sleepiness does not occur within fifteen minutes, repeat the process. Do not panic. Sleep, like sex, becomes more elusive the harder you try to make it happen. You might even use reverse psychology and try to stay awake all night.
14. Try soft wax earplugs if you have trouble sleeping. They block noises that can interfere with sound sleep.
15. A footnote on sex: its aftermath may be relaxing for some men and overstimulating for others. If you are in the former category, sex may be the ultimate "sleeping pill."

If, after three weeks, insomnia still plagues you, see a physician about possible underlying physical causes. If none can be found, he or she may recommend behavior therapy to help you improve your sleep habits, relaxation/biofeedback training to improve stress management, or psychotherapy to explore underlying emotional problems. A physician may also prescribe intermittent use of a sleep medication. If none of these approaches works, you might ask for a referral to one of the approximately two hundred sleep research centers in the United States.

Snore Wars

"Laugh and the whole world laughs with you," British novelist Anthony Burgess once said. "Snore and you sleep alone." Hence residents of a U.S. Army barracks carried a snorer out into the rainy night some years ago and left him, still snoring, on the lawn. Elsewhere, victims of snore wars — sleep-starved spouses, lovers, and roommates — resort to earplugs, elbow jabs, nasal pinches, and separate bedrooms. One woman attacked her snoring husband with a billy club, an outburst he later noted in divorce court.

What, exactly, is this snogczzzzzzz!! thnxxxzzz!!! that drives so many to the edge of madness? Until recently, medical scientists have ignored snoring. Today it is recognized as a true medical problem. A snore is born during deep sleep. The tongue slips to the rear of the mouth, and the soft palate and surrounding throat tissues relax. When this happens, the airway becomes flabby, like the neck of a balloon. The narrowing of the airway is aggravated by enlarged tonsils and adenoids, flaccid soft palates, nasal polyps (protrusions from the mucous membranes in the nose), deviated septums (the cartilage between the nostrils), other nasal deformities and obstructions, allergies, infected sinuses, and nasal congestion.

Lifestyles compound the problem. Snorers tend to be overweight and sedentary. Sometimes they wear loose dentures. Snorers often smoke and drink too much. These last two habits irritate the nasal passages and throat, causing them to swell and block the flow of air. Some people think snoring stems from sleeping on one's back. But snorers are of two basic types: those who snore occasionally and those who snore every night. The former tend to snore in one position — usually on their backs. The latter snore in all positions.

An estimated 30 million people — about one out of every eight Americans — snore. According to Dr. David. N. F. Fairbanks, an otolaryngologist (ear, nose, and throat specialist) who practices head and neck surgery in Washington, D.C., men tend to snore more than women, although the differences decrease with age. At age thirty to thirty-five, for example, 20 percent of men snore versus 5 percent of women. By age sixty, however, 60 percent of men versus 40 percent of women snore. There is no good scientific explanation of this "snoring gap." Anthropologists facetiously suggest it may be a carryover from prehistoric times when men needed to make ferocious noises to frighten off nocturnal predators and protect their families.

The sounds of snoring are infinite in variety. There are sonorous nores (long and rippling) and snarking snores (short and staccato), deep-throated and nasal snores, supine and prone snores, petit and grand snores, and stentorian snores. The latter are named after the mythical character Stentor, whose voice, described in *The Iliad*, equaled those of fifty ordinary men.

The late Sir Winston Churchill, according to a naval officer who measured the sound level, could snore at 35 decibels. *The Guinness Book of World Records*, however, reports that Sir Winston was surpassed by a fellow Britisher whose snore registered 85 decibels, or about the loudness of a diesel engine heard from the back seat of a transcontinental bus.

A common and serious problem of snorers is daytime sleepiness. In a study of eighty-three snoring adults by Dr. Fairbanks, three snorers fell asleep waiting for a red light to change; one fell asleep eating dinner; and one dozed off while talking to his wife. Occasionally, the breathing of habitual snorers is so seriously disturbed during sleep that their hearts, brains, and other organs are deprived of oxygen. This can cause their hearts to pump less efficiently, to slow down, and to beat irregularly. (See the section on sleep apnea, pp. 114–115.)

Hundreds of remedies for snoring have been tried through the years, including exercises to develop the muscles that hold the mouth closed. However, some people snore even with their mouths closed; others snore while lying on their sides or stomachs or even while sitting up.

Among the many cures for snoring that do not work, or are downright dangerous, are more than three hundred devices registered in the U.S. Patent and Trademark Office. These include gadgets that attach to the snorer's back to force him to sleep on his side, chin and head straps, mouth inserts, and electrical devices that emit sounds or shocks during snoring. At least 80 percent of people can be cured of snoring with surgical correction of abnormalities in their noses, soft palates, uvulae, and pharynges. But simple lifestyle remedies should be tried first.

To lessen mild and occasional snoring, Dr. David Fairbanks recommends that you

- Exercise daily to develop good muscle tone and lose weight.
- Avoid alcoholic beverages for at least three hours before bedtime.
- Avoid tranquilizers, sleeping pills, and antihistamines before bedtime because they relax the muscles above the Adam's apple that are supposed to keep the airway open and prevent snoring.
- Sleep on your side rather than on your back (attach a tennis ball to the back of your pajamas).
- Place bricks under the bedposts at the head of your bed to raise it.
- Avoid thick pillows that kink your neck or tuck in your chin. Instead, stuff a pillow under your shoulders so your head is extended.
- Try to keep awake until your bed partner falls asleep first.
- Give your partner earplugs — the soft wax kind are comfortable and drown out snoring, but not telephones, fire alarms, or distress calls.

If snoring is habitual and heavy, see a physician who specializes in ear, nose, and throat problems. The remedy can be as simple as having nasal allergies and infections treated or having a surgeon correct abnormalities of the nose, soft palate, uvula, or pharynx.

Sleep Apnea

Snorers who are chronically sleepy may have obstructive sleep apnea (from the Greek "want of breath"). The official definition of sleep apnea is stoppage of breathing for at least ten seconds more than seven times per hour. Typically, this potentially life-threatening condition causes people to stop breathing for thirty to sixty seconds and then snort loudly as they struggle for a new breath of air. They may stop breathing hundreds of times during the night without ever being aware of their problem, causing inefficient and unrestful sleep. During waking hours — a misnomer since they are apt to be extremely sleepy — their breathing is normal. Only their bedmates are likely to detect the apnea. Indeed, the main reason a person with sleep apnea sees a physician is because "everyone is mad at his snoring, especially his wife." Another common complaint is excessive daytime sleepiness that interferes with work, driving, or personal relationships. Morning headaches also are common.

An estimated 40 to 50 percent of the population over age fifty may have an occasional sleep apnea episode, but that is of little consequence compared with medically significant apnea, which affects four to five million Americans. The typical victim is a somewhat overweight, over-fifty male. But women and children also may have serious apnea. In obstructive sleep apnea, the common and serious form, the muscles of the throat collapse during sleep and *completely* block the air flow, whereas in snoring the blockage is only partial. The causes of apnea and snoring are the same.

Anyone who suspects he or she has apnea should see a physician. Some cases of apnea can be treated with a drug that stimulates breathing. Others require more drastic treatment with a tracheostomy, in which a surgeon opens the windpipe and allows air to bypass obstructions in the throat. This treatment is usually reserved for severe cases. According to Dr. Fairbanks, a surgical procedure known as UPPP (uvulopalatopharyngoplasty) helps about half of the patients with severe apnea recover completely, and helps 80 percent of those with earlier stages of the disease. The procedure involves shortening the uvula and soft palate and removing the tonsils and other masses or flabby tissues in the throat.

In a relatively new nonsurgical treatment, some sleep apnea patients wear a lightweight face mask attached to an air compressor that provides steady air pressure during sleep. But these devices are more successful in theory than in practice. In theory, weight loss could alleviate some cases of apnea associated with obesity, but in practice it is difficult to achieve.

People with sleep apnea should avoid taking sleeping pills or any other type of sedative. Sleeping pills can make breathing difficulties worse and are extremely dangerous. Many of the nation's top sleep researchers believe that apnea — combined with sleeping pills, barbiturates, tranquilizers, antihistamines, alcohol, and other drugs that depress breathing — could be one of the major causes of sudden death in adults at night.

Sleep experts also suspect that sleep apnea may be a major factor in heart disease and stroke. Breathing stoppages that are frequent and prolonged create a serious oxygen lack in the body that places a great strain on the heart and blood circulation. Over half of sleep apnea patients, Dr. Fairbanks says, have developed high blood pressure by the time they come to a physician's attention, and virtually all suffer irregular heart rhythms during sleep. One researcher found that men who stopped breathing in sleep had lower levels of oxygen in their blood than the women with sleep apnea whom he studied. As with snoring, apnea is more common and troublesome in men.

Narcolepsy and Other Sleep Problems

Insomniacs have trouble falling asleep. Narcoleptics have trouble staying awake. They suffer from bouts of uncontrollable sleepiness that make them likely to drop off at odd moments: in midsentence, while laughing at a joke, or while making love. One athlete fell asleep while riding a ski lift, another on the mat while waiting for a wrestling match to begin. These sudden urges to sleep may occur even while driving. Indeed, narcolepsy is a suspected cause of many fatal automobile accidents involving drivers who fell asleep at the wheel.

A common symptom of narcolepsy is abrupt loss of muscle control (cataplexy), usually triggered by emotions such as laughter, anger, surprise, or elation. One man had cataplexy attacks after getting a good hand at bridge. Narcolepsy is often mistaken for other types of daytime sleepiness, such as postlunch lulls and boring lectures. It is also confused with hypersomnia: need to sleep from ten to eighteen hours a day. Nobody knows what causes narcolepsy, although some sleep experts suspect defects in the central nervous systems or "biological clocks" of narcoleptics. There is no evidence of a psychological cause.

The disease usually appears between puberty and age forty and affects men and women equally. Narcolepsy appears to run in families and has no cure, although symptoms can be controlled once a person knows he or she is afflicted. Many narcoleptics spend up to fifteen years seeking help from three to five physicians before their disease is diagnosed correctly. Dr. William C. Dement of Stanford University, a leading authority on narcolepsy, calls it "a condition absolutely destructive to the personality and spirit." The American Narcolepsy Association was founded to help the estimated 250,000 Americans who have this condition. The address is 335 Quarry Road, Belmont, CA 94002; telephone 415-591-7979.

Another sleep problem, myoclonus (from *myo* meaning "muscle" and *clonus* meaning "spasm"), is characterized by strong, involuntary leg jerks that wake the sleeper. Like apnea, it may produce the sensation of not sleeping well and of daytime sleepiness. An anticonvulsant drug can relieve the condition.

Dreams

Some people claim they never dream. But sleep researchers know that most sleepers dream during "rapid eye movement" sleep that occurs four to six times during the night. The first dreams last only a few minutes, while predawn dreams may last an hour. Still, most dreams are quickly forgotten and hence denied.

While the reasons for dreaming remain undiscovered, many people have learned they are handy devices for creating new ideas, changing attitudes and behavior in positive ways, and letting the brain process new information. Robert Louis Stevenson, while writing *Dr. Jekyll and Mr. Hyde*, created complete scenes for his story in his sleep. A nineteenth-century German chemist, August Kekulé, discovered the six-sided shape of the benzene molecule after dreaming of dancing snakes with their tails in their mouths that formed a hexagon.

Some psychologists believe you can select a problem you want to solve, go to sleep, and dream a dream that solves the problem. Others believe you can tune in to your dreams, reverse the action in middream, as it were, and substitute a more satisfying ending. For example, one man continually dreamed that a huge wave had swallowed him up as he walked along a beach. In real life, he felt overwhelmed by job and family responsibilities, and helpless to relieve his burdens. A psychologist convinced him to change the dream: the next time the wave swallowed him up, he dreamed that he popped back to the surface and started swimming. When he awoke, he felt more confident about dealing with his real problem.

To interpret and profit from dreams, you must be able to recall them. Some techniques that may help:

1. Tell yourself before going to sleep that you *will* remember your dreams.
2. Keep a notebook or tape recorder at your bedside.
3. Set your alarm clock back half an hour so you will awaken while dreaming. (Most dreaming occurs during the last part of sleep.)
4. If you have just had a dream, do not move or write it down. Quietly replay it in your mind, starting with the last lingering image. Then reconstruct the whole story.
5. Record the dream, noting facts without making judgments, and dating the entry.
6. Next, describe how you felt as you awakened: angry, depressed, anxious, afraid, excited, elated?
7. Ask what are you telling yourself in this dream. Relate it to recent events and emotional experiences.
8. Remember that dreams express themselves in symbols and that the apparent content of a dream generally is not its only meaning.
9. Try describing your dream to a close friend who might recognize connections you cannot see.
10. Finally, make up a dream you would like to have, in which you are a participant and not an observer. Make sure it includes work, play, sex, and important relationships.

You dream the way you live. By becoming an active participant, you can also start to live the way you dream.

Napping

Naps may be one of the few remaining pleasures that are free, legal, and nonfattening. By one definition, naps are any rest period lasting up to twenty minutes that involves unconsciousness but not pajamas. Some people nap because they like to, but most are making up for sleep lost during the night. Since naps can contribute to insomnia, these individuals often perpetuate the problem they are trying to solve.

People who have no trouble sleeping at night claim to benefit greatly from brief naps. They wake up energized, alert, relaxed, cheerful, and better able to concentrate, even after only a fifteen-minute snooze. Naps help form new perspectives on problems, hence the saying "I'll sleep on it." Studies have shown that people can solve complex mathematical problems more easily after a nap, and college students score higher on skill and memory tests after napping. Even people with Type A personalities, who think they are too busy to waste time sleeping, use brief naps to get even more work done.

Despite these benefits many people, especially men, avoid napping, perhaps because they associate it with being effeminate, passive, lazy, or childish. The objection that naps are for babies is not valid, since babies do not take naps. They engage in a speeded-up version of the sleep/wake cycle that grown-ups follow. And the belief that naps are a feminine behavior is hardly borne out by the historical record.

Thomas Edison's daily four to five hours of sleep included a number of naps, and Winston Churchill, who could doze for a minute or two while sitting upright in a chair, once said, "Nature had not intended mankind to work from eight in the morning until midnight without the refreshment of blessed oblivion." In *The Gathering Storm*, he said that napping an hour or so every afternoon was a good way "to press a day and a half's work into one." President Harry S. Truman often caught five minutes of sleep during the day, and comedian Bob Hope likes to nap between engagements.

Some people can doze in cars, subways, washrooms, and airport terminals. But most people believe they can sleep only under certain conditions and in certain places. Napoleon had no such preconceived notion. He was able to sleep whenever and wherever he felt the need — he could even doze in the saddle in the midst of battle. A modern gambler used to catnap for two or three minutes between deals, which allowed him to stay up most of the night playing poker. Salvador Dalí may be the shortest napper on record. He reportedly sat in a chair with a spoon in his hand and when he dozed off, the sound of the spoon clattering on the plate woke him up. This, he claimed, kept him from overnapping.

Thus naps need not be long to be effective. Scientists once believed that any nap of less than two hours was useless because it takes that long to complete a sleep cycle. Today, sleep experts recognize that naps of about an hour are just as beneficial as longer ones and are less likely to make you feel sluggish. People who have mastered the ten- to fifteen-minute nap technique wake up feeling as if they had a refreshing sleep.

Napping is of greatest value to people who do so regularly. The key to napping successfully is knowing *when* to sleep. Most people naturally feel sleepy and gain the most from napping in midafternoon, which is about eight hours after they get up and eight hours before they go to bed. Midmorning naps, by contrast, usually involve REM (dreaming) sleep and are apt to be perceived by the body as an extension of the previous night's sleep. Late afternoon or evening naps, which involve non-REM or deep sleep, might make your brain think it is going to sleep for the night. That is why you awaken groggy and grouchy from naps taken too early or too late in the day. (Many people consider vigorous exercise after work a good substitute for a nap.)

Tips on Successful Napping

1. Limit your nap to sixty to ninety minutes. (Set a timer if you do not wake up naturally.)
2. Try to develop a "naptitude" for ten- to fifteen-minute naps.
3. Do not nap in the morning, late afternoon, or evening. The ideal nap time is 2:00 to 3:00 P.M. if you get up at 6:00 or 7:00 A.M.
4. Avoid napping if you have trouble sleeping at night.
5. Never force a nap, but set aside time in your daily schedule to take one.

Brief naps are not to be confused with microsleeps, in which your eyes scan a page but your brain does not comprehend what your eyes have seen. These brief sleep episodes are apt to occur in a sleep-deprived person doing paperwork, attending concerts and lectures, or editing dull manuscripts. If microsleeps occur frequently, it means you need more sleep at night, or more naps.

Jet Lag

Jet lag — the disruption of crossing several time zones when traveling east or west by jet — is a late-twentieth-century affliction. In the days of train travel, and even in the prejet days of aviation, travelers had time to adjust their internal clocks to new time zones. Today even twice-a-year changes to or from daylight saving time are enough to disrupt natural body rhythms that regulate sleeping, waking, and other body functions and cause mild "jet lag." Thus jet lag is more than simple travel fatigue.

The classic symptoms of jet lag are trouble sleeping at night and trouble staying awake during the day. This problem may last a day or two. But jet lag disrupts more than your sleep. Digestion, kidney and bowel function, hormone secretion, and body temperature are also affected. Your mind may not work right; concentration and efficiency may be impaired; and you may suffer lapses in judgment and memory. Alcohol goes right to your head. These disruptions last even longer than the insomnia caused by jet lag. Many travelers report that it takes them about one day per time zone crossed to adjust totally.

Some people are susceptible to jet lag; others shrug it off. People who function better in the morning, people who sleep only a few hours at night, and people who do not travel very often are especially vulnerable to jet lag. It also bothers older people more than the young, and people traveling eastward more than westward, because their internal clocks move in a westward direction. Jet lag is more of a problem going than returning: it seems easier to adapt to time-zone changes when you are coming home.

The last-minute frenzy of preparing for a trip makes jet lag even worse. Once on the airplane, you are confronted by an oxygen supply and air pressure that are generally lower than on the ground. Air in an airplane cabin often is warm, dry, and smoky. In addition, you are forced to sit for hours in cramped quarters.

Still, jet lag is more a business risk than a health risk. Many firms require that no contracts be signed within twenty-four hours of arrival across time zones. While Henry Kissinger was secretary of state, he never scheduled a meeting the day of his arrival lest jet lag impair his concentration and judgment. When Lyndon B. Johnson traveled overseas, he did not reset his watch or his schedule, but continued operating on White House time, even if it meant sleeping part of the day and holding meetings at night. Some aircrews on trips of three days or less function on home-base time no matter how many time zones they have crossed. Unfortunately, tourists and business people cannot afford the luxury of doing the same.

How can the ordinary person beat jet lag? One way is to shift sleep patterns and mealtimes in the direction of the trip, but this solution often is impractical. A number of special jet lag diets and drug remedies have been publicized, but none, as of this writing, has been proven effective. A new therapy involving exposure to bright white light may help prevent jet lag, according to a report in the September 13, 1985, *Journal of the American Medical Association*. Such light — which also benefits patients with sleep and mood disorders — may come from either the sun or artificial sources, according to Dr. Alfred Lewy, director of the Sleep and Mood Disorders Laboratory at Oregon Health Sciences University in Portland. Author Lynne Lamberg describes trying this therapy during a trip to Italy. For the first four days after arriving, she and her husband spent as much time outdoors as possible between 9:00 A.M. and 2:00 P.M. local time. After returning home, they got as much sunlight as possible from 2:00 P.M. onward. Both reported that they avoided jet lag.

More Jet Lag Countermeasures

1. If possible, schedule a stopover of several days to a week to break up a long trip, especially if you are crossing four or more time zones.
2. Start adapting to your new time zone on the airplane. Set your watch ahead, and eat and drink according to the clock at your destination.
3. Walk around as much as possible and exercise in your seat since long periods of sitting can hamper circulation, digestion, and flexibility and cause feet to swell.
4. Do in-seat exercises, including deep breathing, stretching, flexing your muscles, rolling your shoulders, rotating your head and feet, and wiggling your toes to increase blood circulation.
5. Avoid overeating, smoking, and drinking alcohol on the plane. Smoking depletes already-reduced oxygen intake in the thin air of the aircraft cabin. And you are twice as vulnerable to alcohol at high altitudes as on the ground.
6. Drink lots of water and fruit juices, even if you are not thirsty, to avoid dehydration caused by dry air in aircraft cabins.
7. When you arrive, try to eat and sleep according to local schedules even if it is dinnertime or bedtime at home.

   NOTE: Concorde jets, which carry you to Europe in about three hours, do not eliminate jet lag because you are still in a different time zone when you arrive. But fast jets do help eliminate travel fatigue.

Adapting to a Bed Partner

Most adults prefer to sleep with somebody else. But many people find it difficult, at least initially, to adapt to a bed partner. Everyone moves about thirty times during sleep. That totals about thirty opportunities to disturb the sleep of someone in bed with you. Yet couples who are accustomed to sleeping together have trouble sleeping apart.

According to Lynne Lamberg's *American Medical Association Guide to Better Sleep*, people who sleep together learn to synchronize their movements — the smaller the bed, the greater the synchrony. They also get less deep non-REM sleep than either would get sleeping alone. Compatibility in sleep habits, thus, may be an important trait to look for in a bed partner. If each of you requires widely varying amounts of sleep, this could be a problem, as could the differing rhythms of a morning person (who rises and goes to bed early) and an evening person (who stays up and gets up late). Such couples, Lamberg reports, have sex less often, go out together less often, and talk to each other less often.

One remedy for the person who wants to watch late television or read — while his bedmate turns in — is to conduct these activities in a separate room, not necessarily a separate bedroom. Different bedtimes are easier to tolerate than separate bedrooms, provided you can agree on other times of day to make love.

How to Improve Nocturnal "Togetherness"

1. Avoid bedtime arguments.
2. Do not ignore snoring problems.
3. Adjust differing sleep cycles.
4. Take your own pillow to her place to help get over the "first night" effect of sleeping in a strange bed.
5. Recognize that multiple sleep partners may adversely affect your ability to sleep well.

Your ability to sleep with a bed partner may be a good test not only of your relationship, but of your "sleep health."

Further Information about Sleep Problems

- Association of Sleep Disorders Centers, P.O. Box 2604, Del Mar, CA 92014.
- *The American Medical Association Guide to Better Sleep*, by Lynne Lamberg (New York: Random House, 1984).

❧ 5

Managing Stress

What Is, Where Is, Stress?

Of all the topics in this book, few have received as much attention as stress. It has been featured on the cover of *Time* magazine and in thousands of articles, books, and other media. The message is that stress is "out there," waiting to get you and make you sick. But what, exactly, is it? Many experts define stress as the body's response to any demand (stressor) placed upon it. The late Dr. Hans Selye, the Austrian endocrinologist, called stress "the rate of wear and tear in the body." Still, many people remain uncertain of whether stress means stressful events themselves or *reactions* to stressful events. As one researcher says, "Stress, in addition to being itself, and the result of itself, is also the cause of itself."

Stress is hard to define because people react so differently. Often the exact same stressor — unpaid bills — can cause one man to lose sleep and another to cope by taking an extra job. A deadline or high-risk job gives one man an ulcer, another a challenge. Reactions differ according to personality traits, state of health, past experience, family relationships, financial status, and other factors. A sense of control also determines how you react to stressful events. Executives who feel they are in command of their organizations do not react as adversely as do workers.

Not all stressors are bad. They are essential for productivity of all sorts. They can stimulate an Olympic athlete to a gold-medal performance, a public speaker to enthrall an audience. Stressors abound in the boardroom and on football fields, and make monster movies and roller-coaster rides more thrilling. Without stress producers, you might be bored to death. In the form of physical exercise, they can relax you.

Stressors also protect your body by priming it for danger. Hearing, smell, and vision sharpen; breathing and heart rate quicken; muscles tense; energy levels soar; sensitivity to pain lessens; and reaction time shortens as you maneuver your car across an icy patch or stop short of a tree lying across the road. This is "eustress," as opposed to "distress."

Yet some situations seem to be universally distressing. Years ago two psychiatrists at the University of Washington, Thomas H. Holmes and Richard H. Rahe, ranked forty-three life events and assigned them scores between 1 and 100, according to how stressful they are for most people. Death of a spouse, the most shattering event, rated 100 points, while divorce rated 73, marriage 50, job change 36, outstanding achievement 28, vacation 13, and Christmas 12 on the Holmes–Rahe Social Readjustment Rating Scale.

Note that ten of the top fifteen stressful events on the Holmes–Rahe Scale involve the family, and the scale does not even include stressors like living together, failing an exam, dropping out of school, fighting with your spouse or parents, infidelity of a sex partner, or hating your job.

THE HOLMES–RAHE "STRESS" SCALE

Life event	Point value
1. Death of spouse	100
2. Divorce	73
3. Marital separation	65
4. Jail term	63
5. Death of a close family member	63
6. Personal injury or illness	53
7. Marriage	50
8. Getting fired from job	47
9. Marital reconciliation	45
10. Retirement	45
11. Change in health of family member	44
12. Pregnancy	40
13. Sex difficulties	39
14. Gain of a new family member	39
15. Business readjustment	39
16. Change in financial state	38
17. Death of a close friend	37
18. Change to different line of work	36
19. Change in number of arguments with spouse	35
20. Mortgage over $10,000	31
21. Foreclosure of mortgage or loan	30

THE HOLMES–RAHE "STRESS" SCALE (continued)

Life event	Point value
22. Change in responsibilities at work	29
23. Son or daughter leaving home	29
24. Trouble with in-laws	29
25. Outstanding personal achievement	28
26. Wife begins or stops work	26
27. Begin or end school	26
28. Change in living conditions	25
29. Revision of personal habits	24
30. Trouble with boss	23
31. Change in work hours or conditions	20
32. Change in residence	20
33. Change in schools	20
34. Change in recreation	19
35. Change in church activities	19
36. Change in social activities	18
37. Mortgage or loan less than $10,000	17
38. Change in sleeping habits	16
39. Change in number of family get-togethers	15
40. Change in eating habits	15
41. Vacation	13
42. Christmas	12
43. Minor violations of the law	11

NOTE: If your score is 150 to 199 in a single year, you stand a 37 percent chance of developing a physical illness or change in health within two years. If your score is 200 to 299, the chances of becoming ill are 51 percent. If your score is higher than 300, you stand a 79 percent chance of illness. One way to lower your score is to defer any changes, such as moving or changing jobs, that are under your control.

SOURCE: T. H. Holmes and R. H. Rahe, "The Social Readjustment Rating Scale," *Journal of Psychosomatic Research* 2 (1967): 213–218.

Job Stressors

One stress producer that seldom appears on rating scales involves day-to-day experience at work. Few other activities, including sleep, consume as much time: forty hours a week at a minimum. If these forty-plus hours are spent in a job that is boring, unrewarding, machine-paced, or marred by nonsupportive supervisors and coworkers, the end result is a new kind of health hazard that only recently has been recognized as such.

Job stressors can harm the health of office and factory worker alike. This phenomenon was described more than fifty years ago in a book titled *Workers' Emotions in Shop and Home*. Author Rex Hersey noted that even blue-collar workers feel the emotional pressures of "the nature of the job, the amount accomplished, plant conditions, treatment by the foremen, [and] relations with one's fellow workers."

Boredom, a common job stressor, afflicts people who have little control over the pace and style of their work. For example, operators of video display terminals are subjected to some of the most relentless physical and psychological pressures in the workplace. Their jobs are paced by machines that impose inflexibility, lack of privacy, and production quotas. Workers sit all day at a keyboard and process checks, insurance claims, address changes, and customer orders under the watchful eyes of supervisors who can verify, on *their* video display terminals, exactly how much work is turned out. It is the twentieth-century counterpart of the nineteenth-century sweatshop.

Burnout is a growing problem among people in the "helping professions" who toil, often under impossible workloads, for long periods without visible results. Physicians, nurses, social workers, police officers, teachers, criminal lawyers, and other human-service workers are especially vulnerable to burnout. So, too, are people responsible for the lives of others — such as air traffic controllers. They often lack either the time or the inclination to take vacations, days off, or memberships in health clubs. They often feel guilty or inadequate when they cannot take on even more work. Burnout occurs in three phases. First comes emotional exhaustion and a feeling of being drained. This is followed by a cynical period of asking, "Why knock myself out?" Finally, the burned-out person becomes depressed and loses vitality and optimism not only about the job, but about other facets of life. Many people who experience job burnout are naive about organizations. When their high expectations about their employers are unmet, they become cynical. If they remain on the job, they usually adopt a more practical view of the complexity and chaos of organizational life.

Another job stressor is the nightmare of working for a *"crazy boss"* who belittles employees (often in front of coworkers), pits one against another, keeps subordinates uninformed and off-balance, bullies, and exploits. Such a boss — who often is character-disordered — inflicts insidious physical and emotional damage. People who derive much of their personal identities from their jobs are especially vulnerable to abuse by a character-disordered boss. The fact that you once depended on your parents for survival and now depend on your job — personified by your boss — for economic survival is no small factor in the powerlessness you may feel when dealing with such a "superior." One way to survive is to adopt this attitude: "I work for the organization, not the boss."

Powerlessness is felt by the head of a public agency who must please pressure groups and legislators and obey so many regulations that he has little control over the organization he supposedly heads. Powerlessness is felt by the midlevel manager who must meet someone else's deadlines and carry out policies he opposes. It is felt even by lower-level workers, such as police officers, who constantly collide with cumbersome administrative and legal systems. Working for a large organization magnifies feelings of powerlessness. Thirty years ago William H. Whyte, Jr., in *The Organization Man*, described an individual who becomes part of a collective for the purposes of work. According to Whyte, individuality is lost not only in the corporate and government workplaces, but in academia, the world of science, and other institutions upon which people depend for survival. Often without realizing it, people expect such institutions to take care of them, according to Dr. Donald S. Jewell, a psychologist in Washington, D.C. Considering the company retirement benefits, health care coverage, life insurance, savings and investment plans, recreation and vacation packages, and discount buying services, institutions appear to do so, he adds. But the individual pays a high psychological price for these false securities.

Job stressors are an increasing problem even for *successful* people who are troubled about what it takes to cope with their jobs. Many individuals trade career success for close personal relationships. Others stifle their own needs in order to develop the character traits encouraged by their employers. Among this group are many "working wounded," who compromise their personal ethics to be successful.

Countless numbers of working people spend time and energy on jobs that do not help them attain their real goals in life. They arrive home physically and mentally exhausted after another day of joyless striving. Victims of the "Sisyphus complex," they resemble the mythical character who offended the gods and was condemned eternally to push a heavy boulder up a hill, only to have it roll down again just as it reached the top. The modern Sisyphus toils for a boss who does not utilize his skills or recognize his accomplishments. His work seems meaningless, and his health, as a result, is at risk.

The Overwork Syndrome

Winston Churchill once said, "Those whose work and pleasures are one are fortune's favorite children." Even when you are satisfied with your job, too much "job" can be harmful. The overwork syndrome afflicts people who have a compulsive need to work. Workaholics seem to lack an inner governor that tells them when they are exhausted, mentally and physically, and when they need rest and recreation. As teenagers, they worked three jobs at once, studied till dawn, and spent Saturdays puttering with their automobiles. As full-fledged adult workaholics, they end up in doctors' offices because they tire easily; cannot sleep, concentrate, or make love; feel irritable, depressed and anxious; and suffer from stomach upsets and assorted aches and pains. Their complaint is not that they are working too hard, but that they cannot work *harder*. Sometimes the "overwork syndrome" causes symptoms that resemble other illnesses: fever of unknown origin, thyroid deficiency, chest pain, and "accidents" caused by lack of concentration. In severe cases, workaholics suffer from memory lapses, confusion, and suicidal thoughts. Overworkers are candidates for more serious medical problems, including alcoholism and drug dependency.

The typical workaholic is a competitive, hurried, perfectionistic male. Overwork and preoccupation with work are common in male physicians, who average about six waking hours a week with their spouses. This time is usually devoted to chores and "crisis conversations." Doctors typically time their vacations to coincide with medical meetings.

Workaholics tend to cope with fatigue and other difficulties by forcing themselves to work even longer and harder to catch up. They forgo all forms of physical exercise and recreation, which makes them even less efficient and able to concentrate. Casualties of Parkinson's Law ("Work expands so as to fill the time available for its completion"), they need to stop and ask these questions:

1. *Am I overworking?* Answer yes if your family and friends complain that they seldom see you, if you avoid social gatherings, if going to a movie or dinner party feels as if you are wasting time, or if you consistently take on more work than you can comfortably handle.

2. *Why do I overwork?* Is it to prove you are worthwhile, to keep from feeling depressed, to avoid your spouse and children? Do you overwork because you feel guilty, cannot delegate chores, or have trouble saying no to the demands of others? Do you work long hours because your spouse does?

3. *Do I want to change?* Change will not be easy, especially if you overwork because of guilt or underlying personal problems, such as avoiding a bad marriage or identifying with a parent who overworked or made unrealistic demands on you.

Workaholism often stems from poor work habits. Time-management experts suggest reassessing your value system and working smarter — not harder — on the things you consider most important. One study of fifteen successful and healthy professionals who worked at least sixty hours a week showed that all were able to recognize and respond promptly to signs of fatigue. All were able to delay thinking about problems until they could actually deal with them. They exercised regularly, avoided drug and alcohol abuse, had stable family lives, maintained friendships, and enjoyed vacations.

An effective remedy for the overwork syndrome is *play,* not to be dismissed as "kid stuff." Dr. George Sheehan, the physician-runner, has written that "play is our first act. If we are lucky, it will also be our last." He defines play as an attitude and a way of living. To make play a part of your lifestyle, you may have to set aside a definite time for adult-style play and lock yourself into dancing lessons, season theater tickets, or advance reservations for a vacation.

Unemployment

Loss of a job usually means loss of status and of identification with society. Besides economic loss, there is loss of daily routine, of human contacts outside the home, of feeling competent, of escape from home pressures and — for many men — of the role of "head of household."

The psychological damage caused by unemployment is directly mirrored in increased disability, disease, and death rates. In a report to the Joint Economic Committee of Congress in June 1984, Dr. M. Harvey Brenner of Johns Hopkins University testified that increased death rates have occurred in three waves after every economic recession during the past century. The first wave comes six to twelve months after a recession and consists of suicides and deaths of men already physically vulnerable. The second wave comes two to three years later, when economic recovery has started and some men realize they have been left out. The third wave comes after seven to fifteen years, when deaths from chronic disease caused by the recession begin to occur.

Dr. Brenner, an authority on the connection between effects of economic recessions and health, reports that each percentage-point rise in unemployment causes about 37,000 deaths over the succeeding six years. More than half the fatalities are from heart disease, which, he says, is aggravated during unemployment by poor diet and adverse reactions to stressors. More than 900 suicides and about 650 homicides occur, both reflecting an increase in stressors and stress reactions, Brenner says. About 500 deaths from cirrhosis of the liver result from alcohol abuse.

Health problems are aggravated as unemployed workers lose their health insurance, postpone medical and dental treatment, and even stop getting new eyeglasses. Violent crime and deaths from auto accidents also rise during recession, drunk drivers abound, divorce rates soar, and depression becomes widespread. Unemployment becomes everybody's health problem, one way or another. Even the employed face increased health risks during a recession. People who have jobs but fear losing them may turn to alcohol or drugs. A study of layoffs among Boston police officers in 1981 revealed that officers who kept their jobs suffered from guilt about having survived the layoff, increased workloads, and greater exposure to personal danger. Mental health counseling services were offered to officers who were fired, but the officers who had *not* been fired most often visited the clinic. A research scientist who observed both groups of police officers concluded that a company that tries to save 10 percent of payroll costs by laying off 10 percent of its people may end up with only 65 or 75 percent productivity because of psychological casualties suffered by those still on the job.

Hidden Stressors

Accumulated daily hassles also are harmful, perhaps more so than job problems and other major life events. High on the "hassle scale" are misplaced car keys, too much to do, yard work, home maintenance, concern about weight, administrative chores, worries about investments and rising prices, and traffic jams. As the saying goes, "Rule no. 1 is, don't sweat the small stuff. Rule no. 2 is, it's all small stuff." The small stuff can erode emotional and physical health over the long run.

Chronic, long-term hassles are even more erosive. Consider the frustration of parents whose twenty-seven-year-old son does *not* leave home, the despair of a man who feels trapped in a bad marriage, or the repression of an executive who can shout at his wife after arguing with the boss, but not vice versa.

Hidden stressors are far more damaging than those at the surface. Most stress-inducing of all are thoughts and feelings — sometimes glimpsed in dreams — that are hidden in your unconscious mind. These trace back to childhood desires to be loved and taken care of. The list includes overwhelming fear, anger, disgust, and hatred (and love) toward family members. These forbidden feelings are like the unseen mass of iceberg that floats below the water line: dangerous and uncontrollable. Consider the man who is fired from his job. He must contend not only with real and immediate loss of status and income, but also with unconscious feelings that he is bad, unworthy, and helpless. When a stress-inducing event, large or small, is unexpected — a man becomes a widower in his thirties instead of in his sixties or seventies — or when such events are cumulative and long-lasting, the consequences may be far more severe. What counts is *how much* you must adapt, and for how long.

Distress Signals

Several years ago, a psychologist meeting with nine corporate personnel directors asked each to describe a particularly stressful event in his life. After giving the executives a few minutes to ponder what intimacies they were willing to reveal, he announced that he had actually wanted them to describe how they had felt at the moment of being asked, since his real intent was to put them under stress. One by one, the personnel directors reported "butterflies," "nervousness," "light perspiration," "internal racing," "heart pounding," and "pressure on the back of the neck."

Predictable body reactions occur in response to a stressful experience. Whether the triggering event or stressor is "good" or "bad," your body undergoes a three-stage reaction: alarm, resistance, and exhaustion. During the alarm stage, when the threat is immediate (an oncoming car or a trip to the podium), your body has a unique ability to release hormones that prepare it almost instantaneously for "fight or flight." Stage two is resistance: your body adapts to the stressful situation and is able to stop the effects of the stressor by releasing hormones. Stage three, exhaustion, occurs if the stressor is excessive or prolonged and your body cannot repair the damage caused by both the stressor and the continued release of hormones. Prolonged adverse reactions to stressors produce unhealthy states that Dr. Hans Selye calls "diseases of adaptation."

The following are primitive, unconscious reactions to stressors that are necessary for survival and warning signals that should be heeded:

- pounding heart, shortness of breath, sweating, dry mouth
- frequent indigestion, diarrhea, or urination
- frequent headaches, backaches, muscle spasms, or fatigue
- susceptibility to colds and viruses
- accident-proneness
- chronically hostile or angry feelings
- tension (a grinding, steady reaction to a specific stressor) or anxiety (apprehension unrelated to any specific stressful event)
- the feeling "That's more than I can take!"

The absence of symptoms does not mean the absence of a stress reaction. Indeed, physical symptoms often are the way that a stress reaction unconsciously expresses itself, especially when symptoms occur suddenly with no apparent physical cause. One way to tune in to these forces is by "inner listening" to your body. A "pounding" headache is a warning, perhaps, that you are taking a pounding at work. Nausea and indigestion might mask distress over "not being able to stomach" the way somebody close is treating you. Your back may hurt because your life hurts. Symptoms of disease often are your body's way of telling you that its needs (which really are *your* needs) are not being met.

Stress Disorders

Volumes have been written about the connection between stress reactions and disease. Boris Pasternak articulated the stress/illness connection in *Doctor Zhivago:*

> Your health is bound to be affected if, day after day, you say the opposite of what you feel, if you grovel before what you dislike, and rejoice at what brings you nothing but misfortune.

Or, as Woody Allen quipped in the film *Manhattan*, "I never get angry; I just grow a tumor."

But what about scientific proof of the mind/body link? It seems reasonable that a headache or upset stomach after an argument with your spouse, or before a sexual encounter with a new partner, might be stressor-related. But what about more serious illnesses — such as heart disease or cancer — that take years to develop and cannot be clearly linked to adverse reactions to stress? Some people think poor health causes stress reactions, not vice versa. While most people undergoing stressful events probably do not get sick, evidence is growing that many disease states — including the top killing diseases in the United States — may be caused by mismanagement of stressful situations.

Scientists have long observed the link between stress and illness. During the Civil War, heart palpitations were so commonplace they became known as "soldier's heart." During World War I, the phenomenon was called shell shock; in World War II, it was battle fatigue. By then, Dr. Hans Selye had suggested that chronic stress reactions cause long-term chemical changes in the body leading to high blood pressure, atherosclerosis, depressed immune function, and many other disorders.

Recent interest in the stress/illness connection began, in part, with crises faced by the hostages of Iran, people living near the radiation accident at Three Mile Island, Vietnam War veterans, earthquake victims, and people threatened by chemical waste hazards at Love Canal. The few available studies of disasters suggest that from 50 to 90 percent of the survivors — who are physically unharmed in the disaster itself — suffer some kind of acute emotional, physical, or psychosomatic consequence, and many suffer long-term changes in health.

The evidence that such emotionally charged events damage health is so compelling that the National Academy of Sciences (NAS), in a 1982 report called *Stress and Human Health,* recommended that scientists move beyond questions of *whether* stress reactions can affect health and explore *how* they have such consequences.

Exposure to a stressful experience does not mean you will get sick. For that to happen, several conditions must be present, according to the NAS report. First, there must be a *stressor:* death of a loved one, loss of a job, marital difficulties, financial crisis, or exposure to dangerous or boring work. Second, a physical *reaction* must take place. It may be, as the NAS report points out, "elevated blood pressure, increased stomach acidity, chemical changes in the body, weakened immunity, or an inability to cope with everyday demands." Third, there must be an absence of *mediators,* such as supportive family relationships, that alleviate the impact of the stressor. Finally, the *health consequence* occurs, often after a lengthy period. Thus, it is not a stressful event, but how you experience it, that eventually can make you sick or well.

Scientific studies have linked adverse stress reactions to colds, minor infections, bronchial asthma, peptic ulcers, hypertension, hyperthyroidism, coronary artery disease, sudden cardiac death, cancer, and liver dysfunction. Consider:

- Type A behavior (unusually aggressive, competitive, work-oriented, time-pressured behavior) raises the risk of (although it does not cause) heart attack and coronary artery disease.

- Digestive problems — such as indigestion, loss of appetite, nausea, constipation, diarrhea, ulcers, spastic colon, and hemorrhoids — often are less a barometer of what you eat than of what eats you.
- In the economically deprived Boston black ghetto of Roxbury and the blue-collar white neighborhood of South Boston, death rates are higher than average for all causes of death, including hypertension-related ailments such as stroke.
- Unprecedented levels of stress-related diseases have affected farmers and their families, especially owners of "century farms" that have been in the family for more than one hundred years. These include heart disease, ulcers, accidental deaths, alcohol abuse, depression, and anxiety disorders.
- The physical consequences of job stressors have been extensively documented in air traffic controllers in the nation's busiest airports. These individuals are significantly more prone to high blood pressure and somewhat more prone to peptic ulcers and diabetes than individuals in less stressful jobs.
- A study by Drs. Suzanne Haynes and Manning Feinleib of the National Heart, Lung, and Blood Institute showed that women clerical and sales workers who had nonsupportive bosses, trouble expressing anger, and lack of job mobility were twice as likely to develop coronary heart disease as nonclerical female workers and housewives. Overall, the women in the study reported more symptoms of stress than did the men.
- A Canadian study of nearly four thousand men, followed for more than twenty-nine years, showed an excess proportion of sudden cardiac deaths on Mondays compared to other days of the week. The men who died had no previous evidence of heart disease. The researchers — noting earlier studies linking psychological stress to sudden cardiac death — concluded that returning to stressors at work after a weekend of respite may have triggered the heart attacks.
- Conversely, studies show that professionals who are satisfied with their jobs — typically, college professors, scientists, engineers, and skilled craftsmen — have lower rates of heart disease than doctors, lawyers, and midlevel executives who choose jobs primarily because of salary or status.
- A 1984 study of bereavement by the National Academy of Sciences' Institute of Medicine shows that loss of a loved one — a

spouse, parent, sibling, child — leaves some survivors more vulnerable to illness and death.

- An earlier study of bereavement in 1977, by Drs. Selby Jacobs and Adrian Ostfeld at Yale, showed excess mortality in the newly widowed, especially in younger persons and men. The elevated mortality continued about two years, but was highest for men during the first six months and highest for women during the second year. Men were at risk of death from influenza and pneumonia, cirrhosis and alcoholism, suicide, accidents, heart disease, and tuberculosis.

- Human loneliness is among the most important causes of premature death in America, according to University of Maryland psychologist Dr. James J. Lynch. In *The Broken Heart: The Medical Consequences of Loneliness*, he notes that divorced, single, and widowed individuals are up to ten times more likely than married people to die prematurely from heart disease, cancer, stroke, accidents, cirrhosis of the liver, suicide, pneumonia, diabetes — in short, just about every leading cause of death. Divorced people, Lynch adds, are particularly vulnerable to all kinds of illness. While their grief is similar to that of the bereaved, the divorced incur the added burden of anger toward a spouse still living.

- Other studies show that people who died suddenly had relinquished control over their environment, had felt helpless and hopeless before their deaths, and had been overwhelmed by the "giving-up/given-up" complex. There also is evidence that people who live in prolonged stressful situations and are powerless to resolve unsatisfactory work or family situations are at increased risk of heart failure. Even healthy individuals, trapped in situations from which there seems to be no escape, have been known to develop slowing of the heartbeat, heart arrhythmias, and loss of consciousness.

- A recent study of healthy Israeli soldiers showed that those who knew how many kilometers they had to march had the lowest levels of the stress hormones, prolactin and cortisol. The soldiers who did not know how many kilometers remained and faced a hopelessly long march had high levels of these hormones in their bloodstreams.

- "Learned helplessness" may weaken the body's ability to fend off disease, while ability to make and execute personal choices is critical to health and well-being. For example, studies show that people adapt better and survive longer in nursing homes if they feel they are in charge of their own fates, rather than ruled by the world around them.

The likelihood of becoming ill following exposure to a single stressor is relatively low. But the cumulative effects of several stressors — as the Holmes–Rahe studies have shown — may be beyond the body's restorative powers. Although the evidence is far from conclusive, some experts believe that prolonged adverse reactions to stressful events play a major role in more than half — and perhaps as high as 80 to 90 percent — of all physical and mental illness, including six of the most common causes of death in the United States: coronary heart disease, lung cancer, emphysema, accidental trauma, cirrhosis of the liver, and suicide.

How Stress Causes Illness

"The trouble with doctors today," Plato quoted Hippocrates as saying around 400 B.C., "is that they separate the soul from the body. They don't recognize that the soul and the body are one." A century ago, Charles Darwin wrote that someday scientists would unearth the physiological mechanisms of emotion. Only during the past fifty years have scientists even attempted to systematically study the stress/illness link, and only in the past few years have they begun really to understand its complexities.

More than forty years ago, Dr. Hans Selye described how the mind and body act on each other in response to physical or mental stressors, good or bad. The brain's hypothalamus ("old brain") signals the pituitary gland, which in turns signals the adrenal gland to secrete the hormones involved in physical arousal to a stressor. The adrenal gland then signals the pituitary to end the stress response. While this classic model of the response is still considered accurate, research scientists have discovered a more sophisticated network of interactions. For example, Dr. Julius Axelrod, biochemist at the National Institute of Mental Health, won the Nobel Prize in 1970 for his discoveries of how a group of chemicals called neurotransmitters fine-tune this network. And in late 1981 scientists at the Salk Institute characterized the corticotropin-releasing factor (CRF), a hormone produced in the hypothalamus that triggers the release of pituitary and adrenal stress hormones.

These discoveries helped clarify the workings of the "stress axis," consisting of the hypothalamus, pituitary gland, and adrenal gland. When the brain perceives something as stressful, it signals the hypothalamus to secrete CRF, which stimulates the pituitary gland to release ACTH (adrenocorticotropic hormone), which travels through the blood to the adrenal glands. The adrenals, in turn, produce a chemical called cortisol that helps the body gear up for the "fight or flight" stress response. Also, the sympathetic nervous system is activated and secretes norepinephrine and epinephrine. These hormones quicken heartbeat and breathing, slow digestion, increase perspiration, and dilate the pupils. Stress hormones are protective in small doses. But long-term stress and prolonged secretion of the "Big Three" stress hormones — norepinephrine, epinephrine, and cortisol — can promote disease states, such as high blood pressure, atherosclerosis, and digestive problems, and can suppress the immune system.

More recently, as Dr. Julius Axelrod reported at a Science Writers' Seminar on the molecular basis of stress, sponsored by the National Institutes of Health in July 1983, scientists have discovered that CRF is only one of several substances that regulate the pituitary's secretion of ACTH. Dr. Axelrod noted that different types of stressors seem to activate different mixes of interrelated neurochemicals, and that vulnerability to stress-related illness may stem from a breakdown in the fine-tuning of this intricate network. Scientists have also discovered that CRF may have a broader role in coordinating the stress response than previously suspected.

Psychiatrist Philip Gold of the National Institute of Mental Health and endocrinologist George P. Chrousos of the National Institute of Child Health and Human Development have suggested that CRF may play an important role in certain forms of human behavior and disease. A persistent excess of CRF in experimental animals causes stress-related behavior, poor feeding, decreased sexual activity, and unregulated secretion of catecholamines and cortisol. The NIH investigators have documented excessive CRF secretion in depressed patients, suggesting that they may be living in a state of chronic stress, and that CRF may contribute to their symptoms. Dr. Gold theorizes that uncontrolled stress reactions in early life may be relived throughout life, perhaps leading to major psychiatric illness in adulthood. Studies by Drs. Gold and Chrousos also show that CRF appears to influence the marked elevations of cortisol found in patients with Cushing's syndrome, which is often associated with depression.

Other stress hormones that act upon the body have been discovered. For example, the body produces the beneficial opiumlike chemicals called beta endorphins, which are released during exercise and may produce "runner's high." They also raise the pain threshold and may explain why seriously injured athletes often feel no pain.

Although scientists have long known that stressors can trigger chemical changes in the brain, only recently have they begun to trace pathways by which stress hormones and chemicals affect behavior and connect the brain with the immune and other body systems. One group of scientists at the National Institute of Mental Health, for example, is exploring how dozens of newly discovered brain-produced proteins called neuropeptides affect behavior and how stress causes disease. Such investigations are still beset by the difficulties of isolating adverse reactions to stressors from all the other factors that contribute to disease. Thus an editorial in the June 13, 1985, *New England Journal of Medicine* questioned the assumption that mental state is a major factor in causing and curing specific diseases, and noted the absence of "scientifically sound studies of the relation, if there is one, between mental state and disease."

Behavioral medicine and its close relatives, psychoimmunology and neuroimmunomodulation, are relatively new fields. Those who discount them should recall that biochemistry — once considered weak chemistry by chemists and weak biology by biologists — today is the foundation of biomedical research. Similarly, the field of genetics was hardly thought, only a few years ago, to have the importance it occupies in medicine today. As Dr. Meyer Friedman notes in *Treating Type A Behavior and Your Heart*, "Very few things worth measuring can be measured."

Men at Risk

Stressors may be harder on men than on women in the physiological sense as well. Still, men have some advantages over women in dealing with stressful situations. Men are less handicapped by culturally induced "learned helplessness," which makes them more likely to act against adversity. But many men, raised to hide their feelings, become victims of the "Pagliacci Syndrome." Like the operatic hero Canio in *I Pagliacci* (The Clowns), they cover despair and sadness with the characteristic light manner and smile of a clown. This cultural conditioning to ignore such feelings as grief, despair, anger, anxiety, jealousy, boredom, and uncertainty can leave a man chronically out of synchrony with what he really feels behind his mask and what he expresses.

A case in point, according to Dr. Herb Goldberg in *The New Male*, is the man who would rather learn that his impotence is caused by physical disease than by an emotional reaction. Such a man, according to

Goldberg, does not have to "take responsibility for his reaction or go about the painful process of becoming self-aware in order to deal with it." Those at risk include the following:

Bereaved Men. Each year some eight million Americans lose a family member. According to the Institute of Medicine's 1984 report on bereavement, men under age seventy-five who lose a mate or family member incur increased risk of death from accidents, cardiovascular disease, and some infectious diseases, especially during the first year. Suicide rates rise during the first year, particularly among older widowers and single men who lose their mothers. Widowers who do not remarry incur an above-average death rate for six years. Health problems tend to be worse among survivors who already are in poor physical or mental health, who abuse alcohol or drugs, and who lack a social network.

Divorced Men. Mortality from all causes of death is consistently higher for divorced, single, and widowed individuals of both sexes and all races. Moreover, epidemiological studies and data from major life insurance companies show that divorced men have higher rates of mortality and suicide than any other marital group.

Lonely Men. People who are socially isolated and whose human attachments are weak are more prone to illness and early death, according to the NAS report *Stress and Human Health* in 1982. A study by the California Department of Mental Health found that loners are two to three times more likely to die prematurely and face even greater odds of serious physical or mental illness. Persistent, severe loneliness is defined as emotional and social isolation, lack of meaningful social contact, and inability to share feelings or sustain close relationships. "Quite literally," says Dr. James J. Lynch in *The Broken Heart: The Medical Consequences of Loneliness,* "we must either learn to live together or face the possibility of prematurely dying alone." Many men rely on wives and girlfriends for social relationships and intimacy. When death or divorce occurs, they have no confidants. Men who are workaholics or have highly successful careers often disconnect from their personal lives and are unable to sustain emotional relationships. This makes them more vulnerable to illness.

Men under Job Stress. Heavy workloads, too much responsibility, conflicts with coworkers, and mismatches between skills and job requirements raise the risk of illness, according to *Stress and Human Health.*

Men Undergoing Multiple Stressors. Accumulated events such as getting married, moving, buying a house, and changing jobs can increase the risk of illness.

Men with Emotional Problems. The severest life strains supposedly befall women, the young, blacks, and people with low incomes. But results of the most comprehensive survey of mental disorders ever conducted in the United States, announced by the National Institute of Mental Health in October 1984, refuted the myth that men are somehow exempt from psychic distress. The survey showed that men and women suffer equally from serious emotional disorders, including anxiety and phobias, alcohol or drug abuse, and depression.

The Depressed Male

Winston Churchill called depression his "black dog." F. Scott Fitzgerald described it as the "dark night of the soul." Abraham Lincoln wrote in 1841: "If what I feel were equally distributed to the whole human family, there would not be one cheerful face on earth." Clinical depression, which probably causes more misery than any other single medical or emotional illness, is among the most treatable — yet least treated — of all human afflictions. Depression, contrary to myth, is an illness, not a personal weakness. It affects at least one in four Americans at some point in their lives. Yet most people fail to recognize depression in themselves or in others.

Like the common cold, periodic depression, sadness, "emptiness," or "the blues" is a normal part of the human condition. But when depression interferes with normal daily activities and lasts longer than two weeks, it is a more serious matter. While nobody is immune from clinical depression, some people are more vulnerable than others, especially those who respond adversely to stressful events. The depression-prone include adolescents entering adulthood, the physically ill, people with drinking problems or family members with histories of depression, and people undergoing widowhood, separation, divorce, changes in job or residence, and other significant changes or losses. Even normally happy events, such as marriage, childbirth, or success, can trigger depression. Yet some people become depressed without a precipitating event. The peak years for depression are the twenties to forties overall, and the mid-fifties and sixties for men.

There is no single cause of clinical depression. Early studies of the fitful and shallow sleep of depressed people suggested that depression involves disturbances of brain and central nervous system functioning. Scientists have long associated a disturbance in the brain chemical serotonin with clinical depression. People diagnosed as manic-depressives have alterations in their norepinephrine levels during the depressed and manic phases. Scientists have discovered a variety of neurotransmitters that help regulate emotions and other body processes. Perhaps the best evidence that depression at least partially stems from defects in body chemistry is the fact that certain drugs so effectively treat it, while others so effectively produce it. Studies of fraternal and identical twins and of siblings show that tendencies toward some kinds of depression, such as manic-depressive illness, are inherited. Illnesses such as influenza, infectious hepatitis, and mononucleosis often are associated with depression, as are certain antihypertensives, corticosteroids, and other drugs. Other factors leading to depression include learned behavior (such as holding in anger) that "runs" in families, social and economic class, culture, and stressful life events. Scientists have also long suspected — but have not proven — that depression is linked with personality traits such as interpersonal dependency, low self-esteem, and unfulfilled or uneven personal relationships in which one person feels that "I love her (him) more than she (he) loves me."

Whatever its causes, severe depression affects the entire body. Depressed people tend to feel hopeless, worthless, guilty, pessimistic, helpless, and withdrawn from others. They often become anxious and irritable and have trouble concentrating, reading, writing, conversing, and getting started in the morning. They may lose energy, ability to feel pleasure, and interest in their usual activities and in sex. In some people, periods of depression alternate with periods of mania, during which they may become frenzied rather than passive. They may work fourteen to eighteen hours a day, eat incessantly, and/or shift sexual activities into high gear. Depression also can cause insomnia, hypersomnia (too much sleep), fatigue, appetite loss, stomach upset, constipation, heightened sensitivity to emotional and physical pain, and thoughts — sometimes translated into action — of suicide (see chapter 7, pp. 198–201). Depressed people are hard to live with. Having so little joy in their own lives, they bring little to others. As the poet John Donne observed, "No man is an iland, entire of itselfe; every man is a peece of the continent, a part of the main. . . ." What the depressed need is reassurance that loved ones will stand by them and that the pain is a normal and — in all likelihood — temporary interlude.

To relieve temporary depression:

- Do not increase depression-causing stressors by changing jobs or residence while going through a divorce, for example.
- Be aware that certain holidays (like Christmas) and anniversaries can trigger the blues. Depression also is more likely to strike when you are tired, undernourished, or in poor physical condition.
- Share your feelings with a trusted family member or friend. Find better ways to express your wants, your needs, and especially your negative feelings, such as anger, which, when bottled up, can turn into depression. Many men "tough out" difficult situations or escape via the bottle or illegal drugs. "When a woman gets the blues, she hangs her head and cries," the song goes. "When a man gets the blues, he takes the train and rides."
- Avoid people and situations that make you feel bad about yourself.
- Exercise regularly. Moderate exercise can enhance the brain's production of mood-elevating endorphins.
- Avoid naps. They worsen the insomnia that often accompanies depression.
- Avoid alcohol and illegal drugs. They offer at best a temporary escape and ultimately might make you feel even more depressed.
- Get involved in activities you enjoy, and try to remain active even though you do not feel like it. A change in pace — a vacation for example — can break the cycle of depression.

If the blues last longer than two or three weeks, are severe, and cannot be related to an obvious event or loss, seek professional help from a physician, psychologist, health clinic, or local mental health association. Some people feel as if they were "born depressed," but fail to recognize that something is amiss because they have felt terrible all their lives. Serious depression of this kind will not go away of its own accord. Yet only about half of the 10 to 14 million individuals who have a diagnosable depression seek treatment. The cost of this neglect is high: illness, disability, lowered productivity, absenteeism, and human misery beyond measure. Research scientists now theorize that many cases of depression are chronic and that people who avoid treatment and wait for their depression to "lift" may be inviting it to recur in the future.

Tricyclic antidepressants have saved as many as 70 to 85 percent of depressed individuals from the depths of despair. Generally, moods begin to lift within two to three weeks of initial dosage. Recent studies show that psychotherapy is just as effective as standard drug treatment in relieving acute depression. One study demonstrated the effectiveness of two forms of psychotherapy: (1) interpersonal therapy that focuses on problems with relationships, and (2) cognitive/behavioral therapy that helps patients change negative ways they have been thinking about themselves and their futures, and reinforces positive thinking and behavior they find more satisfying. (See the section on psychotherapy, pp. 148–150.)

The bottom line is that depression can be overcome. Many people who seek treatment testify that recovery from depression is like emerging from a long tunnel. They become productive and enjoy life more than ever before, confirming the lines:

> The deeper the darkness, the brighter the morn;
> The spirit's rare gladness of sorrow is born.

Putting Pressure in Its Place

People who handle pressure well understand what is happening to them and know how to minimize its worst effects. One way to get a quick reading of your vulnerability to stressful events was developed by Drs. Lyle H. Miller and Alma Dell Smith at Boston University Medical Center. Their "Vulnerability Scale" measures such lifestyle factors as how often you eat at least one hot, balanced meal a day, exercise to the point of perspiration, attend club or social activities, confide in friends about personal matters, speak openly about feelings when angry or worried, do something for fun, and take some quiet time during the day. For a copy of Dr. Lyle Miller's booklet *Stress: What Can Be Done? A Guide to Reducing the Strain Caused by Mismanaged Stress*, send $2.00 to Biobehavioral Associates, 1101 Beacon Street, Brookline, MA 02146.

Psychologist Albert Ellis suggests a practical way of looking at stress: the A-B-C theory of emotion. Individuals, he says, are the creators both of stressors and of their consequent reactions in the form of stress. For such an emotional reaction as tension or anxiety to occur, there must be the following:

A. An Activating Event or stress producer, such as a job problem.
B. A Belief System — which often is subconscious — about that event.
C. Consequent Feelings or actions.

Ellis's theory is that A doesn't cause C. It's B — or what you *believe* about A — that causes C. For example, you learn that you have been passed over for promotion. This is the Activating Event. Next your Belief System about the meaning of A comes into play. First you feel frightened, then angry. Then you start worrying. You might even worry about the fact that you are worrying, further increasing your emotional load.

But you have options. You can decide that being passed over means you are inadequate and the victim of office politics. Or you can decide that being passed over means that (1) your performance *does* need improvement; (2) you need new job skills; or (3) you might be happier in another job, with another boss, or even in another line of work.

Your belief about A determines your Consequent Feelings. You can become depressed and dead-ended as you decide to hold on to your job while others pass you by. Or you can feel sad and disappointed about being passed over, and even anxious about a job or career change. But in the second case your distress will be temporary, will not endanger your health, and will spur you to change.

There are other ways to minimize stress reactions besides altering your perceptions about what is stressful. One is to recognize the power of concentration as a stress reducer. Think of the times when you are most tense. Often many things are happening at once, preventing you from focusing attention on any one task. The next time you feel pressured or "pulled" in several directions, select one activity, concentrate on it, and notice how the tension seems to drain away. Sports like skiing and tennis, meditation, and even playing bridge require tremendous concentration, which is why they — or any activity you can "get into" — are so relaxing. Another way to reduce tension is to adopt certain attitudes and habits common to people who handle stress well. They seem to have four major sources of strength: fitness, friends, fun, and flexibility.

Fitness

If you are physically fit, you will probably feel mentally fit and able to handle stressful situations well. Therefore:

1. Exercise regularly to build fitness and let off steam. Physical exertion raises the body's level of beta endorphins, natural opiumlike substances that reduce anxiety and help make you feel "mellow."

2. Control your weight and eat well, including at least one hot, balanced meal a day.

3. Get enough sleep: seven to eight hours at least four times a week. To sleep less is to run on four cylinders instead of six or eight.

Friends

Recent research suggests that people with many social ties — whether through marriage, close friends and relatives, church membership, or other group activities — are better able to keep stress reactions within tolerable limits. A nine-year study of seven thousand persons in Alameda County, California, by epidemiologist Lisa Berkman showed that low-income men in their fifties with strong social networks lived far longer than high-income men with weak social networks. So:

1. Keep in touch with others, not only through family and intimate relationships, but through self-help and other groups, and nonsexual friendships with men and women whom you trust.

2. Speak openly when you feel grief, anger, disappointment, and other important emotions. Avoid sulking. Allow yourself to cry. As Charles Dickens wrote in *Oliver Twist*, "It opens the lungs, washes the countenance, exercises the eyes, and softens down the temper."

3. Give and receive affection regularly. Many experts have observed that touching can relieve pain and stress and promote more rapid healing. An arm around the shoulders, a pat, a handclasp, a hug, can create a sense of well-being. But many people, especially men, suppress their desire to be held.

4. Learn to listen. Psychologist James J. Lynch, in *The Language of the Heart*, writes that most people — especially those with high blood pressure — experience a significant rise in blood pressure when they speak, followed by a rapid drop in blood pressure and heart rate when they listen attentively to others.

Fun

Enjoyment is the most neglected way to break the negative power of a distressful situation.

1. Balance work with recreation. Schedule breaks during your day. Spend lunch hour or an evening doing something you enjoy.

2. Take a "mental health" day off at least once a month and escape to a pleasant environment: in the woods, along a beach, beside a lake or river, near grazing horses, or in your own home. There is evidence that even thinking about such peaceful surroundings can alleviate stress reactions.

3. Learn to laugh. Laughter is a uniquely human behavior that may stimulate release of the same brain chemicals that cause "runner's high." Even a smile has therapeutic value, according to psychologist Paul Ekman of the University of California, who asked actors to produce facial expressions of happiness, anger, fear, disgust, sadness, and surprise. Results showed that each of these "faces" elicited the same changes in heart rate, sweating response, and skin temperature that the emotions themselves would have produced. In the words of King Solomon, "A merry heart doeth good like a medicine."

Flexibility

Flexibility means you are open to change because you have a basic sense of control over your life.

1. Decide what you really want out of life, set attainable goals, and undertake one thing at a time according to a checklist with priorities.

2. Give in once in a while. You do not always have to be right.

3. Develop options. The person who feels "trapped" experiences more stress than the person who has a repertoire of healthy escapes and alternatives.

4. Cultivate emotional resilience. Research shows that moods of people under intense distress one day tend to bounce back to normal the next. Scarlett O'Hara was right: "Tomorrow is another day."

And Finally

1. Concentrate on managing your own life rather than wasting energy trying to change or "fix" family and friends.

2. Do not try to alleviate stress with alcohol, drugs, smoking, coffee drinking, overeating, overworking, fast driving, or fighting. These "solutions" keep you from functioning on your own and lead to even greater problems. Liquor and drugs reduce the perception of stress, but not stress itself.

3. Learn stress reduction and relaxation techniques such as meditation, deep breathing, stretching and relaxing muscles, and brief naps. Relaxation is more than the absence of stress; it is a positive and satisfying feeling of peace of mind and simply of *being*.

Dr. Herbert Benson, a cardiologist who has studied the body's innate ability to alleviate or prevent stress-related diseases, has written a book, *The Relaxation Response.* This response evokes a drop in blood pressure, heart rate, oxygen consumption, and metabolism, and increases alpha brain waves associated with feelings of well-being.

- Sit in a comfortable position in a quiet place.
- Close your eyes.
- Tense, then relax, successive sets of muscles, one at a time, from the tips of your toes to the muscles in your forehead and neck.
- Breathe through your nose, saying the word "one" silently to yourself each time you breathe out.
- Continue for ten to twenty minutes. You may open your eyes to check the time, but do not use an alarm clock.
- Maintain a passive attitude and let the relaxation occur naturally. When distracting thoughts occur, do not dwell on them, and keep repeating "one."
- Sit quietly for a few minutes after you finish.
- Practice relaxing once or twice daily, but not within two hours after a meal, since digestion seems to interfere with the relaxation response.

Hundreds — even thousands — of stress management techniques exist. They all work in the sense that by trying any one of them, you move from passivity to action against stress, from immobility to creativity, from helplessness to control, from despair to optimism, from ignoring to meeting your personal needs. You refuse, in other words, to give up.

Author Norman Cousins provides the classic example of how refusal to give up and positive thinking can affect health. Told that he had a 1-in-500 chance of recovering from ankylosing spondylitis, a disease that was causing the connective tissue in his spine gradually to disintegrate, he decided to beat the odds. He reasoned that if adverse stress reactions could cause illness, then positive emotions, such as love, hope, faith, confidence, laughter, joy, and the will to live, might promote health. He started the process of self-healing by checking out of the hospital and into a nearby hotel where his physicians could visit him. He then rented films of "Candid Camera" and old Abbott and Costello movies. He discovered that twenty minutes of laughter afforded him a few hours of pain-free sleep. He then expanded his self-healing program with other measures that, during the next year, restored his health. "Since I didn't accept the verdict," Cousins later wrote, "I wasn't trapped in the cycle of fear, depression, and panic that frequently accompanies incurable illness."

Psychotherapy

Some people suffer anxiety, depression, and other emotional reactions because they have complex psychological problems. The danger signs:

1. Undue, prolonged anxiety
2. Severe, long-lasting depression
3. Abrupt changes in mood and behavior
4. Persistent tension-caused physical symptoms
5. A feeling of being trapped
6. Suicidal thoughts
7. Misuse of alcohol or drugs

When psychological pain becomes great enough — often after a job crisis, divorce, or loss of a loved one — millions of men and women have sought professional help from psychiatrists, psychologists, social workers, psychiatric nurses, or other qualified counselors. The seekers are not insane, irrational, or even unable to function. They *are* depressed, anxious, and unwilling to continue leading lives of quiet (or in some cases noisy) desperation.

They progress according to how much effort and money they are willing to spend, how successfully they select a therapist who is interested but objective, and how well they develop a trusting relationship with that person. This relationship is the basic tool of psychotherapy.

There are two approaches to psychotherapy: (1) as short-term intervention for an immediate crisis such as death or divorce, or (2) as long-term therapy to explore underlying emotions, increase self-knowledge, modify behavior, build self-esteem, learn to manage stressful situations, and acquire a whole new set of tools for handling life's problems, large and small.

Psychotherapists might use behavioral, cognitive, or short-term psychotherapy; psychoanalysis; group, marital, and family therapy; biofeedback; hypnosis; relaxation training; behavior modification; or sex counseling. Some problems, such as exploring your past, are better solved in individual therapy sessions. Difficulties getting along with other people are better handled in a group. Some therapists combine individual and group therapy.

An individual therapy session usually lasts fifty minutes and is scheduled weekly or more often if needed. Group therapy can last from one to several hours and usually includes eight or more people. Therapy may continue for months or, when problems are severe, for years. One study of three thousand individuals involved in various types of therapy showed that twenty-six to fifty-two sessions of psychotherapy — assuming the patient actively cooperates in his treatment — are sufficient for most emotional ailments. Other evidence shows that twenty cognitive therapy sessions in ten to twelve weeks will suffice for treating depression.

Costs of private psychotherapy vary according to geographic area and type of practitioner. A session with a psychiatrist costs $75 or more for fifty minutes. Group therapy costs less. Unfortunately, health insurance usually picks up no more than half of the bill. Less costly psychotherapy, on a sliding scale basis, may be available in selected mental health clinics.

Because psychotherapy is so expensive and personal a process, great care should be taken in choosing a therapist with whom you feel comfortable:

- Shop around for a qualified professional. Get referrals from respected friends, private physicians, county medical or psychological societies, local medical schools, health clinics, hospital psychiatric departments, family service/social agencies, community mental health clinics, or local chapters of the mental health association.
- Discuss fees, hours, and schedules. State what you expect to gain from therapy, ask what method the therapist will use, and explore the therapist's background and values.
- If, after a few sessions, you feel uncomfortable with the therapist, it is perfectly appropriate to look elsewhere. But remember that three or four changes of therapists after treatment begins may mean the problem lies with you, not with the therapist.
- Over the long run, expect a sense of progress despite the emotional discomforts of therapy.

Entering and staying in psychotherapy is a major life decision that deserves careful consideration and commitment. Perhaps the best analogy to what therapy offers in return appears in *The Wizard of Oz*, in which the Scarecrow, Cowardly Lion, and Tin Woodman finally realize that they already possess what they have traveled so far to find: brains, courage, and a heart.

People who gain the most from psychotherapy

- recognize how they cause or contribute to their problems
- can define a single problem instead of saying, "Everything always goes wrong"
- feel more comfortable with people who are struggling than with those who think they have "arrived"
- are motivated to work toward personal change

Many people who undergo therapy find that it improves both their mental and physical health. According to a study of health insurance claims by federal employees, sponsored by the National Institute of Mental Health, the use of mental health coverage may be an important way to reduce general health care costs.

Successful management of stressors and stress, by whatever means, can produce "emotional hardiness," according to the National Academy of Sciences' *Stress and Human Health*. The emotionally hardy have a sense of purpose, feel in control of themselves, are open to change, and see stress-producing events as challenges rather than as threats.

By mastering stressful challenges, they build skills for handling stressors the next time they come around. Putting pressure in its place may be as important as good nutrition, adequate exercise, satisfying work, and intimate relationships with others in defending against some of the leading killers of men. Thus the way you manage stressful events is an essential survival skill that can affect your health and longevity, over the long term, as much as the way you eat, exercise, sleep, and enjoy your working day.

Where to Get Help in Managing Stress

- The National Health Information Clearinghouse has published a list called "Stress Information Resources." For a free copy, write to NHIC, P.O. Box 1133, Washington, D.C. 20013-1133.
- The National Institute of Mental Health has published an excellent booklet, *Depression: What We Know,* available from the Consumer Information Center, Pueblo, CO 81009.

- Two books that may be helpful in managing stressful situations are *The Relaxation Response,* by Herbert Benson (New York: Morrow, 1976), and *How to Get Control of Your Time and Your Life,* by Alan Lakein (New York: New American Library, 1973).

For further information about stress and depression, contact the National Institute of Mental Health, Public Inquiries Section, Parklawn Building, Room 15C-05, 5600 Fishers Lane, Rockville, MD 20857; telephone 301-443-4513.

II

DISEASES OF MEN

6

Heart Disease and Cancer

This section presents bottom-line basics needed to prevent and deal with the ten diseases for which men are most at risk: heart disease, cancer, accidents, stroke, chronic lung diseases, pneumonia/influenza, suicide, liver disease and cirrhosis, homicide, and diabetes. These diseases reduce men's life expectancy by seven years compared with women's and kill men at rates three or more times greater. Yet most of these diseases can be prevented, treated, and — in many cases — arrested or reversed.

The following table gives numbers of deaths and death rates per 100,000 population for the top ten killing diseases of men in the United States in 1984.

Cause of death	Number of men who died	Rate per 100,000
1. Heart disease	397,097	345.2
2. Cancer	242,790	211.1
3. Accidents	64,053	55.7
4. Stroke	61,697	53.6
5. Chronic obstructive lung disease	44,013	38.3
6. Pneumonia/influenza	29,440	25.6
7. Suicide	22,689	19.7
8. Liver disease/cirrhosis	17,558	15.3
9. Homicide	15,038	13.1
10. Diabetes	14,859	12.9

SOURCE: National Center for Health Statistics.

Heart Disease: Good News and Bad

Upon starting to write this chapter, I realized that during twenty-five years of medical writing I had never written much about heart disease. My father died prematurely of rheumatic heart disease, and the risk of heart disease runs in my family, higher for my brother than for me, but I am increasingly at risk as I grow older. We all, in our own ways, avoid dealing with what threatens us.

Heart disease actually threatens fewer Americans than in the past. Deaths from heart attacks, angina, and related ailments have consistently declined since 1968, particularly in men. Better medical care has probably contributed to the decline. But the major reason, many researchers believe, is decreasing incidence of the disease itself, probably reflecting that men are smoking less, eating less cholesterol and fat, controlling high blood pressure, and making other healthful changes in their lifestyles.

Still, the United States continues to have one of the world's highest rates of heart disease, which remains the leading cause of death in the United States and kills one in five American men. Men of all ages remain four times as likely to contract heart disease as women, and twice as likely to die of it.

Recognizing Heart Disease

What is this ailment that seems to single out men? Heart disease affects not only the heart itself, but also blood vessels, especially the arteries that carry blood throughout the body, hence its name, cardiovascular disease — "cardio" meaning heart and "vascular" meaning blood vessel.

The healthy heart, which weighs well under a pound and is only a little larger than your fist, is a hollow organ with a tough, muscular wall called the myocardium. The heart has four chambers. Two on your right side receive blood from the body and pump it to the lungs, where it picks up oxygen. The chambers in the "left heart" receive the oxygen-rich blood from the lungs and pump it to the body through the largest artery in the body: the aorta.

Although you are scarcely aware of it, your heart

- beats 70 to 90 times a minute, or about 100,000 times a day
- pumps 5 quarts of blood through 60,000 miles of arteries, veins,

and small blood vessels (a pumping capacity of 4,300 gallons a day)

- sends blood from the heart to the big toe and back in less than sixty seconds
- increases its output by nearly five times during vigorous exercise, when the body needs more oxygen- and nutrient-rich blood

The myocardium is the strongest muscle in the body. But it needs an unceasing supply of oxygen and nutrients or it will almost instantly die. The myocardium cannot obtain these essentials from the blood within its own chambers. Blood vessels that nourish the heart muscle — the right and left coronary arteries — must provide the needed oxygen and nutrients. They are called the coronary arteries because they appear to sit atop the heart like a crown.

The most common type of heart disease is called coronary heart disease. It is caused primarily by atherosclerosis, a form of arteriosclerosis, or hardening of the arteries. Atherosclerosis is a buildup of fatty deposits in the coronary arteries leading to the heart. This buildup impedes the flow of blood and may eventually lead to coronary heart disease (CHD) or, if the buildup affects blood flow to the brain, a stroke. Although nobody knows what causes the underlying atherosclerosis, scientists have found that a diet high in cholesterol and saturated fats is statistically associated with high blood cholesterol levels and an increased risk of heart attack and stroke. (See the section on stroke in chapter 7, pp. 189–193.)

Because more than two-thirds of a coronary artery may be filled with atherosclerotic deposits without causing symptoms, too often the first warning sign of coronary heart disease is a heart attack or sudden blockage of one of the arteries that supplies the heart muscle with blood. This irreversibly injures the heart muscle and causes a surrounding area of injury or inflammation called a myocardial infarction (MI). A heart attack is also called a "coronary" if the obstruction is in one of the coronary arteries, or a "coronary thrombosis" if a blood clot, rather than narrowed artery, is the specific obstruction.

Sometimes, diminished blood flow in the coronary arteries causes not a heart attack but angina pectoris, a chest pain that occurs when blood supply is adequate to meet normal heart needs, but not the increased demands of running or shoveling snow. Diminished blood supply can also cause changes in heart rhythm — another warning sign of coronary heart disease.

The average heart attack victim waits three hours before deciding to seek help, according to the American Heart Association. About a third of the time, victims do not realize they have suffered a heart attack.

Not all of the warning signs of a heart attack are always present, so if only one of the following occurs, get help immediately:

- A dull, heavy squeezing pain in the center of the chest that lasts two minutes or more. Heart attacks seldom cause massive, immobilizing pain, but they do cause enough pain to make you stop what you are doing. Sharp, stabbing pains that last a few seconds usually do not indicate a heart attack.
- Pain that spreads to the shoulders, arms, neck, or jaw.
- *Severe* pain, dizziness, fainting, sweating, nausea, or shortness of breath.

  NOTE: Do not attempt to drive yourself to a hospital. Get someone else or call an ambulance, and ask to be taken to the coronary care unit.

Some people having a heart attack feel only mild, indigestionlike discomfort. Others have no symptoms at all. Still others have heart attack–like symptoms caused by angina pectoris (transient chest pain), racing heartbeat, excessive caffeine, stress, or a panic attack. It is better to seek medical attention than to assume nothing is wrong.

About 70 percent of cardiac arrests occur in the home. Thus it is important for middle-aged and older women who might be living with a man at high risk of a heart attack to learn cardiopulmonary resuscitation (CPR). This emergency procedure has saved the lives of thousands of heart attack victims and other persons in whom heartbeat and breathing have stopped.

- CPR combines external chest massage to restore heartbeat with mouth-to-mouth resuscitation to restore breathing.
- CPR should be used only by persons thoroughly trained in its use. It can be learned in three to four hours.
- If CPR is started for a heart attack victim within one minute of collapse, chances of recovery are estimated at 98 percent. A four-minute delay lowers chances of recovery to 50 percent (most emergency vehicles take at least this long to respond), and a seven-minute delay means only an 8 percent chance of recovery.

- Information about CPR courses is available through local heart associations and American Red Cross chapters.

Some heart specialists recommend "do-it-yourself" CPR. In case you have a heart attack while alone, cough vigorously about once every second. This helps keep blood flowing through the heart and to the brain and helps you stay conscious for a minute or longer. This may be enough time to pull your car off the road, make a phone call, and get life-saving help.

Sudden Cardiac Death

Many people — especially men — do not know they have heart disease until they suffer a heart attack. Of 550,000 deaths from heart disease each year in the United States, two-thirds occur without warning. Most of these sudden cardiac deaths strike men aged thirty-five to sixty-five.

By definition, sudden cardiac death (SCD) occurs without symptoms or with symptoms of less than an hour's duration. Often sudden death is the first sign of underlying heart disease. But some of those stricken may have had previous "silent heart attacks," according to data from the Framingham Heart Study, an ongoing survey of factors that correlate with the occurrence of heart attacks and strokes in more than five thousand men and women. These findings, reported in the November 1, 1984, *New England Journal of Medicine,* revealed that more than 25 percent of heart attack patients do not realize they have just suffered a heart attack. But these silent heart attacks are just as likely to later cause stroke or heart failure as recognized heart attacks.

It is well established that at least 75 percent of the victims of sudden cardiac death have significant atherosclerotic heart disease, usually involving two or three coronary arteries. The remainder usually have other types of heart disease. Sudden cardiac arrest is also associated with "electrical failure" of the heart or degeneration of the heart's electrical signals. The disorganized electrical signals may lead to disturbances in the heart's rhythm (arrhythmia). Some arrhythmias are not life-threatening, but one, known as ventricular fibrillation (VF), completely disrupts the heart's orderly contraction or beating and is deadly if not reversed within a few minutes.

Other studies suggest that sudden cardiac death is associated with depression, a sense of psychological entrapment, recent loss of a loved one or other significant emotional distress, unaccustomed physical activity, or even a heavy evening meal. But these may be triggers rather than basic causes.

The "Big Three" Risk Factors

What can be done to prevent the sudden deaths and slower declines from heart disease? The answer lies in risk factors, which explain, to some extent, why heart attacks occur and therefore suggest some ways to prevent them. Some risk factors cannot be changed. These include

- heredity (especially a father, grandfather, brother, or uncle who died of a heart attack before age sixty
- maleness (especially men between thirty and forty-nine)
- age: over sixty for men and after menopause for women

Of all the risk factors that *can* be modified, the three most important are smoking, high blood cholesterol, and high blood pressure. These "Big Three" risk factors are additive in their impact. Each increases the risk of heart attack by two to three times. A person with two risk factors has three to four times the risk of someone with none. A person with all three has eight to ten times the risk. Eliminating any of the "Big Three" risk factors also lowers the likelihood of heart attack to the same degree.

Smoking is the primary risk factor for sudden cardiac death and heart disease. It stimulates heart rate and the oxygen needs of the heart, and infuses the blood with carbon monoxide. Smokers are two to three times more likely to have heart attacks than nonsmokers and two to four times more vulnerable to sudden cardiac death. Smoking also is the number one risk factor for peripheral vascular disease — narrowed blood vessels in the leg and arm muscles that can lead to gangrene and leg amputation. No matter how long you may have smoked, stopping greatly reduces your risk of heart disease, even when there is a family history of heart disease. According to the American Heart Association, if you have smoked a pack a day or less, ten years after quitting your risk will be the same as if you had never smoked. (For more reasons to stop smoking, see chapter 9, pp. 244–247.)

High blood cholesterol is another leading risk factor for atherosclerosis and coronary heart disease. A desirable blood cholesterol level is 200 mg/dl or less in a person over age thirty. Most heart attacks occur in persons with cholesterol levels between 210 and 265 mg/dl, the American Heart Association says. Although atherosclerosis is not part of the natural aging process, in this culture people rarely escape it as they grow older. Yet, theoretically, there is no *age-related* reason why a healthy man in his eighties should not have far clearer arteries than he is likely to have today, given current dietary habits. Blood cholesterol levels can be lowered by reducing cholesterol and saturated fat in the diet (see chapter 1, pp. 14–18).

It is hard to control your blood cholesterol level if you do not know what it is. Many physicians advocate a routine cholesterol test during your twenties and, if normal (i.e., below 200), at least every five years until age forty, and every two to three years thereafter. Abnormal blood cholesterol should be treated immediately, and checked yearly until normal and every two to three years thereafter.

High Blood Pressure

Blood pressure is the force blood exerts against the walls of blood vessels throughout your body as your heart pumps blood. Muscle cells in small arteries called arterioles regulate blood pressure. When they contract so that blood cannot pass through easily, your heart must pump harder to maintain blood flow and your blood pressure rises. When elevations in blood pressure continue, the result is a disease known as hypertension or high blood pressure. In nine out of ten cases the underlying cause is unknown. Hypertension does not mean you are tense or nervous, although severe stress can cause temporary elevations in blood pressure.

High blood pressure seldom causes symptoms, which is why it so often goes undetected. Meanwhile, this silent killer makes the heart enlarge from working harder than normal. Constantly elevated blood pressure is thought to accelerate atherosclerosis because it stresses the linings of major blood vessels. High blood pressure also increases the risk that a blood clot may lodge in a narrowed artery, and it prevents narrowed arteries from delivering enough blood to the body's organs. This may damage blood vessels that supply vital organs such as the brain, heart, eyes, and kidneys, and may lead to strokes, heart attacks, blindness, and kidney disease.

High blood pressure contributes directly or indirectly to about one million deaths in the United States each year. Yet recent studies show that only half of 58 million Americans with high blood pressure are aware of their condition, and only 10 percent satisfactorily control the condition.

Blood pressure is measured in milligrams on a column of mercury (mm/Hg). The pressure reading has two numbers: the first number —

the systolic, or pumping, pressure — measures pressure in the blood vessels during a heartbeat; the second — diastolic, or resting, pressure — measures the pressure during the rest between beats. Of the two measurements, diastolic pressure is considered more important. According to the National High Blood Pressure Information Center, a blood pressure below 120/80 mm/Hg is considered normal for people under eighteen. Between ages eighteen and fifty, a blood pressure reading *up to* 140/90 is considered normal. Blood pressure above 140/90 in people of any age increases the risk of heart disease and other complications and should be treated by a physician. Even one or two elevated blood pressure readings should not be ignored, according to the National Heart, Lung, and Blood Institute. High blood pressure can be detected easily and painlessly. Many physicians recommend that everybody aged eighteen or older have an annual blood pressure check by a physician or health professional. Yearly checkups are especially important for people in high-risk groups. These include blacks (who are affected three times as often as whites), people over fifty, postmenopausal or pregnant women, women taking contraceptives, and people whose parents or other close relatives are hypertensive.

One high reading does not necessarily mean trouble, but it does mean *check again* with your doctor. If readings remain high during at least two subsequent visits, your doctor may advise you to take steps to control high blood pressure:

- Maintain a normal weight.
- Reduce intake of high-fat, high-cholesterol foods and eat balanced meals (see chapter 1).
- Stop smoking.
- Exercise vigorously three to four times a week for thirty to forty minutes.
- Lower salt consumption if you are salt-sensitive (see chapter 1, pp. 21–23).
- Most important, take high blood pressure medication if prescribed, and do not "double up" if you miss a dose.

Blood pressure medication often causes frequent or urgent urination, dry mouth, or dizziness. Certain medications may cause headache, fatigue, or impotence. Many patients discontinue medication because of these side effects and do not tell their physicians about it. There are many different drugs for high blood pressure, and people react differently to them. The blood pressure of white people, for example, can respond to certain drugs differently from that of blacks. By trial and error, a physician and patient nearly always can find the right combination that controls blood pressure and minimizes side effects.

Low blood pressure of 110/70 mm/Hg or less is normally considered safe for most people unless it is a symptom of an underlying disease, shock, or internal bleeding. The lower your blood pressure, the lower your chances of developing a stroke, heart attack, or kidney failure. People with low blood pressure (hypotension) usually live long, normal lives, as insurance companies recognize in the lower premiums charged for such individuals. However, people with hypotension may tire easily or feel faint in a hot room or after a few alcoholic drinks.

Suspected Risk Factors

There are several suspected — and controllable — risk factors for heart disease.

Obesity places a heavy burden on the heart and is associated with high blood pressure, high blood cholesterol, and other diseases and risk factors. No hard evidence shows that losing excess weight will prevent heart disease. But safe, gradual weight loss can reduce the effects of other risk factors and improve overall health.

Physical inactivity leads to obesity and all its associated risk factors. Although there is no proof that exercise delays or prevents a heart attack, inactive people tend to have more heart disease than physically active people. Regular, vigorous exercise also improves heart efficiency and general health.

Diabetes is a risk factor, especially for diabetics between age forty and fifty-nine who do not keep their disease under control. Because diabetes is associated with high blood pressure, high blood cholesterol, and obesity, controlling diabetes may help reduce these risk factors for coronary heart disease. (See chapter 7, pp. 206–209, on diabetes.)

Alcohol in moderation does not appear to increase the risk of heart attack. But some studies show that heavy use of alcohol — 3 to 4 ounces of 100 proof whiskey, 12 to 18 ounces of wine, or 36 to 48 ounces of beer per day — can significantly raise blood pressure.

Stress: There is no hard proof that stress leads to heart disease. Yet physicians have known for many years that heart attack victims are more likely than healthy persons to report periods of prolonged stress and that emotional disturbances can trigger angina. In *The Broken Heart: The Medical Consequences of Loneliness,* psychologist James J. Lynch shows that the incidence of premature death from heart disease is significantly higher among loneliness-prone people, many of whom are widowed, divorced, or separated, and among people who lack human companionship.

The Type A Personality

One popular — and controversial — theory is that people with Type A personality have a higher risk of heart disease. The link was first reported by Drs. Murray Friedman and Ray Rosenman of Mount Zion Medical Center in San Francisco. They noticed, during the 1950s, that the chair seats in their waiting room were worn only on the front edges. Investigating further, Drs. Friedman and Rosenman discovered that many of their heart patients seemed to be impatient, competitive overachievers who were always "on edge," as it were, racing against the clock, and ready to erupt into anger at almost any target.

To identify patients with Type A behavior, Drs. Friedman and Rosenman used, among other techniques, a voice analysis test, and asked their patients to read the following passage silently and then aloud:

> This is the way that you and me, every God damned one of us are going to lick the hell out of whoever stands in our way. And I don't give a damn whether you like what I'm telling you or not. This is the way I say it's got to be done. First, we're going to smack them hard with mortar fire, understand? I want you to pour it on them! Let the bastards feel it get hot. . . . After the mortars, I'll tell you when to advance. And when I give the signal, don't crawl, you run forward! Remember, it's your skin or theirs! All right, enough talk, now let's get the lead out of our pants and get going. Hey! One more thing, good luck!

Subjects were then told to read the text again and imagine that they were officers giving this speech on the battlefield. Analysis of voice-prints showed that Type B's (who are more easygoing and noncompetitive) rarely inflected their words, while Type A subjects read in harsh rhythms that caused the voice-print needle to oscillate wildly.

People with Type A personality ("hurry sickness") tend to

- try to do two things at once
- walk, eat, and talk fast
- have trouble sitting and doing nothing

- often use gestures of impatience, such as jiggling knees, tapping fingers, pounding fists, and talking with their hands
- often sit on the edge of their chairs, have hostile, jarring laughs, speak explosively, use obscenities, and display obvious facial tension
- get irritated if kept waiting for any reason
- always play to win, even in games with children
- distrust other people's motives

NOTE: Some studies have shown that Type A behavior is more common in men than in women.

Type A's are more likely to have a heart attack than Type B's, Drs. Friedman and Rosenman reported in 1959. A study by Friedman and colleagues, published in the August 1984 *American Heart Journal*, demonstrated, moreover, that Type A behavior can be altered in people who have suffered heart attacks, and that such alteration significantly reduces a susceptible individual's risk of suffering another one. In Dr. Friedman's Type A behavior modification program, participants learn to recognize Type A behavior first in others, then in themselves. They learn alternatives to Type A behavior, including physical and mental relaxation techniques, and discover the root causes of their Type A behavior.

Some people enjoy being Type A's and have no desire to change. If you wish to modify Type A behavior, however, you must essentially relearn how to live, says Dr. Friedman. He recommends these "homework" exercises for unlearning the time urgency aspect of Type A behavior:

- Listen to somebody without interrupting or thinking about something else.
- Do nothing but listen to music for fifteen minutes.
- Concentrate on one task at a time. Even Einstein, when tying his shoelaces, thought chiefly about the bow, Dr. Friedman says.
- Drive in the slow traffic lanes.
- Stand in the longest line at the supermarket.
- Spend at least ten to fifteen minutes each day taking "miniholidays" to meditate, daydream, or nap.
- Read books that demand concentration.
- Whenever you can, buy time with your money.
- Walk, talk, and eat more slowly.

- Listen to at least two persons talking on separate occasions without interrupting even once.
- Tell yourself at least weekly that few enterprises ever fail because they are executed too slowly or too well.

  SOURCE: Murray Friedman, *Treating Type A Behavior and Your Heart* (New York: Knopf, 1984).

Other researchers have since found that Type A behavior is associated with elevated blood cholesterol levels, increased clot formation, high blood insulin levels, and high levels of the adrenal hormone norepinephrine, which may trigger abnormalities in heart rhythm. In 1981 a panel meeting at the National Institutes of Health concluded that Type A behavior is as serious a risk factor for coronary heart disease as smoking, high blood cholesterol, and hypertension.

Despite these findings, the Type A theory is not universally accepted among heart disease experts. A report in the March 21, 1985, *New England Journal of Medicine* noted no relationship between Type A behavior and recurrent acute myocardial infarction. This study, however, did not explore the effects of *modifying* Type A behavior. Recent textbooks on heart disease and the American Heart Association rank Type A behavior secondary to the "Big Three" risk factors mentioned earlier.

Living with Heart Disease

Today there are treatments — many of which did not exist fifteen to twenty years ago — that help people with heart disease thrive and survive. They include

- nitroglycerin and new drugs that relieve angina by slowing heart rate, dilating blood vessels, relaxing arteries, and preventing the heart from absorbing too much calcium
- clot-dissolving agents, such as tissue-type plasminogen activator (TPA), that prevent recurrent heart attacks
- pacemakers with surgically implanted batteries that produce electrical impulses for regulating abnormal heart rhythms, and new heart-assist devices that help remove the burden of work from a diseased heart
- coronary bypass surgery — the grafting of healthy blood vessels to arteries leading to the heart — to provide a new path for blood flow to the heart and relieve disabling chest pain and other symptoms caused by coronary heart disease

- balloon angioplasty, or widening the inside of arteries with a tiny balloon-tipped instrument to improve blood flow
- lifestyle modifications, especially smoking cessation, dietary changes, and control of high blood pressure

Some heart attack and angina patients take aspirin each day to prevent blood clots that might cause another heart attack. This treatment has been so successful that the FDA now allows aspirin sold over the counter to be so labeled. Although it is not proven that aspirin will do the same for *healthy* adults, many physicians, including the Surgeon General of the Public Health Service, informally advise male patients, in particular, to take one-half to one 5-grain aspirin daily, and their female patients to take half an aspirin every other day (because women produce fewer clot-promoting hormones than men). People with ulcers should not take aspirin, and those who take it regularly should do so during or following a meal.

About twenty-two thousand physicians in the United States are taking aspirin and beta-carotene (a substance that causes the orange color in carrots and turns into vitamin A compounds in the intestines) on alternate days in a study to determine whether they can lower their risk of developing heart attacks and cancer.

Perhaps the best way to conquer heart disease is to avoid risk-taking coronary-prone behavior: skipping high blood pressure medication or continuing to smoke. Many men associate heart disease with aging, helplessness, dependency, loss of masculinity, and a curtailed sex life. But author James Michener's life illustrates that these need not be the outcome. After Michener suffered a heart attack in 1965 at fifty-eight, the late Dr. Paul Dudley White, the heart specialist who took care of President Eisenhower and who himself lived to the age of one hundred, advised Michener to

> do everything you've ever done before: work, exercise, sex, travel, obligations. . . . Don't ever again drink whole milk. Cut out eggs. Go light on cheese. . . .Learn to walk away from tense situations. . . . Exercise to the limit of your endurance, but also take a nap every day.

Dr. White added: "I may not have placed sufficient emphasis on psychological factors." In an article in the *New York Times Magazine*, August 19, 1984, Michener wrote that White's precepts were the key to some of the best years I've had. . . . I was able to get out of bed after a prolonged recuperation, play vigorous tennis again, circumnavigate the globe four or five times, write 10 books and serve the Government in various ways. I do not smoke, drink or eat the things he forbade. . . . Each night at dusk I walk two miles up some very steep hills. I have realized since my final meeting with Dr. White that I live on borrowed time, and I have done so in accordance with the simple, optimistic rules he laid down.

Dr. White's advice — which calls for no less than learning a new way to live — continues to make sense today, whether you have had a heart attack or are trying never to have one.

Cancer: The Good News

Few words cause greater fear than cancer. Cancerphobia feeds on myths that cancer is incurable, inevitable, and contagious. Fear of cancer causes many people to avoid screening tests that could detect it, ignore symptoms, and even refuse to seek proper treatment. Yet many cancers are curable, and many are preventable by avoiding behaviors known to raise the risk of cancer.

About half of patients with newly diagnosed cancer are alive five years later, thanks to improved detection and treatment methods. Some of the most "curable" cancers of men are Hodgkin's disease, melanoma skin cancer, and cancers of the testes and thyroid. The least curable are cancers of the pancreas, esophagus, lung, stomach, and brain. Depending on the type of cancer, some patients who have no evidence of disease for five years after treatment are considered cured and generally have the same life expectancy as someone who has never had cancer. Others are considered cured after one to three years, while some have to be followed longer than five years. The best news about cancer involves prevention. The National Cancer Institute (NCI) reports that about 30 percent of all cancer deaths could be prevented if people stopped smoking. Dietary changes could reduce cancer deaths by another 35 percent.

What Causes Cancer?

Cancer is not one but perhaps one hundred different diseases, all characterized by uncontrolled growth and spread of abnormal cells. Since it takes twenty to thirty years for most cancers to develop — lung cancer may take even longer — their causes are difficult to determine.

All humans appear to have within their cells normal growth genes with the potential to be transformed into cancer genes, probably because of damage to DNA, the genetic material that controls all functions in cells. This damage can result from repeated or long-term exposure to cancer-causing agents called carcinogens. Scientists hypothesize that a normal cell must undergo at least two steps — initiation and promotion — before it becomes cancerous. During *initiation*, normal cells are exposed to carcinogens (X rays, chemicals found in cigarette smoke, viruses, and possibly other agents) that cause irreversible damage. During the *promotion* phase, certain chemicals such as asbestos and dioxin, drugs such as synthetic estrogens, alcoholic beverages, dietary fat, and radiation allow "initiated" cells to reproduce and form tumors. This phase is sometimes reversible; if exposure to the promoter is stopped, the initiated cells may not survive and grow to become tumors. Scientists theorize that both initiation and promotion must occur to produce cancer.

Many people worry that air pollution, pesticides, and artificial sweeteners, nitrites, and other food additives can cause cancer. But only a small percentage of cancer has been proved to be caused by such agents. Some cases of cancer of the colon, brain, and skin (malignant melanoma) appear related to genetic factors. The best way to reduce cancer risk, advises Dr. Peter Greenwald, director of the Division of Cancer Prevention and Control for the National Cancer Institute, is "Don't smoke, change your diet to increase fiber, reduce fats, and keep trim. The other things that you hear about almost every day either are unproven or are of trivial importance to most people. They just do not affect the cancer risk of the average citizen."

It has been estimated that diet is linked to about 35 percent of cancer deaths; tobacco, 30 percent; occupation, 4 percent; viruses, 3 percent; alcohol, 3 percent; excess sunshine / X rays / environmental pollution / food additives / industrial products, 8 percent; and unknown, 3 percent.

Who's at Risk?

Cancer occurs more often in men than in women, and more often in black men than in white. Cancer is primarily a disease of middle and old age; for example, cancer of the prostate seldom strikes men under age fifty. "Familial susceptibility" poses a much greater cancer threat than genetic inheritance because it includes not only genes but shared lifestyle and environment. Generally, individuals whose mother, father, or siblings developed cancer of the stomach, breast, colon, uterus, or lung have a two- to three-times-greater chance of developing the same type of cancer.

Adult men in the United States are at greatest risk of death from cancers of the

- lung (death rates for men are nearly two and a half times those of women)*
- colon/rectum
- prostate
- blood/lymphatic system
- pancreas
- urinary tract
- stomach
- kidney
- oral cavity
- esophagus

* Differences in lung cancer mortality are expected to narrow because women's death rates from lung cancer have risen markedly in recent years while death rates for white men have been leveling off.

Breast cancer affects several hundred men each year. This rare disease in men is associated with testicular disorders and with Klinefelter's syndrome, a disorder of men characterized by poorly developed sex organs, hormonal abnormalities, and gynecomastia (breast swelling).

Ten Ways to Beat Cancer

Never before has scientific evidence shown so clearly that cancer can be prevented. About 80 percent of all cancers are linked to lifestyle. Cancer-preventing changes in lifestyle need not be drastic. Most do not even require a trip to the doctor. These changes can be beneficial at any age — even during middle age or later. Step 1 is to know the warning signs of cancer; steps 2 through 5 involve simple screening practices that can reduce your cancer risk. Steps 6 through 9 involve anticancer lifestyles. Step 10 describes what to do if you are diagnosed as having cancer.

1. Know the Warning Signs of Cancer

Many cancers can be detected early — and probably cured — if you listen to your body's signals:

- Change in bowel or bladder habits, such as diarrhea or constipation lasting more than two weeks
- A sore that does not heal
- Unusual discharge or bleeding, especially blood in the urine or stool
- Thickening or a lump in the breast or elsewhere
- Indigestion or difficulty swallowing
- Changes in a wart or mole
- Nagging cough or hoarseness
- Unexplained weight loss lasting two or more weeks

These symptoms do not necessarily mean you have cancer. But if a symptom persists longer than two weeks, see a physician without delay. Equally important, follow medical recommendations for further examination and treatment. In general, the American Cancer Society recommends a cancer-related checkup, including examination of the testes and prostate, every three years between ages twenty and forty, and annually thereafter.

2. Examine Your Testicles Monthly

For years, women have been urged to examine their breasts each month to detect early breast cancer. No comparable self-examination has been recommended for men. Even today most men have not even *heard* of testicular self-examination, let alone practiced this little-known life-saver regularly. Testicular cancer, although rare, is one of the most common tumors of men aged fifteen to thirty-five; of white men, who have more than four times the risk of black men; and of men with a family history of testicular cancer. Men who have an undescended testicle also are at a much higher risk of developing testicular cancer than other men. The risk increases with increasing age at correction, with the highest risk for men whose undescended testis was never surgically corrected. Several research studies have suggested a relationship between testicular cancer and inguinal hernia at an early age, but the link has not been well established.

Testicular cancer is nearly 100 percent curable if detected and treated early. However, most testicular cancer is far advanced when finally seen by a physician. In many cases, this needless tragedy could be prevented by a simple three-minute testicular self-examination that can detect the common symptoms of testicular cancer: lumps, swelling, and pain.

If you are a man aged fifteen to forty-five, pick a day each month to examine yourself during or soon after a warm shower or bath, when the scrotum is relaxed and abnormalities are easy to feel:

- While standing, gently roll one testicle between your thumb and fingers and check for lumps, swelling, or other changes.
- Repeat this exam on the other testicle.
- See a doctor immediately if you notice a small, hard lump about the size of a pea; scrotal swelling, pain, unusual tenderness; or a feeling of heaviness in the scrotum.

Although these symptoms do not necessarily mean cancer (some difference in the size or shape of the testicles is normal), only a physician can tell the difference. Some men, even after discovering an abnormality in a testicle, delay seeing a doctor. Cancers of reproductive organs tend to spread quickly. Even a two-month delay is dangerous. If you have an undescended testis, ask your doctor to perform a simple procedure to correct it.

3. *Examine Your Skin Monthly*

Learn what your skin looks like and note where birthmarks and moles are located. Examine your skin monthly, using a mirror for such hard-to-see areas as the back, scalp, between the buttocks, and genitals. If you have a family history of melanoma, ask your spouse or a friend to help you inspect these areas. Pay attention to moles (the average person has about fifty of them) to see if they are enlarging or spreading, changing colors (especially to dark brown or black), bleeding, or healing slowly. Some early skin cancers look like sharply outlined, flat, red patches. Others resemble pale, waxy nodules that may ulcerate and crust. They occur in areas that usually receive the most sun exposure: forehead, neck, backs of the hands, forearms, and tops of the ears. Malignant melanomas — cancers that spread quickly and can cause death in six to twelve months — usually start as dark brown or black molelike growths that increase from the size of a freckle to that of a pencil eraser or larger. They are asymmetrical, have irregular borders, uneven surfaces, and/or a mixture of colors, especially black, gray, or blue. If you notice any suspicious changes in your skin, see a physician immediately. Delays of even a few days can be dangerous.

4. Get Tested for Colon Cancer

Colorectal cancer is the second most deadly cancer in men after lung cancer. Yet it may be the most preventable through early detection. The American Cancer Society recommends three examinations to detect cancers of the colon and rectum:

1. A digital rectal examination every year after age forty
2. A proctosigmoidoscopic ("procto") exam every three to five years after age fifty, following two annual exams with negative results
3. A stool blood test every year after age fifty

> NOTE: These guidelines apply *only* to people who are symptom-free. Those with rectal bleeding or changes in bowel habits should see a doctor immediately.

During a "procto" exam, a physician inserts a lighted tube into the first twelve inches of the rectum and lower colon to detect tumors and other abnormalities. Digital and "procto" examinations combined can detect 60 percent of all colorectal cancers, since most tumors occur in the lower third of the colon. Cancers detected by these tests have a high cure rate.

A slightly lower percentage of colon cancers can be detected by a screening test for hidden blood in the stool. Although these tests are designed to be performed at home, they have a high false positive rate and should be used under the guidance of a physician. You eat a meat-free diet and avoid iron, aspirin, and vitamin C for forty-eight hours. You continue this regimen until you have collected specimens from three consecutive stools on a paper slide that can be mailed to your doctor. Test kits are available from your physician or local health department.

Some people need more extensive testing and should be under a physician's care if they have

- ulcerative colitis (inflammation of the inner lining of the large intestine) for ten years or longer
- a family history of colon or any other form of cancer
- polyps (small, cherrylike growths on the intestinal wall that tend to become cancerous if not removed)

5. *Have Your Prostate Examined Annually After Age Forty*

Prostate cancer is so common in men over age fifty-five that it is some-times called the male equivalent to breast cancer. Although prostate cancer tends to cause no symptoms in its early stages, a physician, during a digital rectal examination, can feel the prostate through the rectal wall and detect irregular or unusually firm areas that may indi-cate a tumor. The American Cancer Society recommends that men over age forty have a prostate exam annually. Early detection is not only life-saving, it can ensure that treatment does not disrupt tissues near the prostate.

The following symptoms, most involving urinary difficulties, should be checked by a physician promptly. Most indicate enlargement or inflammation of the prostate (see chapter 8, pp. 225–228) rather than cancer.

- weak or interrupted flow of urine
- inability to urinate or difficulty starting urination
- need to urinate frequently, especially at night
- blood in the urine
- urine flow that is not easily stopped
- painful or burning urination
- continuing pain in the lower back, pelvis, or upper thighs

SOURCE: American Cancer Society, *Facts on Prostate Cancer.*

6. *Do Not Smoke*

Although many smokers do not get lung cancer, from 10 to 20 percent of all smokers do. Tobacco smoke contains forty or more known car-cinogens. The more cigarettes you smoke, the younger you start, the more you inhale, and the longer you smoke, the greater your chances of eventually developing lung cancer. In humans, the process usually takes thirty-five to forty years. Although smoking one or two cigarettes daily may not appreciably increase the risk of developing lung cancer, smoking nine to ten cigarettes a day raises your lung-cancer risk to about four times that of a nonsmoker. Smoking a pack or more of cigarettes a day multiplies the normal risk of lung cancer by ten. Cig-arettes also contribute to cancers of the mouth, larynx (voice box), esophagus, pancreas, urinary bladder, kidney, and possibly the stom-ach.

Pipe and cigar smokers are less likely than cigarette smokers to de-velop lung cancer. But they stand the same risk of developing cancer of the mouth, lip, tongue, pharynx, and esophagus. Snuff and other forms of "smokeless tobacco" that are increasingly popular among teenage and young adult males increase the incidence of cancers of the mouth and throat. Low-tar and low-nicotine cigarettes can reduce the risk of lung cancer, provided the smoker does not compensate by inhaling more deeply, taking more puffs, or smoking more cigarettes. But these smokers still have an increased risk of developing other cancers. According to the Surgeon Geneal of the Public Health Service, there is no such thing as a safe cigarette. People who smoke *and* drink heavily increase their risk of cancers of the mouth, throat, larynx, and esophagus more than people with either habit alone. But people who quit, even after smoking for decades, reduce all these risks almost to zero within ten to fifteen years after quitting.

7. Eat More Fiber and Less Fat

Hundreds of studies of laboratory animals and human populations from around the world suggest that cancers of the colon and rectum, breast, and prostate are associated with the type of diet most Americans eat: low in dietary fiber and high in total fat, saturated fat, simple carbohydrates, and sugar. Although the scientific evidence against fat is not conclusive — results from twenty-four clinical intervention trials are not expected until 1989–1992 — it seems needlessly risky to delay acting on the accumulated evidence. The National Cancer Institute and American Cancer Society recommend a balanced diet that is high in fiber (fresh fruits, vegetables, and whole grain cereals) and low in fat. This diet is consistent with well-established recommendations to reduce the risk of heart disease and stroke.

Specifically:

- Eat more fiber-rich foods, such as whole grain cereals, fresh or frozen fruits and vegetables, and dried peas and beans (see chapter 1, pp. 18–19).
- Eat a variety of foods low in fat: fish, poultry without the skin, lean meats, and low-fat dairy products, salad dressings, and desserts.
- Eat fresh fruits and vegetables containing vitamin A, vitamin C, and beta-carotene.*
- Eat dark green and deep yellow vegetables such as cabbage, broccoli, brussels sprouts, and turnips (see chapter 1, p. 19).
- Keep trim.

- If you drink alcoholic beverages, have no more than two drinks daily.
- Eat fewer salt-cured, smoked, nitrite-cured, and charcoal-broiled foods.
- Avoid obesity.

* This recommendation is based on studies showing that diets low in vitamin C may be associated with stomach cancer and that diets low in vitamin A are associated with cancers of the lung, bladder, and larynx.

For further information, see the National Cancer Institute's *Diet, Nutrition & Cancer Prevention: The Good News,* available by calling, toll-free, 800-4-CANCER.

8. *Avoid Overexposure to the Sun*

In a culture that values the well-bronzed look, advice to cover up or stay in the shade is hard to sell. Yet there is no medical benefit from tanning, and repeated overexposure to the sun's ultraviolet rays can cause skin cancer. The damage is cumulative and slow. Risk groups include people with fair, ruddy, or sandy complexions and those who are repeatedly overexposed to great amounts of sunlight: farmers, sailors, and cab and truck drivers. Even dark-complexioned and suntanned people need protection against ultraviolet rays, although they do not burn as easily.

The most common, and least harmful, skin cancer is basal cell cancer — the kind that affected President Reagan's nose in 1985. It grows slowly and rarely spreads beyond the skin itself. Squamous cell cancer is more dangerous because it tends to spread to other tissues and organs. Even so, 90 percent of patients survive this skin cancer if they detect it early enough. Malignant melanoma, a deadly and rare form of skin cancer that has been steadily increasing in incidence for the past forty years, is also thought to be related to sun exposure.

You can protect your skin against premature aging *and* reduce the risk of skin cancer by covering up and using chemical sunscreens containing PABA (para-aminobenzoic acid). Select sunscreens according to their sun protection factor (SPF): the higher the SPF number, the longer you can stay in the sun without burning. An SPF of 15 affords the best protection. But even the strongest sunscreen does not protect you indefinitely from skin damage. Use a sunscreen several times daily, especially after swimming or sweating. Limit sun exposure to fifteen minutes daily the first day, adding five minutes daily until a protective suntan is established. Wear protective clothing the rest of the time: hats, long-sleeved shirts, pants. The sun's rays are strongest between 11:00 A.M. and 3:00 P.M., and at higher altitudes, beaches, and poolsides. For more information about tanning safely and protecting your skin against premature aging and wrinkling caused by overexposure to the sun, see chapter 8, pp. 222–224.

Avoid artificial suntanning methods such as tanning booths. They emit high-intensity ultraviolet radiation that can cause skin cancer, premature aging of the skin, and cataracts and damage to the retina of the eye. The American Medical Association's Council on Scientific Affairs has disputed claims that new-style tanning beds and booths are safer than earlier types of sunlamps. The newer devices do block out ultraviolet beta (UVB) rays, which cause burning and skin cancer, in favor of ultraviolet alpha (UVA) rays, which cause skin aging. But exposure to UVA radiation is just as hazardous as exposure to UVB, the AMA warns, especially since users are less likely to restrict themselves to short tanning periods. If you insist on artificial suntanning, wear protective eye goggles, limit tanning sessions, and avoid exposure while using antibiotics or other drugs that make your skin more susceptible to sun damage.

9. Adopt an Anticancer Lifestyle

Everybody should avoid smoking, eat well, limit exposure to the sun, and get cancer-related checkups. In addition, individuals whose jobs or lifestyles expose them to additional cancer risks should

- minimize exposure to pollutants and hazardous substances at work by using masks, respirators, coveralls, gloves, and other protective clothing, and by handling hazardous substances only if properly trained
- learn which chemicals are considered carcinogenic, such as asbestos, creosote, arsenic compounds, radium, coal tar, vinyl chloride, and pitch
- avoid unnecessary X rays

10. Do Not Panic If You Get Cancer

What happens if you are diagnosed as having cancer? First of all, do not panic. Fear can immobilize you so that you do not seek proper treatment, while intelligent decisions can prevent many cancers from spreading, recurring, or threatening your life.

Second, tell your family. Sharing feelings and openly discussing the diagnosis, treatment, and chances for survival can ease emotional strain both for you and for them.

Third, ask questions. This will help relieve anxiety and provide facts you need to make treatment decisions that affect survival.

Fourth, get second opinions on the diagnosis and pathology report. A competent physician will not object, and any delay in treatment is better than getting the wrong treatment.

Finally, seek treatment from a physician in whom you have confidence. Specialized cancer centers may be the "best" source of treatment for cancers that are rare or that require technically difficult procedures by an oncologist (physician specializing in cancer treatment) with special experience, judgment, and skills. More common cancers of adults — bowel, pancreatic, stomach, and most forms of lung cancer — are best treated by a local physician who specializes in the treatment of cancer. Above all, avoid quack treatments, such as laetrile and coffee enemas, and clinics south of the border. For information on where to get the best cancer treatment, ask your doctor or nearest medical school, or call the National Cancer Institute's Cancer Information Service, toll-free, at 800-4-CANCER. You might also ask your physician to check the NCI's Physician Data Query (PDQ) computer information system for the latest information on clinical trials of new cancer treatments and names of consulting experts using each treatment. PDQ can be checked from a library or personal computer. The American Cancer Society has local chapters throughout the United States that provide information and support for people with cancer.

Cancer treatments that have recently emerged from research labs include new combinations of radiation, chemotherapy, and surgery; new ways of delivering radiation to cancer cells; and nontoxic radiation therapy. Promising new approaches that are *still experimental* include monoclonal antibodies (genetically engineered protein substances) that can be programmed to seek out cancer cells; new anticancer drugs; manipulation of oncogenes that switch on cells to be cancerous; biological agents, such as interleukin-2, which helps turn the body's own natural disease-fighting system against cancer, or interferon, which may reduce tumor growth; hyperthermia or the use of heat to kill cancer cells; and chemoprevention in which high-risk patients are given certain substances to prevent cancer or its recurrence.

One controversial cancer treatment combines psychotherapy with standard cancer treatment. At the Cancer Counseling and Research

Center in Fort Worth, Texas, Dr. Carl Simonton, a radiologist, and Dr. Stephanie Simonton, a psychologist, encourage positive thought processes in patients, who are asked to draw pictures of what their cancers look like and how the cells of their immune systems are destroying the cancer cells. Dr. Simonton reports high cure rates, but critics say his results have not been subjected to rigorously controlled studies.

While it is not proved that positive mental attitudes can cure or even help prevent cancer and other illnesses, negative attitudes can keep cancer and other patients from dealing with their diseases effectively. This negativism is more pronounced in men than women, according to a study of 181 adult cancer patients. Women in the study, funded by the National Cancer Institute, tended to be more devastated than men by a diagnosis of cancer. But, unlike the men, the women adjusted emotionally and improved their outlook on life as they underwent treatment. Men tended to give up. If this finding reflects the population at large, it may help explain why men die from cancer at one and a half times the rate of women. It may also suggest a way to improve these odds.

7

Other
Leading Man-Killers

Accidents: How Accidental?

Few people think of accidents as a disease, yet they are the third leading cause of death for men. Only heart disease and cancer take a greater toll. Half the 92,500 accidental deaths that occurred in 1985 — or about 46,000 deaths — involved motor vehicles. Since 1941, more than three times as many Americans (1.8 million) have been killed in traffic accidents as in World War II, Korea, and Vietnam combined (519,000). Most of the deceased are men. The average American has a one-in-three chance of suffering a disabling injury in an autombile collision during his or her lifetime. On the average, everybody can expect to be in a crash once every ten years. For one person in twenty, it will be a serious crash. For one in sixty, it will be fatal.

Accidents — especially those involving the automobile — may be the most predictable of all leading causes of death. You can predict *when* most automobile fatalities will happen: on New Year's Day and on spring and summer weekends between 8:00 P.M. and 4:00 A.M. You can predict *where* these accidents will happen: mostly within twenty-five miles of home. You can predict *to whom* these accidents will happen: mostly to white males aged sixteen to twenty-nine, although males in all age groups are at high risk. Experts even know *why* automobile accidents happen:

- *Alcohol* is involved in about half of the 46,000 motor vehicle fatalities each year.
- *Falling asleep at the wheel* is the second most common cause of one- and two-car accidents, according to the Association of Sleep Disorders Centers.

- *Speeding over the posted limit* is involved in 35 to 40 percent of all accidents in automobiles and other vehicles.
- *Night driving* is involved in two out of three accidents and more than three times the fatalities of daytime driving. A person with 20/40 daytime vision may have only 20/100 vision at night.

Fortunately, there is evidence that the highway death toll may be leveling off, contrary to previous higher predictions. What has helped prevent tens of thousands of deaths on the highway?

- The 55 mph speed limit has influenced more than half of the nation's drivers to drive more safely.
- Highways and automobiles have become safer.
- As the population grows older, there are relatively fewer young drivers, who tend to have more accidents than older drivers.
- Higher gas prices during recent years may have caused people to drive fewer miles.
- Most important, there are significant reductions in drinking-while-driving incidents, especially among fifteen- to twenty-year-olds.

Drinking and Driving

Alcohol affects the faculties you need most for safe driving: judgment, vision, motor coordination, and reaction time. Drinking distorts your ability to judge how fast you are going, how far away the car in front of you is, and whether you have time to pass. The effect of alcohol on vision is not so obvious, yet 85 to 90 percent of the information upon which you base driving decisions comes through your eyes. Alcohol reduces control over the amount of light entering your eyes, distorts focus, can cause double vision, impairs depth perception, narrows peripheral vision, distorts color vision, and reduces night vision and visual acuity. Alcohol-impaired drivers are less likely to wear seat belts and — contrary to myth — are two to four times *more* likely to suffer serious injury than sober drivers who have accidents. Alcohol also makes diagnosis and treatment of injuries more difficult.

The National Highway Traffic Safety Administration reports far more male drivers involved in alcohol-related crashes than female drivers, in part because social customs call for men to drive more than women, especially at night, when most drinking occurs. Male drivers aged twenty-one to twenty-four are most likely to have alcohol-related road crashes. A combination of inexperience in using alcohol and in driving puts these young males at especially high risk. Among adult drivers, heavy social drinkers, "escape" drinkers, and male alcoholics have more alcohol-related traffic fatalities than other drivers.

Alcohol is a hidden cause of many other kinds of accidents as well. High blood alcohol concentrations have been recorded in people who died from falls, burns, drowning, and accidents at home and work. On the waterways, 35 to 38 percent of fatal recreational boating accidents may involve persons with high blood alcohol concentrations. In the skies, at least one in ten pilots killed in general aviation accidents between 1975 to 1981 tested positive for alcohol.

None for the Road

Many people wonder how much alcohol they can safely drink before driving. There is no simple answer. In most states a blood alcohol concentration (BAC) of 0.10 percent is the legal definition of intoxication. For comparison, a person with a BAC of 0.50 (or five times as much) would be in deep coma and near death. Drivers with a 0.10 or higher BAC are three to fifteen times more likely to have fatal accidents than nondrinking drivers. But alcohol impairs driving skills even at 0.05 percent BAC or lower, according to a 1980 report, *Alcohol and the Driver*, by the American Medical Association's Council on Scientific Affairs. For a 160-pound man, that means one drink per hour over a six-hour period. One drink is defined as 5 ounces of 12 percent wine, 12 ounces of 5 percent beer, or 1½ ounces of 80 proof liquor. The latter contains 40 percent alcohol. The AMA recommends that all states adopt a BAC of 0.05 percent as evidence of alcohol-impaired driving.

The numbers and kinds of drinks that will intoxicate vary widely. Even in the same individual, alcohol's effects depend upon how fast you drink, what you drink, what and when you have eaten, medications, body weight (heavier people can "hold" more alcohol than featherweights), sex (women's blood alcohol concentrations rise faster than men's), drinking history and experience, and what kind of day you have had. According to the AMA report *Alcohol and the Driver*, there is "no 'safe' drinking level for drivers." A Washington, D.C., journalist who was involved in an alcohol-related fatal traffic accident in 1984 makes the point:

> The night of the incident, I drank no more than others and felt in control. I stopped drinking an hour and a half before heading home . . . yet it still happened. Why? Because . . . even a little

too much was too much when poured onto fatigue. . . . One must realize one does not have to feel drunk to be a threat behind the wheel.

When has someone had too much to drink? When

- people offer to drive him home
- he cannot remember how many drinks he has had
- he has trouble walking or talking
- he seems to be the only one drinking

NOTE: An intoxicated person probably cannot tell when he is in no condition to drive because alcohol distorts judgment.

How long does it take to detoxify and become a safe driver again? The answer varies. There is no way to sober up quickly. It takes the liver about two hours to completely metabolize the alcohol in each average drink. Black coffee, a cold shower, exercise, fresh air, or even a whiff of pure oxygen are not effective sobering agents. All they achieve is a wide-awake drunk.

Drivers with hangovers may be just as dangerous as drivers who are drunk. In a study by two Swedish research scientists, twenty-two volunteers with hangovers were tested for driving ability on an obstacle course. Nearly all scored about 20 percent lower than when they were sober. Test yourself someday when you are hung over, and try backing your car into a parallel parking space.

Next to alcohol the most dangerous drugs, according to extent of usage, are marijuana, Valium and other mild tranquilizers, and barbiturates. Driving ability is not regained for at least four to six hours after smoking a single marijuana cigarette. Using multiple drugs or mixing alcohol and drugs — including many prescription and certain nonprescription medications — can be even deadlier. Unfortunately, the knowledge about how such drugs affect driving is not yet sufficient to develop legal guidelines such as those that exist for alcohol and driving.

Deterring Drunk Driving

Three defenses against alcohol intoxication are food, time, and amount consumed. Eat high-protein and fatty foods before drinking since they stay in the stomach longer than carbohydrates and slow the absorption of alcohol. Sip your drink slowly. Limit yourself to one or two alcoholic drinks, measured with a jigger. Use noncarbonated mixers to slow alcohol absorption. Before driving, wait one to two hours for each alcoholic drink you have had. If you have overindulged, get someone to drive you home or spend the night. If someone else has overindulged, invite him or her to spend the night, or drive that person home, even if you have to pay for a cab or take the car keys away. Anything — including physical restraint or even calling the police — that prevents an intoxicated person from driving is the right thing to do. If you *must* ride with an alcohol-impaired driver:

- drive only as far as necessary to seek other transportation
- wear seat belts
- check the speed frequently
- do not distract the driver with music or conversation (alcohol impairs ability to concentrate)
- remind the driver to keep his or her eyes moving (eyes tend to fixate on the road when you drink, instead of scanning from side to side)

Another way to combat drunk driving is to report to local or state police the vehicle description, license number, place last seen, and direction of travel of any automobile that

- turns with a wide radius
- straddles the center or lane marker
- has a driver who appears to be drinking
- almost strikes an object or vehicle
- weaves or swerves
- drives on other than the designated roadway
- drives more than 10 mph below the limit
- drives with open windows in bad weather

These, in descending order of probability, are signs of a drinking driver.

Seat Belts

Americans were first introduced to seat belts back in the late 1960s when federal regulations required that all American-made cars be equipped with these devices. Since 1972, lap-and-shoulder belts have been mandatory in all new cars. Still, they are not *widely used*, even though they could prevent half of all deaths from automobile accidents and 65 percent of all injuries.

In 1976–77, a National Highway Traffic Safety Administration (NHTSA) survey of 84,000 drivers in sixteen U.S. cities showed that most seat-belt wearers were women. Drivers of small cars buckled up almost twice as often as drivers of luxury cars. Cadillac drivers were among the least inclined to wear seat belts. More drivers used belts during evening rush hour than at other daylight hours. The survey showed that one in five drivers used seat belts. Today, mainly because of laws requiring the use of seat belts in half the states, seat-belt usage has increased to one in three, according to a NHTSA survey of 51,000 drivers during the first six months of 1986. That survey also showed that 31 percent of men, versus 40 percent of women, wore seat belts.

What keeps people from buckling up? Many seem to believe a number of myths:

Myth 1: Seat belts trap you in a burning or sinking car.

Fact: Fewer than one-half of 1 percent of all accidents involve fire or submersion in water. Seat belts, rather than trapping you, can keep you conscious so you *can* escape from your car.

Myth 2: Seat belts are hazardous because they keep you from being thrown clear of an accident.

Fact: If you are thrown out of a car, you are twenty-five times more likely to die.

Myth 3: Seat belts cause injuries.

Fact: Seat belts help reduce the force of impact and distribute it across the strongest parts of your body. They *can* cause injuries, especially if the belt is worn incorrectly, but such injuries are far less serious than those caused by *not* wearing belts.

Myth 4: Seat belts mean you are a bad driver.

Fact: Even an excellent driver can be killed by other bad drivers, especially drunk drivers.

Myth 5: Seat belts keep you from avoiding an accident.

Fact: To the contrary, seat belts help you stay behind the wheel and maintain control during a collision. They also keep driver and passengers from colliding with one another, which causes one in four serious injuries.

Myth 6: Seat belts are a hassle.

Fact: Buckling up takes less time than adjusting the mirrors and car seat, which many drivers do routinely. Belts also reduce driver fatigue and the need to brake at every sharp turn. Regular wearers claim they are uncomfortable *without* seat belts.

Myth 7: Seat belts are unnecessary when driving slowly or going only a short distance.

Fact: Eighty percent of serious injuries and deaths occur in cars traveling 40 mph or less. Nonbelted occupants have been killed at speeds as low as 2 mph. And three out of four crashes occur within twenty-five miles of home.

Myth 8: Seat belts cannot keep you from striking your head against the dashboard because they do not lock when you tug on them.

Fact: Belts made since 1974 lock to keep your head from striking the dashboard, steering wheel, or window *only* during a collision or sudden stop. At other times, they allow you to lean forward.

Myth 9: Seat belts are unnecessary since you can brace yourself with your hands.

Fact: At 30 mph, the force of impact is several thousand pounds, or the same as jumping from a third-story window. Human arms and legs cannot withstand such forces.

Myth 10: You will offend passengers if you ask them to fasten their seat belts.

Fact: Polls show that nine out of ten passengers will willingly wear seat belts if you, the driver, ask them.

Every motor vehicle accident involves at least two collisions. The first occurs as a vehicle traveling 30 mph, say, crashes into an oncoming car traveling at the same speed. In the second collision, the unbelted occupant continues to move forward in the car at 30 mph. He or she slams into the car's steering wheel, windshield, instrument panel, or roof, or onto the outside road surface if ejected. In addition, physicians have defined a third collision that follows the second: that of the brain hitting the inside of the skull or of abdominal organs colliding within the abdominal cavity.

Anybody who has ever wandered through a junkyard will notice that the part of a car, however mangled, that stays reasonably intact is the seat. Seat belts anchor you to the seat, which is anchored to the frame, which is your best anchor during a crash.

Cycling Safety

Helmets are the motorcyclist's/bicyclist's version of seat belts. At one time many states required motorcyclists to wear helmets. One by one, state legislators repealed these laws under pressure from motorcyclists. Yet these individuals die in accidents at eight times the rate of automobile occupants. Motorcycle riders without helmets are twice as likely to suffer head injuries (and consequent paralysis, brain damage, and coma) and three times as likely to die as riders with helmets, according to a University of Southern California study. The main casualties are young men, aged seventeen to thirty. Had they worn helmets — as soldiers do in training and combat — these road warriors might still be around.

Some riders object that helmets are too hot and, in the case of bicycling, could raise internal body temperature to a level that could cause heat injury. But a study at the University of Iowa College of Medicine in Iowa City in 1986 showed no differences in internal body temperature, heart rate, or skin temperature when six competitive bicyclists rode a stationary bicycle for two hours while bareheaded, compared with wearing a helmet with minimal ventilation.

Road rash and broken bones heal. Brains may not. To prevent brain injury under extreme impact, a helmet should have

- a hard outer shell to spread impact energy (white, yellow, or orange affords the best visibility)
- a liner of stiff, nonspringy foam to absorb shock
- a strong strap and fastener that keeps the helmet snug while riding

  NOTE: If you are wondering whether to buy a cheap versus a high-quality helmet, let the price of your helmet reflect the value you place on your head. Helmet and seat-belt use equate to eating a healthy diet, exercising, and driving only when sober as behaviors that preserve health and life.

Are Men Accident-prone?

Men die in accidents — primarily automobile accidents, but also falls and drowning — at almost three times the rate of women. Twice as many male as female drivers have fatal accidents. Five times as many men as women drown. Teenage boys and older men are particularly vulnerable to fires, explosions, gun mishaps, and, later in life, falls.

Why do men have more accidents than women? Society seems to urge men toward stress- and thrill-seeking behavior, such as auto racing, skydiving, scuba diving, hang gliding (which becomes riskier the more proficient you become), and boxing (which kills or causes brain damage to thirteen out of fifteen professional boxers), football, and other violent contact sports. Although such challenges can promote personal growth, they also can cause a false sense of indestructibility, leading to injury and death.

Psychologists observe that accidents tend to happen to people who are angry, frustrated, or grieving. One early study of ninety-six drivers showed that one in five who had fatal accidents had "acutely disturbing experiences" — usually quarrels — within six hours before the accident. Accidents are two to three times more common in families under stress from recent deaths, divorces, unemployment, and other unhappy events. Some researchers claim it is even possible to see an accident coming years ahead. Dr. Hanna Levenson and colleagues at the University of California College of Medicine in San Francisco studied 110 men and 54 women who had accidents at work, and found that many had been worn down by years of escalating stresses that finally exploded in an "accident." The people who did not suffer as many accidents had more vacations, personal achievements, and other positive life changes than did the 164 who had accidents.

Sports injuries often result from psychological pressures to excel, to "prove" one's self, or even to avoid the possibility of failure. In extreme cases, accidents, especially those that occur in automobiles, may even reflect unconscious or conscious self-destructive behavior that could be labeled as suicide. (See the section on suicide, pp. 198–201.)

Lesser emotions also can cause accidents. People who are too tired, hurried, uninterested, or unwilling to do the task at hand often are the casualties. Accidents frequently are an expression of a person's health and physical condition. Sensitivity to glare; poor night vision, eyesight, and hearing; weak or inflexible bodies; poor coordination and balance; slow reaction time; and lack of physical endurance can be offset by driving fewer miles, less often, and more slowly, and by driving less at night, during rush hours, and in the winter.

Another precursor of accidents is risk-taking behavior. At one extreme, driving home drunk after spending an evening drinking is part of some men's lifestyles. And many men take risks on a lesser scale when they routinely drink coffee, eat sandwiches, smoke cigarettes, make phone calls, and dictate memos while driving. They speed, tailgate, lane hop, and run yellow lights. At home they are careless with ladders, lawn mowers, chainsaws, power tools, house chemicals, liquid fuels, and hammers.

The Norwegian explorer who was first to reach the South Pole, Roald Amundsen, led himself and four companions through miles of frozen peril by adhering to his paramount rule of safety: to conserve physical and mental energy. He recognized that accidents are expressions of how a person feels — physically and mentally — at the time they occur. The key to survival is recognizing that accidents seldom happen *to* you. For whatever reasons, you let or make them happen. This means that most accidents are under your control and not really accidental at all.

Stroke: Good News and Bad

Stroke — a sudden loss of brain function caused by disruption of blood flow to an area of the brain — has declined in incidence for nearly a decade. In the United States, death rates from stroke have declined 5 percent per year since the early 1970s. The reasons, stroke experts suggest, may include better diagnosis, treatment, and control of stroke risk factors such as high blood pressure.

Still, stroke kills 150,000 Americans each year and is the fourth leading cause of death for men. Stroke also remains one of the most disabling diseases. Almost two million Americans have had strokes and survived with varying degrees of physical and mental impairment, emotional stress, and medical expense.

Most strokes are caused by clots or bleeding, specifically thrombosis (a local clot within an artery in the neck or brain), embolism (a clot that wanders from another part of the body to block a blood vessel in the brain), or hemorrhage (rupture and bleeding of a blood vessel in the brain).

Clots often occur in arteries damaged by the same disease process that blocks coronary blood vessels and causes heart attacks: atherosclerosis. Blocked arteries leading to the brain — usually the carotid arteries in the neck — eventually deprive part of the brain of blood and oxygen. Hemorrhagic strokes — the deadliest kind, which cause blood to pool in one area of the brain while starving other areas — often are associated with high blood pressure. When brain tissue is deprived of oxygen, nerve cells stop functioning and die, causing impaired speech, vision, or movement.

A stroke of any type is a medical emergency that demands immediate expert care: the faster, the better the chances of recovery. Stroke warning signs include

- sudden, temporary weakness or numbness in the face, arm, and leg on one side of the body
- temporary difficulty in speaking or understanding speech
- temporary dimness or loss of vision in one or both eyes
- unexplained dizziness, unsteadiness, or sudden falls

"Little Strokes"

Sometimes major strokes are preceded by "little strokes" — also known as transient (temporary) ischemic (lack of blood) attacks (TIAs) — which occur days, weeks, or months before a more severe stroke. A TIA is a temporary lack of blood supply to the brain, probably caused by a thrombus or embolus briefly blocking an artery before melting or washing away. A TIA causes the same changes in vision, language, or limb movement and sensation that occur during a stroke. The difference is the temporary nature of these symptoms: usually from five to ten minutes, although they sometimes last from a few seconds to several hours.

People often ignore TIA symptoms because they quickly fade. It is also easy to assume they are caused by overwork, lack of sleep, a skipped meal, or some other minor cause. This assumption could be fatal, since about 25 percent of TIA patients later have major strokes. Conversely, a TIA may herald an approaching stroke in time to prevent it through dietary changes, aspirin and other anticoagulant drugs, high blood pressure medication, or surgery.

Most stroke victims are men. Black Americans are at higher risk than whites, possibly because of the greater prevalence of high blood pressure among blacks. Age also is a risk factor for stroke. The incidence of stroke more than doubles each decade after age fifty-five. Nobody is certain whether or not stroke runs in families.

Reducing the Risk

Stroke, medical experts emphasize, is the end of a chain of events set in motion many years earlier. The number one reducible risk factor for stroke is *high blood pressure*. Studies have shown that stroke is ten times more likely in people with high blood pressure than in people with normal pressure. To prevent stroke, have annual blood pressure checkups and keep high blood pressure under control.

Heart disease is two to three times more prevalent in stroke patients than in the general population. Good medical care of heart disease prevents clots that may break loose, travel to the brain, and cause a stroke.

A marked increase, as well as moderate elevation, in *red blood cell count* may be a risk factor for stroke because excessive red blood cells thicken the blood and cause it to clog small blood vessels. This condition can be treated medically.

Diabetes is associated with destructive changes in blood vessels throughout the body. In addition, if a diabetic's blood sugar is high when a stroke occurs, brain damage may be more severe.

Among the secondary risk factors for stroke are *high blood fats/high cholesterol*. Although this condition causes coronary heart disease, which is a major risk factor for stroke, and may increase stroke risk in people under age fifty, in older groups the risk is not well documented.

Cigarette smoking, until recently, had not been directly linked to stroke. But a report in the September 18, 1986, *New England Journal of Medicine* indicates that cigarette smoking is a risk factor for all forms of stroke. A study of 8,000 men in the Honolulu Heart Program, 3,435 of whom were cigarette smokers, showed that the smokers had two to three times the risk of stroke. Subjects who continued to smoke during the same twelve-year follow-up period had four to six times the risk of stroke, while those who stopped smoking reduced their risk of stroke by more than half. Smoking by women who have used birth control pills for many years has long been an established risk factor. In addition, smoking is a major risk factor for atherosclerosis, which leads to stroke.

Obesity is associated with heart disease, high blood pressure, and diabetes, all of which are risk factors for stroke.

Physical inactivity is not a cause of stroke per se, but often accompanies obesity. Moderate exercise may strengthen the heart, improve blood circulation, and help dissolve atherosclerotic deposits in blood vessels.

Excessive alcohol consumption: A study of 8,006 men in the Honolulu Heart Program, reported in the May 2, 1986, *Journal of the American Medical Association*, showed that high alcohol intake nearly tripled and light drinking nearly doubled the risk of hemorrhagic stroke. Heavy drinking was defined as 40 ounces or more of hard liquor or the equivalent per month. Light drinking was defined as 1 to 14 ounces per month. The study also showed that those who reduced alcohol intake reduced their risk of stroke. This study provides the first evidence that alcoholism is directly related to stroke, even when high blood pressure does not occur.

Research studies suggest that aspirin protects against stroke by lessening the severity and incidence of subsequent TIAs. Other studies suggest that small daily doses — from 40 mg (half a baby aspirin) to 1,300 mg (about four adult aspirin) — can protect against heart attack and stroke, perhaps by making clots less likely to form and obstruct blood flow to the heart and brain. Many physicians advise patients at risk for heart attack or stroke to take one-half to one adult aspirin a day, unless they have ulcers. This dosage is safe for most people and has potential value for preventing heart attacks and stroke. (See chapter 6, p. 167.)

Recovering from a Stroke

For many years, little could be done for a person who had a stroke. Today the outlook has improved. Of nearly two million stroke survivors in the United States, about a third recover enough to resume normal prestroke activities, and half can conduct the activities of daily living with some assistance. The remainder are so severely handicapped that they require hospitalization or constant care.

Rehabilitation — resumption of activities a stroke patient can perform and substitution for those he cannot — should begin in the hospital immediately after a stroke and continue at home. Recovery is greatest during the first few weeks. Then it tapers off. It may take nine months or more to reach maximum recovery. Neurologists once thought that after a stroke, alternate pathways in the brain would gradually restore lost functions. Now there is evidence that damaged brain cells recover to some degree and that restored function comes from healed areas of the brain as well as from undamaged areas.

Stroke patients need encouragement and optimism from their physicians and families. They must contend not only with loss of physical abilities, but with depression, which commonly occurs after a stroke.

Stroke patients should participate as much as possible in family life and in planning for their own care.

Stroke support groups also are helpful, according to a physician recovering from a stroke. Told he would never walk again, he found that one visit to a support group bolstered his confidence and helped him learn to walk with a cane. A list of stroke support groups is available through the American Heart Association, 7320 Greenville Avenue, Dallas, TX 75231.

A book called *Stroke,* by Joseph Jaffe and Dr. Charles Clay Dahlberg, who had a stroke and recovered, offers this advice for families and friends:

- Do not try to change the stroke victim's personality. If he is obsessively neat, messy, lazy, or hypochondriacal, let him remain that way.
- Do not minimize or exaggerate the patient's symptoms.
- Do not invalidate his problems by noting that you have similar ones.
- Try to stimulate the patient's interests, even in his own body and its recovery.
- Recognize that some depression is very likely if recovery drags on or if improvement slows. Allow yourself and the patient to express it freely.
- Invent activities that even a patient who cannot speak can join in by nodding or blinking.
- For the patient, the authors advise that "extended discussions of your illness will drive [friends] away. And you do need friends."

Emphysema and Chronic Bronchitis

A healthy person breathes about fifteen times a minute. A person with emphysema may breathe twice as often and still hunger for air. Although emphysema and chronic bronchitis are considered separate diseases, they almost always coexist. However, one may predominate. Together these conditions are known as chronic obstructive lung, or pulmonary, disease (COPD).

The typical patient is a male smoker over age forty who is prone to colds, wheezing, and other bronchial problems. Although chronic obstructive lung disease is vastly more prevalent among cigarette smokers, the disease strikes nonsmokers as well. More than 10 million Americans are affected by this fifth leading cause of death for men. In addition, each year chronic obstructive pulmonary disease turns thousands of people into bedridden invalids who cannot breathe freely without the help of medications and oxygen.

Think of the respiratory system as an inverted tree with two main branches, one leading to the right lung, the other to the left. Increasingly smaller branches spread throughout the lungs, ending in microscopic air sacs called alveoli. Through the ultra-thin walls of 300 million of these tiny pockets, oxygen from inhaled air passes into the bloodstream. Waste carbon dioxide from the blood is picked up and expelled from the body along the same route in reverse.

Normally elastic and resilient, the walls of the alveoli are broken down by destructive body chemicals when a person has emphysema. Groups of ruptured alveoli combine to form larger sacs that trap stale air. The result is permanent overinflation of the lung, often causing a "barrel chest" appearance. As less normal lung tissue is available to exchange oxygen and carbon dioxide, and as more air is inhaled and trapped in the alveoli, the body must work harder to get enough oxygen.

Chronic bronchitis causes excessive mucus secretion in the larger air passages in the lungs (the bronchi), and inflammation and thickening of the bronchial walls. This causes narrowed air passages and a persistent cough that produces sputum.

Symptoms of emphysema and chronic bronchitis begin gradually with mild shortness of breath and a slight morning cough. The sputum is usually clear. During "colds" and other acute respiratory tract infections, shortness of breath and coughing may become more noticeable. The sputum frequently turns yellow or greenish.

Later, as chronic obstructive lung disease progresses, shortness of breath becomes more obvious. Severe episodes may occur after even modest exertion. This may be accompanied by increased fatigue, a feeling of tightness in the chest, difficulty breathing while lying down, waking at night feeling "choked up," urges to cough, and wheezing during or after colds. Minor respiratory tract infections may become incapacitating and prolonged.

Anyone who notices such symptoms should see a doctor since emphysema and chronic bronchitis steadily worsen if left untreated. Although nothing can reverse damage already done, proper care — including medication, good nutrition, adequate rest, daily physical exercise, avoiding colds and air pollution, and, above all, stopping smoking — can keep symptoms under control and slow the damage these diseases cause.

The person at highest risk for emphysema is a middle-aged male who smokes a pack or more of cigarettes a day and who has close relatives with chronic obstructive lung disease. The risk for pipe and cigar smokers is less than that for cigarette smokers, but higher than that for nonsmokers. There is no evidence in human subjects as yet about the relative risks of low-tar, low-nicotine cigarettes in causing chronic obstructive pulmonary disease. However, some studies suggest that low-tar cigarettes — although safer in terms of cancer risk — may pose a higher risk for emphysema. Smokers of these cigarettes often compensate by increasing the number and volume of puffs. Although chronic obstructive lung disease is still more common in men than in women, the greatest increase in death rates from all diseases since 1968 has been from COPD among white females, reflecting the increased number of women who smoke cigarettes.

No cure has been found for chronic obstructive lung disease. But almost all cases can be prevented by giving up smoking. This habit causes 80 to 90 percent of all deaths from emphysema and chronic bronchitis each year. Indeed, emphysema, like lung cancer, would hardly exist were it not for cigarette smoking, according to the Surgeon General of the Public Health Service. Heavy smokers die of lung disease at thirty times the rate of nonsmokers. Within a few years, many smokers develop inflammation of their small airways. Such changes can revert to normal if the smoker quits. But the longer he smokes, the deeper he inhales, and the more cigarettes he consumes, the greater the decline in lung function. Once maximum lung growth is attained in early adulthood, everybody loses lung function at a small, but measurable, rate. Cigarette smokers tend to lose lung function at a faster rate than nonsmokers. Although lost lung function cannot be replaced, the decline in lung function can slow to approximately that of nonsmokers when the smoker quits.

Preventing Chronic Obstructive Lung Disease

- Avoid air pollutants, particularly the self-inflicted one: cigarette smoke.
- Do not neglect colds that hang on, a throat with a perpetual tickle, sneezing and coughing spells that turn into spasms, or shortness of breath after mild exercise.
- Stay healthy through good nutrition and exercise.

Influenza / Pneumonia

You are at a country and western dance. You set your drink on a table, and when you return, you reach for the wrong glass. Or you have just met an attractive woman who — unknown to you or herself — is coming down with flu. You are directly in the path of virus-containing fluids she expels into the air as she talks. Twenty-four to seventy-two hours later, you notice sudden fever, chills, headache, aching muscles, extreme malaise, cough, and perhaps a sore throat. You recover within a week, although you continue to feel unusually tired for days longer.

In the aged or chronically ill, flu is no weeklong lapse in health. It is a life-threatening illness. The most frequent complication of flu is bacterial pneumonia, particularly that caused by the pneumococcus bacterium. This is the most serious form of pneumonia, an infection of the lungs that causes inflammatory cells and fluid to collect and interfere with breathing. Influenza and pneumonia together are the sixth leading cause of death for men and are the only infectious diseases remaining among the top ten causes of death. Influenza and pneumonia kill tens of thousands of Americans each year; 80 to 90 percent of them are sixty-five or older.

Those at greatest risk of severe illness and death from influenza and pneumonia include

- people over sixty-five years of age
- adults and children weakened by chronic heart and lung disease, diabetes, kidney failure, impaired spleen or liver function, sickle-cell disease, and conditions that compromise the immune system
- residents of nursing homes or other chronic-care facilities
- physicians, nurses, and others who have extensive contact with high-risk patients

The Immunization Gap

There is a way to reduce mortality by nearly 80 percent: pneumonia and influenza vaccines. But only 20 percent of individuals at high risk have been vaccinated against these diseases. The immunization gap threatens to widen as the proportion of elderly persons in the population increases. The Public Health Service has recommended a one-time vaccination against pneumococcal pneumonia since the vaccine was introduced in 1977. An improved pneumococcal pneumonia vaccine that gives longer-lasting protection was introduced in 1983. But persons who have had the earlier vaccine should not be revaccinated, even with the improved vaccine, because revaccination could cause severe side effects.

Mankind's Last Great Plague

Since 1963 the Public Health Service has also urged that high-risk individuals be vaccinated against influenza each fall before the influenza season. Annual flu shots are necessary because the influenza virus constantly changes. Influenza has been around for a long time. As far back as 412 B.C., Hippocrates, the father of medicine, described a respiratory disease that resembled flu. Through the centuries, it has been known as "Russian fever," the "Chinese sickness," "the Bolshevik disease," and "the black whip." It was "Blitzkatarrh" to the Germans, "wrestler's fever" to the Japanese, and "the too muchee hot inside sickness" to residents of Hong Kong.

The influenza pandemic that swept the globe in 1918–19 was known primarily as "Spanish" influenza since it originated in Madrid. Before it ran its course, it killed 20 million people throughout the world, including 500,000 in the United States. Sixteen times during the past twenty-eight years, influenza has become epidemic. About every ten years, the virus undergoes major mutations. Entirely new strains caused worldwide epidemics of Asian flu in 1957 and Hong Kong flu in 1968. That is why people at risk need to be vaccinated yearly. But nearly half of elderly persons mistakenly believe that influenza vaccine is unnecessary and that influenza is not a threat to their health. Even though vaccination does not guarantee protection to each person who receives it, it does guarantee overall reductions in influenza and its complications. An improved live-virus influenza vaccine is being developed and, when it becomes available on a wide scale, may be administered in nose-drop form. Normally you should get a flu shot during the fall, although the vaccine is still effective later. It takes two weeks for the protective effect to develop.

In recent years an antiviral drug, amantadine, has been used to prevent and treat influenza A — the most prevalent and destructive type of flu virus — particularly in high-risk individuals. Often, when a vaccine against a new strain has not yet been produced, amantadine is the only preventative available. Prompt treatment with amantadine also reduces the severity of influenza in high-risk individuals who have not been vaccinated or for whom the vaccine has not prevented infection. The drug causes mild side effects.

Penicillin and other antibiotics cure 95 percent of cases of pneumonia in individuals aged two to fifty, but the disease remains deadly for older people. These drugs have no effect on influenza or other viruses, although they may help combat certain complicating infections, such as bronchitis. Antibiotics should be used only when necessary, since overuse of an antibiotic such as penicillin could lead to the development of bacteria resistant to it, making the drug useless when you need it.

The worst part of flu lasts two or three days, but fever can last up to five, and fatigue, sweating, and shortness of breath can last for several days or even weeks, according to the National Foundation for Infectious Diseases. The foundation recommends that adults relieve flu symptoms with

- bed rest
- increased fluid intake
- aspirin for fever and headache
- a humidifier to reduce breathing discomfort
- nourishing foods to maintain body strength
- a cough syrup if cough is severe

Suicide: A Matter of Degree

Somebody once remarked that if a little switch in your arm would let you die immediately and painlessly, everyone might sooner or later commit suicide. Many people think, at one time or another, of ending their lives. But the suicidal person makes it more than just a passing thought.

An estimated 250,000 individuals attempt suicide each year. In 1984 nearly 30,000 succeeded — including nearly 23,000 men. Men kill themselves at more than three times the rate of women. Moreover, in recent years the suicide rate for males has risen, while it has declined for females.

The traditional suicide victim is a middle-aged, white male who lives alone and is unemployed or retired. In many ways he resembles the character Richard Cory, who was envied by all who knew him and who, in Edwin Arlington Robinson's famous poem, "one calm summer night, / Went home and put a bullet through his head." The contemporary Richard Cory seems to have everything in life, but is secretly obsessed by what so often is lacking: a sense of self-esteem.

Why are so many people, especially men, bent on self-destruction?

Alcoholism, which predominates among men, is a leading predictor of suicide: as many as 50 percent of all suicides may be alcohol-related. Suicide is also strongly associated with depression, especially depression that is untreated. About 15 percent of people who are clinically depressed eventually commit suicide. Other studies show a strong link between suicide and loss of a parent through death, divorce, or separation. There also is evidence that close relatives of individuals who commit suicide are significantly more vulnerable to suicide.

The incidence of suicide among twins and first-degree relatives suggests a genetic component to suicide. A study of the Amish, who rarely kill themselves, revealed that nearly all of twenty-six individuals who committed suicide from 1880 to 1980 in an Old Order Amish community in southeastern Pennsylvania belonged to families with higher rates of depression, manic-depressive illness, and other major emotional disorders. The study was reported in the August 16, 1985, *Journal of the American Medical Association.* Suicide experts have also reported studies showing that patients with low levels of the brain chemical transmitter serotonin attempted and committed suicide more often than individuals with normal levels of serotonin.

Suicidal individuals tend to exhibit the "three H's" of suicide proneness: they feel hapless (out of luck), helpless to improve themselves or their lives, and hopeless about the future. Some people resort to suicide because they feel rejected, hurt, and angry or want to get back at someone close. Others kill themselves out of impulsiveness or loss of face. Throughout history, suicide has been committed to maintain personal honor, to express loyalty (such as soldiers slaying themselves on the pyre of their commanders), or to save the lives of others (such as covering a grenade with one's body). For centuries, people have killed themselves after learning they had a terminal illness. The late Nathan Pritikin of Pritikin Diet fame, for example, slashed his wrists and bled to death after becoming despondent about having incurable cancer.

Suicide methods have been as varied as the motives. Historically, the Greeks drank hemlock, and the Romans fell on their swords or cut their wrists in hot baths. Eighteenth-century gentlemen used pistols to take their lives, while members of the lower classes hanged themselves. Later, drowning became fashionable, along with cheap poisons like arsenic and strychnine. Alfred Alvarez wrote, in *The Savage God: A Study of Suicide*, that a nineteenth-century Viennese man killed himself by driving seven three-inch nails into the top of his head with a blacksmith's hammer. A Polish girl whose lover spurned her swallowed, over the course of five months, four spoons, three knives, nineteen coins, twenty nails, seven window bolts, one hundred and one pins, a stone, three pieces of glass, a brass cross, and two beads from her rosary.

In modern times, drugs and domestic gas have placed painless, relatively easy means of suicide within everybody's reach. For males, firearms remain the most commonly used method of direct suicide in the United States, followed by hanging, strangulation, and suffocation. The suicide "season" peaks in March, April, and May. This may reflect a similar pattern in episodes of depression among some individuals who seem especially sensitive to the absence of light and the changing seasons.

Parasuicide

The completed suicide act is only the tip of the iceberg of self-destruction. For every successful attempt, there may be ten unsuccessful attempts; for every suicide completed, two or three more go unrecorded. Suicide statistics omit the single-car accidents without skid marks, the people with alcoholism who drink themselves to death, those addicted to drugs who die of overdoses, those with heart disease who refuse to stop smoking, those with hypertension who refuse to take high blood pressure medication, those with diabetes who stop taking insulin, and others who refuse to take care of their health.

In *The Many Faces of Suicide: Indirect Self-Destructive Behavior*, Dr. Norman L. Farberow, the noted suicide expert, writes that time and awareness are the distinguishing features of "indirect" self-destructive behavior. The person usually does not consciously intend to die, but is at least moderately aware that death could result from his behavior. He does not consider himself a suicide.

Many people who are indirectly self-destructive subscribe to the "play now, pay later" philosophy and use indirect self-destructive behavior to distract from deep emotional pain. The immediate benefits — pleasure (from smoking), relaxation (from alcohol), or a psychological lift (from drugs) — are powerful motivators. Pain may motivate still other people who need to atone for failed marriages by seeking partners who will make them feel bad. (See chapter 9 for more information on addictions.)

Dr. Thomas M. Vogt of the Kaiser Foundation Hospitals in Portland, Oregon, who has studied heart disease prevention in men, has written:

the most impressive observation of this study has been the high level of misery among the middle-aged male participants. This unhappiness took time to recognize. It was initially masked by bravado, fear, and an inability to communicate effectively. One will not read about the joyless lives of these men when the results are published — only about their respective diseases — and will not know how many of them simply refused to make changes because they had no wish to prolong their lives.

Spotting the Suicidal Person

How can you recognize and help the suicidal individual? The task is not easy since even the directly suicidal person seldom talks about his feelings. Yet studies show that up to 75 percent of people who commit direct suicide have repeatedly, although subtly, communicated their intent. They may show sudden changes in behavior and become more agitated or withdrawn than usual. They may ask about the hereafter, talk about "somebody else's" suicidal thoughts, give away favorite possessions because they "won't be needing them anymore," make a will, pay up insurance, and/or put personal affairs in order.

Such actions often are cries for help. The best response is as follows:

- Listen and encourage the distressed person to talk about his or her feelings.
- Always take suicide threats seriously.
- Take positive action. Remain, or have somebody else stay, with the distressed person until the crisis passes.
- Beware of sudden "recoveries." The underlying problem is probably still present.
- Get professional help from a physician, psychologist, clinic, hospital, minister, or suicide crisis center as soon as possible.

There are about five hundred local crisis centers throughout the United States. Trained volunteers at these centers counsel callers and guide them to service agencies that can address their specific needs. Resources nearest you can be located by looking under "Suicide" or "Crisis" in your local telephone directory.

Cirrhosis: The Drinking Man's Disease

For years scientists have pondered what causes cirrhosis of the liver, a disease in which the cells of that organ degenerate and die. Even before the time of the Greek physician Hippocrates (400 B.C.), physicians suspected that alcohol could somehow injure the liver. A medical text published in 1802 suggested that the most common cause of "scirrhous livers" is intemperate use of "spirituous liquors." Studies in the 1940s suggested that even small amounts of alcohol — so-called social drinking — could cause accumulations of fat or "fatty liver," a common precursor to cirrhosis. It was later established that excessive alcohol is directly toxic to the liver. Many experts now associate alcohol abuse with 90 to 95 percent of deaths from cirrhosis.

Still, nobody knows how much alcohol is needed to produce cirrhosis. (By one definition, a "heavy drinker" is someone who drinks more than his doctor.) Apparently, the length of time one drinks has a greater effect than the amount. Cirrhosis usually develops only after many years of heavy alcohol consumption. Studies show that of individuals who drink the equivalent of ten drinks daily for fifteen years or more, about 8 percent develop cirrhosis and about 25 percent develop alcoholic hepatitis, an acute inflammation of the liver. Fatty liver occurs in nearly all individuals who drink heavily and is generally not considered a serious condition. Some experts note that three to four years are sufficient to produce fatty livers among a small number of "social drinkers" who drink as little as two to three drinks a day. In a few cases, two days of heavy drinking have been enough to increase liver fat.

Alcohol is not the only cause of cirrhosis. Teetotalers get it, too, as do people with viral hepatitis, certain inherited diseases, severe reactions to drugs, and prolonged exposure to environmental toxins. Cirrhosis also may occur in children who have cystic fibrosis and in people with long-term obstruction of the bile ducts.

Silent Symptoms

The earliest signs of cirrhosis are barely noticeable. As it develops, so do weight loss, nausea, vomiting, stomach upsets, and inability to digest fats. Often a physician is the first person to discover an enlarged liver by feeling it during a physical examination. In some cases a fatty liver visibly protrudes on the right side of the abdomen.

If liver disease has progressed, the skin and eyes may turn a yellowish color, and the person may pass dark urine. Hepatitis may develop if heavy drinking continues. This stage of alcoholic liver disease causes the liver to become enlarged and tender, and may cause jaundice (yellowed skin and whites of the eyes).

In stage three, the cirrhotic liver stops helping the body digest food, and bile backs into the bloodstream, causing severe jaundice. Spidery blood vessels appear on the face and neck, the belly swells, palms turn red, blood refuses to clot, male breasts enlarge, impotence occurs, and — if drinking continues — hemorrhage or liver failure eventually causes death.

Chronic liver disease and cirrhosis comprise the eighth leading cause of death for men in the United States. Twice as many men as women die from liver disease. Cirrhosis usually strikes people in their forties and fifties, but teenagers have been known to develop the disease. Cirrhosis is legendary among the French, whose *crises de foie* (liver attacks) send them to the mineral waters of Vichy to partake of "the cure." Among Jewish people, cirrhosis is virtually nonexistent.

Preventing Liver Disease

The remedy for cirrhosis is to stop drinking. Although scarring of the liver cannot be reversed, it can be slowed down and even stopped. Depending on how far their disease has progressed, many people with alcoholic cirrhosis who give up alcohol are alive and well five years later. Close to 100 percent of those who continue drinking are dead or near-dead by then. People who stop drinking at the earlier fatty liver or hepatitis stages can recover completely.

Prolonged exposure to environmental toxins also can cause cirrhosis. The American Liver Foundation recommends these precautions when using chemicals at work, home, or in the yard:

- Make sure there is good ventilation.
- Follow directions on the label.
- Never mix chemical products.
- Avoid getting chemicals on your skin. If you do, wash them off immediately before they are absorbed.
- Do not inhale chemicals, and wear protective face masks and clothing when using them.

Homicide

In the conventional view, homicide — the killing of one human being by another — is a legal matter and no topic for a health guide. Presumably, it happens only to people from the wrong side of town who tangle with criminals and who have little or no control over their fates. This theory pales before evidence that nearly 60 percent of the 19,000

(in 1985) people who are murdered each year are related to or acquainted with their killers.

Because so many homicides are perpetrated by relatives or persons
acquainted with the victims (41 percent in 1985), the FBI for many years
has held the view that "murder is primarily a societal problem over
which law enforcement has little or no control." Yet only recently have
homicide and other violence been recognized as a health problem as
well as a law enforcement problem. The Surgeon General of the United
States, Dr. C. Everett Koop, in 1985 called violence a "serious issue
affecting the health and well-being of millions of Americans." Homicide is the ninth leading cause of death for men. Murder claims men's
lives at more than three times the rate of women, one of the greatest
sex differences in mortality among the top ten causes of death for men.
Homicide victims tend to be young (under thirty-five years old), poor,
and urban-dwelling. Black males have higher death-by-homicide rates
than any other race/sex group. The black-on-black murder rate is eight
to twelve times that of the white-on-white rate. If males are the victims,
who are the offenders? According to the FBI's Uniform Crime Reports,
most are men using handguns and other firearms.

Unemployment, stress, racism, social isolation, hopelessness, drug
and alcohol abuse, and inability to get along with others can breed
destructive behavior and uncontrolled rage. Some experts believe homicide often substitutes for suicide in lower socioeconomic classes where
males are brought up to vent their anger on others rather than on
themselves. The National Institute of Alcohol Abuse and Alcoholism
has estimated that about half of all homicides in the United States are
related to use of alcohol, and an estimated 10 percent are related to use
of illegal drugs. Domestic violence in all its forms — from family fights
at one extreme to spouse and child abuse at the other — is a major
contributor to the homicide death toll.

Domestic Violence

Each year more than one million children are seriously abused —
physically, sexually, and emotionally — by their parents, guardians,
or other adults, according to the AMA Council on Scientific Affairs. Of
this number, between two thousand and five thousand die from their
injuries.

The roots of child abuse reach far back in history. Aristotle wrote in
the fourth century B.C. that "a son or slave is property, and there can
be no injustice to one's own property." In ancient Rome, a father could

sell, abandon, or kill his children. Until the twentieth century, the rights of parents over their children were still paramount in the United States. By the 1960s, all the states had enacted laws protecting children against abuse and neglect, and physicians finally began recognizing what the unexplained welts, bruises, burns, strap marks, swellings, lost teeth, and fractured bones in young patients really meant. It also became apparent that child abuse is not just a blue-collar crime. It occurs among the well educated, well housed, and well heeled, and often is committed by a parent who was abused as a child.

Yet child abuse is not the most frequent form of violence in the family. Serious violence among adults is even more prevalent. An estimated two million American women are severely beaten each year by their husbands, ex-husbands, or lovers, according to a survey in 1985 by the National Institute of Mental Health. The familiar term "wife beating" has fostered the myth that spousal violence is always against women. The NIMH survey showed, however, that women nearly as often severely assault their husbands/lovers.

Few people can cause as much anger as those who are close. Spouse murders often result from romantic triangles or lover's quarrels. In many cases, murder serves as a form of divorce for people who can find no other way out of an unhealthy relationship. Violence at home also serves as a training ground for violence outside the home.

Preventing Homicide

Experts on victim-offender relationships note that many homicides are preceded by nonfatal violence that comes to the attention of police and health care providers. In one study of domestic homicides conducted in Kansas City, it was found that during the preceding two years police had responded to one or more disturbance calls at the addresses of 90 percent of the homicide victims and suspects. To an as-yet-unknown — but probably significant — extent, child abuse, spouse abuse, and other assaults that bring victims to hospital emergency rooms eventually lead to homicide.

Homicide prevention requires attention to high-risk situations and personal relationships. Easy access to firearms may be particularly dangerous in households where domestic violence prevails. Violence-prone individuals need to learn, through counseling, to get along with a spouse/lover, raise a family, control rage, redirect anger, and break the cycle of child/spouse abuse that thrives best in shadows. At the community level, homicide prevention requires domestic-crisis-intervention programs, child-care facilities, design of structurally safe environments, promotion of neighborhood ties, counseling to help parents and children deal less violently with stresses they face, and educational programs to change attitudes in communities that view homicide as normal.

Diabetes

Everybody has sugar, mainly in the form of glucose, in his or her bloodstream. Blood sugar tends to soar after a heavy meal, especially one rich in easily digested simple sugars. In response, the pancreas automatically secretes more insulin, a hormone that helps the body turn glucose into energy or store it for later use. When the pancreas is unable to secrete enough insulin to lower blood sugar to the normal range, or when it secretes insulin but the body cannot respond, unused glucose collects in the blood and blood sugar remains elevated. The result is diabetes, a complex disease in which cells cannot get enough glucose to function properly.

Type I, or insulin-dependent, diabetes — once known as juvenile-onset diabetes — usually occurs in children and adolescents, although it may strike at any age. People with Type II, or non-insulin-dependent, diabetes represent about 90 percent of the 10 to 11 million people who suffer from diabetes in the United States. This form of the disease once was known as adult-onset diabetes because it usually occurs after age forty. But it, too, may strike at any age.

Diabetes is the tenth leading cause of death for men. In addition to shortened life expectancy, many people with diabetes have serious health problems, especially when their disease is not treated properly. For example, the abnormal metabolism of diabetes can alter tissue development and lead to deterioration of small blood vessels throughout the body. This, in turn, can lead to loss of vision, kidney and nerve damage, and other life-threatening complications. People with diabetes are twenty-five times more likely to develop blindness or visual impairment than nondiabetics. The former are seventeen times more prone to kidney disease, five times more prone to gangrene requiring the amputation of a limb, and at least twice as prone to coronary heart disease and stroke. In addition, people with diabetes frequently develop atherosclerosis, severe periodontal (gum) disease, infection, depression, and, in 50 to 60 percent of diabetic men, impotence.

Fortunately, you can prevent or reverse much of this damage by recognizing the symptoms of diabetes, having periodic medical checkups to detect "hidden diabetes," maintaining normal weight, and — if you have diabetes — learning to take good care of yourself and keep blood glucose at or near normal levels.

The early warning signs of diabetes include
- excessive thirst
- frequent urination
- extreme hunger
- rapid weight loss
- fatigue, weakness, irritability, and nausea

Advanced cases of diabetes may cause
- frequent infections of the gums, skin, or urinary tract
- change in vision or blurred vision
- pain, cramps, or tingling in the legs, feet, or fingers
- cuts and bruises that are slow to heal
- intense itching
- drowsiness, tiring easily

If you notice any of these symptoms, see a physician promptly.

The Hidden Diabetic

Four or five million Americans who have diabetes do not know it. People with Type II diabetes, in particular, tend to have few or no symptoms. Many cases are detected only after heart, kidney, nerve, or eye problems develop. Often the only way to detect diabetes is through periodic blood or glucose tolerance tests, in which blood is tested at intervals after you drink a measured amount of a glucose solution. These tests are simple and painless, and may be done during a routine physical examination.

Who Gets Diabetes?

People at risk for diabetes tend to be
- overweight
- over forty
- relatives of people with diabetes, especially overweight relatives
- black or Hispanic

The greatest risk factor is obesity. Eighty percent of all diabetics are overweight. The chances of developing diabetes increase even with moderate obesity. Moreover, obesity aggravates and increases the risk of death from existing diabetes, while sensible weight control increases glucose tolerance and decreases the need for oral medication.

Taking Care of Diabetes

Diabetes cannot be cured, but it *can* be controlled. People with Type I diabetes need to keep blood-sugar levels as near normal as possible by closely synchronizing diet, exercise, and daily injections of insulin. They should always have easily absorbed sugars, such as hard candy or fruit juice, within reach, in case insulin causes a too-rapid drop in blood sugar. This can cause hypoglycemia or more serious insulin shock.

The main treatment for Type II diabetes is weight control through diet and exercise, supplemented by oral hypoglycemic agents if necessary. Although they have been called "oral insulin," they actually are related to the sulfa drugs and increase insulin secretion and the body's sensitivity to insulin. The sulfonylurea compounds, especially tolbutamide, are also used. Insulin itself may be needed when neither diet nor oral medication can control Type II diabetes.

There is no single diet for people with diabetes. They should eat the same normal, healthy diet described in chapter 1. Like everybody else, people with diabetes should eat more complex carbohydrates and fiber, avoid simple sugars, and limit intake of cholesterol and saturated fats. The main difference is they must schedule meals regularly to maintain glucose levels. People with diabetes can tolerate small amounts of alcohol taken with food and small amounts of sugar if their disease is well controlled. The American Diabetes Association advises that up to 5 percent of total carbohydrate intake may be consumed as sucrose, as long as it is part of a mixed meal and is spaced throughout the day.

To control weight, people with diabetes need regular exercise (see chapter 2). They should work out *at least* three times a week for thirty minutes minimum. Each session should include warm-up and cool-down periods, followed by aerobic exercise, such as dancing, cycling, swimming, or walking, that raises pulse rates to 75 percent of maximum. Exercise reduces the need for medication, helps maintain normal weight, and protects against heart disease. People with diabetes also need to refrain from smoking since it doubles the risk of cardiovascular disease, have their blood pressure checked periodically, and have an annual eye examination.

Whether blood-sugar levels should be carefully controlled is still controversial, especially for Type II diabetes. Studies in animals have shown that "tight control" helps prevent cardiovascular, kidney, nerve, and eye damage. Recent studies in humans suggest that careful control of blood-glucose levels with insulin or oral agents might prevent damaging changes in linings of blood vessels, which can be early indicators of diabetic complications. But other studies show that insulin helps prevent only life-threatening diabetic coma in Type I diabetes, not other complications of the disease. Many experts note that tight control — especially when it requires a rigid diet and frequent insulin injections — unnecessarily impedes the patient's lifestyle. The National Institutes of Health are sponsoring a ten-year study of "tight" versus conventional treatment in preventing or delaying serious complications in Type I diabetes. Results are expected in 1993.

Despite the known benefits of weight control, healthy diet, and exercise, only 10 to 20 percent of diabetics successfully maintain such regimens in the long run. Often the most difficult task is sticking to a diet. It is tempting for people with diabetes who have no symptoms to lose motivation and forget to eat and exercise properly, skip medication, and even go on food sprees and refuse to take care of themselves. Those who successfully adapt their lifestyles to their disease need family support in treating diabetes as a problem that involves everybody, not just the patient as an isolated entity. In other words, a person with diabetes needs to do the same things to stay healthy as other people do.

Sources of Help for People with Diabetes

- American Diabetes Association
  Council on Nutrition
  2 Park Avenue
  New York, NY 10016
- American Dietetic Association
  Council on Practice
  430 N. Michigan Avenue
  Chicago, IL 60611
- National Diabetes Information Clearinghouse
  Box NDIC
  Bethesda, MD 20205

The Clearinghouse has booklets on fast food, ethnic foods, dining out, and parties for diabetics.

Life's Problems,
Small and Large

In a more tolerant world, bad breath, belching, borborygmus, body odor, dandruff, ear wax, and intestinal gas would not rank among life's problems, small or large. But society views these smells, sounds, and secretions not as normal bodily functions, but as embarrassments. How many quiet hand-holding moments have been disrupted by the sound of something sloshing in your loved one's, or *your*, stomach? How many times have you passed gas in mixed company? Such happenings are disastrous mainly because nobody is willing to talk about them. They are not only life's little problems, they are life's *unspeakable* problems.

Bad Breath

So you remain unaware that your biggest little problem is halitosis. An 1873 dental journal suggests why: "No one detects the smell he is used to, and by consequence, since each one is accustomed to his own breath, he will regard it as odorless, though its vapors be loaded with a dozen different stenches." Dentists, the journal added, are among the worst offenders.

About 80 percent of bad breath is caused by poor oral hygiene: decaying food, unclean dentures, tooth decay, bleeding and diseased gums, and plaque — an invisible bacterial film on the teeth. A coated tongue can cause bad breath, especially when the back portion is coated. So can dry mouth, which occurs when you are dehydrated or hung over. Breathing from the mouth also can cause bad breath because the saliva dries and cannot wash away odor-causing bacteria. Early-morning halitosis is common because the tongue has been inactive, whereas its constant motion all day helps keep your mouth clean. Bad breath may also be caused by smoking, emotional upset, and skipping meals. Food passing over the tongue cleans it and stimulates the flow of saliva. You can also get halitosis from eating onions, garlic, and foods loaded with fats, sugar, and spices.

If you want to clean up your breath, forget about mouthwashes or breath mints. They may hide halitosis for a few hours, but they do not eliminate its causes. What does prevent halitosis is brushing every tooth surface, as well as your gums and your tongue as far back as possible, three times a day. To prevent gum disease and remove plaque, clean between each tooth with dental floss at least once a day. Most important, have a dental examination every six months so a professional can polish your teeth and remove hardened plaque and calculus. This will help prevent tooth decay, gum disease, and, as a result, bad breath.

Gas

Halitosis is a problem of proximity, while belching and intestinal gas span great distances. These two by-products of digestion are often, although not necessarily, related. Most belching is caused by swallowing air. The air either returns via your esophagus or passes into (and eventually out of) your intestine.

Intestinal gas, also known as flatulence, is most often caused by eating gas-producing foods, such as beans, cabbage, cauliflower, brussels sprouts, onions, and — for people who are sensitive to them — milk and milk products. If you are normal, you pass from less than a pint to a little over a quart of gas each day. This approximates the volume of one to three 12-ounce cans of beer.

The easiest way to get rid of gas is to exercise. Gas pains, caused by the combined pressures of food and suppressed gas, also can be relieved by (1) rocking back and forth while holding your knees close to your chest; (2) lying facedown with your stomach on several pillows; or (3) standing on your head. (Gas tends to rise.)

Borborygmus

A related gut reaction — borborygmus — is caused by air and liquid sloshing around in your stomach and intestine during digestion. Borborygmus has nothing to do with an empty or overfilled stomach, as many people believe. Although borborygmus occasionally results from a stomach abnormality or disease, swallowing air usually is the cause. Nervousness and drinking carbonated beverages can make the problem worse. To make it better, eat some food to quell the anticipation of eating, which can generate borborygmic rumblings. Avoid carbonated beverages, or lie down on your back or right side and apply pressure to your abdomen.

Body Odor

Ever since the first deodorants came on the market in the early 1900s, body odor and its first cousin, sweat, have received bad press. The value of sweating in cooling your body, keeping your skin moist, and helping maintain your water and salt balance has been discounted, while myths about the odor of sweat have thrived:

> *Myth 1:* If you sweat, you automatically have body odor.
> *Myth 2:* You need a deodorant more in summer than in winter.
> *Myth 3:* Antiperspirants are unhealthy, since sweating rids your body of wastes.
> *Myth 4:* You can become immune to one deodorant and should periodically switch to a new one.
> *Myth 5:* Men need a stronger deodorant than women.

All of these statements are myths mainly because of the differences between eccrine and apocrine sweat glands. Myth number 1 is untrue because sweat from eccrine glands — the kind found all over your body — is odorless. Apocrine sweat — the kind produced in the groin, armpits, soles of the feet, and palms — produces odor and is stimulated by emotions rather than heat. Apocrine sweat is as profuse in winter as in summer, contrary to myth number 2. Sweating cools the body; it does not serve as a means of waste disposal as suggested in myth number 3. Myth number 4 is incorrect because deodorants and antiperspirants do not lose effectiveness, and people do not build up immunity to them, as they do to antidandruff shampoos (see the section on dandruff, pp. 213–214). As for myth number 5, apocrine secretion and odor are about the same for both sexes, although people with hairy armpits must work a little harder to keep body odor at bay.

Eccrine sweat is essentially odorless because it is 99.5 percent water, and the remainder is salt and trace amounts of ammonia, glucose, iron, calcium, and potassium. So inoffensive is this kind of sweat — known in athletic circles as "sport sweat" — that Dr. George Sheehan, a long-distance runner and author of many books about running, says he skips taking a shower after a sweaty hour on the road. He just towels off, puts on a suit, and goes back to work. Sheehan does say that to prevent B.O., you need to change your clothes daily and take a Saturday night bath, provided you are sweating only from your eccrine glands.

The problem is that your apocrine glands pour forth a milky, pale gray fluid whenever you feel fear, anxiety, guilt, apprehension, or sexual excitement, or sometimes for no apparent reason at all. Even this kind of "psycho sweat" would not smell if confined to a cool, clean environment. The men who explored the South Pole with Ernest Shackleton found that their skin remained odorless after almost *two* bathless years of living in the same clothes. Body odor is caused by millions of bacteria that live on the skin and thrive in a dark, moist environment. They nourish themselves with apocrine sweat, then decompose it into a smelly deposit that, when dried, forms shiny, gluelike granules.

To prevent apocrine sweat odor, you can mask it or use antiperspirants to remove the moisture needed for bacterial growth. For best results, do not apply an antiperspirant when you are already sweating, or when your body is warm just after a shower or bath. Wait until you are cooled down so the product can penetrate into your sweat ducts. Since antiperspirants and deodorants do not remove bacteria that are already present, you will also need to shower regularly and often with a deodorant or antibacterial soap.

Aside from odor, many people worry about *how much* they sweat. A normal person loses about a quart of water a day through sweating and skin evaporation. Men usually sweat more than women, whites and blacks sweat more than Orientals, and athletes sweat more efficiently and profusely than nearly everybody else.

Dandruff

Dandruff, also known as *furfuraceous desquamation* (shedding of skin), usually occurs between puberty and middle age, more often in men than in women. Healthy scalps constantly shed small, dead surface cells that go unnoticed. When dandruff occurs, these cells are clumped by gummy secretions that bind them into visible scales.

Dandruff is a form of seborrheic dermatitis, a skin disorder that occurs when the normal shedding of dead skin cells accelerates. Seborrhea affects hairy and oily areas: the scalp, behind the ears, around the eyebrows, sides of the nose, and sometimes the chest, buttocks, and pubic area. Severe dandruff may cause the face to develop seborrhea. This condition, often mistaken for dry skin, usually clears up when dandruff is brought under control.

Washing the hair with an ordinary shampoo will control most dandruff problems if you use it several times weekly or even daily. If this fails, try a nonprescription dandruff shampoo containing any of the following ingredients: zinc pyrithione, sulfur, tar, selenium sulfide, or salicylic acid. *The secret of dandruff control is playing musical shampoos.* Dr. Laurence Miller, a dermatologist in Washington, D.C., advises buying a different brand whenever your previous supply runs out because each dandruff shampoo loses its effectiveness with repeated use. Follow directions and leave the medicated shampoo on the scalp five to ten minutes so it can loosen dandruff scales. Then reapply the shampoo for another five to ten minutes and rinse thoroughly.

When dandruff persists and makes the scalp red, itchy, and unsightly, ask a physician to prescribe a stronger shampoo or cortisone preparation to relieve scalp inflammation. If dandruff shampoos make your hair dry, use a hair conditioner to replace oils removed during shampooing. Dry hair is far less serious than dandruff itself, which, when severe, can cause moderate but reversible hair loss.

Diarrhea

Aretaeus of Cappadocia, an ancient Greek physician, defined diarrhea as "the discharge of undigested food in a fluid state . . . no part of the digestive process having been properly done, except the commencement." Diarrhea ranges from occasional loose stools and cramps to the profuse, watery discharge that requires trips to the bathroom six to perhaps twenty-four times a day.

The enemy below could be a virus that causes "stomach flu," a bacterium or parasite lurking in your food, a physical disease, bowel obstruction, antibiotic, laxative habit, a reaction to psychological stress, oral-anal sexual contact, allergy to certain foods, or improper digestion of food in the small intestine.

"Stomach flu" is one of the most common causes of diarrhea. This acute viral infection of the digestive system is surpassed only by the common cold as a cause of illness in the United States. Actually a form of gastroenteritis, stomach flu causes fever, chills, stomachache, nausea and vomiting, abdominal cramps, and diarrhea in varying combinations. It usually lasts one or two days and is rarely serious.

If you are traveling and get diarrhea, the most likely cause is *Escherichia coli* (*E. coli* for short), which produce more severe diarrhea than viruses. Normally you harbor these bacteria in your intestines, but when traveling you may ingest one of a tremendous number of alien strains that populate the earth. In your intestine *E. coli* produce a substance that injures the intestinal wall and makes it "weep" and pour fluid into the stool, causing cramping, abdominal pain, and diarrhea. Viral or bacterial diarrhea takes hours or days to develop, depending on the cause, how much of the organism you have consumed, and how quickly it multiplies and produces toxins in your gut. If vomiting and diarrhea occur soon after you eat, you probably have diarrhea caused by food poisoning. Thus diarrhea protects you by getting rid of harmful bacteria and their toxins. The gastrocolic reflex also can cause diarrhea. About five minutes after eating, wavelike involuntary contractions, known as peristalsis, are triggered in your intestine, causing the food that you ate several days earlier to pass.

Thousands of diarrhea remedies exist, but many do not work. Some work but should be used only occasionally. Kaopectate, a nonprescription drug, may relieve mild cases of diarrhea. Prescription drugs such as Lomotil or preparations containing paregoric, a narcotic that slows down the action of the digestive tract, are stronger but may cause retention of harmful organisms and their toxins. Overuse of Lomotil can cause constipation and both physical and psychological dependence. One remedy that seems to relieve diarrhea is Pepto Bismol. Its active ingredient — subsalicylate bismuth — also alleviates upset stomach, indigestion, and nausea. But the dosage required is large: about one 8-ounce bottle daily.

Dealing with Diarrhea
- Get plenty of physical rest.
- Avoid solid foods.
- Drink fluids containing sugar and salt, such as Gatorade or a home mixture of ½ teaspoon table salt, ½ teaspoon baking soda, ¼ teaspoon potassium chloride, and 2 tablespoons glucose. You may need a physician's prescription for the potassium chloride.
- As you improve, add soups, applesauce, rice, toast, saltines, and Jell-O.
- Avoid milk and high-fiber fruits and vegetables, fatty or spicy foods, sweets, and carbonated drinks or beer.
- Work up slowly to a normal diet.
- If a clear liquid diet does not work, try a tablespoon of Kaopectate after each loose bowel movement.

- If Kaopectate does not work, try Parapectolin or Parelixir, which may be available without a prescription.
- If vomiting and diarrhea are severe or last longer than two to three days, see a doctor.
- To prevent traveler's diarrhea, wash your hands thoroughly before eating.

Ear Wax

There are only two things you need to know about ear wax: (1) it will not make you go deaf, and (2) it does not mean you are a slob who does not clean his ears. Ear wax is secreted by glands in the outer ear canal. Most of it dries and drops out in tiny pieces while you sleep. Ear wax usually causes no problem unless it is produced too rapidly and becomes a hard plug filling the outer ear canal. Then it may become impacted and cause a feeling of fullness in the ear, difficulty in hearing, mild earache, or ringing and other strange sounds in the ears. Only a physician should remove impacted ear wax.

To safely remove normal amounts of ear wax from your ears, clean them gently with a washcloth. Commercial softening agents are safe and effective for removing wax accumulated in the external ear canal. *Never* try to clean your ears with cotton-tipped sticks. These products not only damage the protective skin barrier in the ear, they can push the wax deeper into the ear canal, where it can become impacted and cause infection. Never use a paper clip, bobby pin, matchstick, toothpick, nail, or other hard object to remove ear wax. In other words, never put anything smaller than your elbow in your ear.

Potbellies

Potbellies may look charming on stoves, but on people they are unattractive and — their owners may not realize — bad for health. Among other things, the protruding gut cannot properly protect such underlying organs as the liver, gallbladder, stomach, spleen, bladder, and genitals from sharp blows and other injuries. Strong abdominal muscles keep these organs in place inside the body and help them work well mechanically. Even men in their twenties can develop potbellies, usually because of weak abdominal muscles and body fat. And while potbellies are not necessarily a sign of aging, redistribution of weight to the abdomen does progress as the years pass.

Exercise or weight loss alone cannot flatten the protruding gut, but exercise *plus* weight loss can. There are many ways to strengthen the major muscles comprising the abdominals. One isometric exercise is to stand or sit up straight, take a deep breath, pull in your abdomen while slowly exhaling to a count of ten. Relax and repeat ten times. Do this frequently during the day: in elevators, in line at the bank, at stop lights, and at your desk.

Some people do sit-ups by the score to flatten their abdominals. But traditional sit-ups, in which you lie flat on the floor and rise to a sitting position, can injure your back, as can leg lifts. Neither is as effective as newer versions of this exercise: curls, reverse curls, and twists. Many variations make these calisthenics more intense and less boring, but here are the three basic movements:

Curl: Lie flat on your back, knees bent, feet on the floor. Place your hands behind your head and slowly lift your head and shoulder blades just enough to make your upper abdominal muscles contract. Lower your head slowly, keeping the small of your back flat against the floor. Exhale while raising your head, inhale while lowering. Work up to twenty to thirty repetitions.

Reverse curl: Lie in the same position as for the curl, but keep your hands at your sides. Raise your bent knees slowly toward your chest. Exhale while raising, inhale while lowering the knees. A more difficult version of this exercise is to raise your knees halfway toward your chest and then toward the ceiling. Work up to twenty to thirty repetitions.

Twists: Lie in the same position as for the curl, with knees bent and feet flat on the floor. Straighten your arms and clasp your hands together in front of you. Raise your head and shoulders about the same amount as in the curl, but twist either to the right or left as you do so. Your hands will extend toward the outer right or outer left side of your knees. Work up to twenty to thirty repetitions. Do one to three sets of each of these exercises three to five times a week. If you feel pain in your back, discontinue.

A potbelly will not disappear quickly. But if you combine a proper diet, regular workouts with curls and twists, and vigorous aerobic exercise three to five times a week, you should begin to notice some difference in your body shape and firmness (i.e., your pants should fit looser) in four to six weeks, depending on your starting point. Some individuals — because of the way their bodies respond to exercise — may never achieve a "washboard" look. The average person should, however, be able significantly to reduce — if not totally eliminate — a potbelly.

A flat belly takes time and effort to achieve. In return, it

- helps prevent low back pain by supporting the delicate structures of the lower spine
- supports and protects organs inside the abdominal-pelvic area
- promotes regular bowel habits
- supplements weight-reducing programs
- makes you feel and look better, in and out of your clothes

Baldness

"A hair in the head is worth two in the brush," the saying goes. Or, as George Bernard Shaw suggested, balding heads are good examples of what is wrong with capitalism: oversupply in some sectors and poor distribution. Most of the baldness, or alopecia, that occurs in the world — whether a rising forehead, a Kojak-type pate, or a shining island surrounded by a sea of hair — is known as "male pattern baldness." Over 40 percent of all men inherit a predisposition to it.

Male pattern baldness, and women's near-universal immunity to it, is explained by the presence of male sex hormones, such as testosterone. Men who lack these hormones, including eunuchs, do not develop male pattern baldness. Castration early in life can delay — although it cannot ultimately prevent — baldness. Yet a full head of hair does not mean a man is testosterone-deficient, nor does hair loss mean he has high levels of the hormone.

The average healthy human scalp grows about one hundred thousand hairs, each growing from a follicle beneath the skin. A hair on your head is genetically programmed to grow about half an inch a month for three to five years. (Other body hair is programmed to grow to shorter lengths.) Scalp hair growth then stops for several months and the hair falls out. After a three-month "resting" phase, a new hair emerges from the same follicle.

Normally you lose fifty to one hundred scalp hairs per day as the old make way for the new. This means that most of your scalp's hair is growing and a tiny percent is resting at all times. But often the percentage of hairs in the resting phase rises sharply, and the number of hairs lost exceeds the number gained. As more and more hair falls out, male pattern baldness sets in.

This condition afflicts about 12 percent of twenty-five-year-old men, 37 percent of thirty-five-year-old men, 45 percent of forty-five-year-old men, and 65 percent of sixty-five-year-old men. Thus, if you are a male over age thirty, your chances of becoming bald are about equal to your age. If the men on both sides of your family have bald spots, you are likely to have them, too. Baldness can be passed along on either the mother's or father's side of the family, contrary to the prevailing impression that it comes only from the mother's side. Caucasians are the most prone to baldness, and Asians are the least prone.

Some hair loss is only temporary. High fever, major illness, general anesthesia, anticancer and other drugs, X rays, drastic weight loss, severe emotional upset, childbirth, or rubbing or pulling the hair too hard can cause it to fall out, sometimes by the handfuls. But it regrows several months later. There is no evidence that frequent washing or brushing the hair causes (or prevents) baldness. Nor do hats, wigs, hairpieces, oily hair, or dandruff cause baldness.

For centuries, bald men have grasped at hairs, as it were, and rubbed their scalps with special shampoos, oils, and ointments. Others have tried vitamins, hormones, radiation, and special foods. Some have tried electrical stimulation to increase blood circulation to the scalp. These hair-raising remedies have one thing in common: they do not work. The Food and Drug Administration is considering removing from the market such products claiming to grow hair or prevent baldness because none of these products has been found effective. Some of these products contain female hormones that can cause male breasts to enlarge.

One promising — but still experimental — treatment for baldness was discovered when some bald men taking minoxidil for high blood pressure in the early 1970s noticed that the drug caused hair to grow on their scalps. The drug just as often caused hair growth on the eyebrows, trunk, or other parts of the body. The treatment works best on men who have been bald less than ten years or who are just beginning to lose their hair. In a clinical trial conducted by the Upjohn pharmaceutical company in 1983–84, nearly two thousand bald men applied minoxidil in liquid form directly on their scalps in hopes of confining hair growth to that area. Results of the trial showed that 76 percent of a group of 619 men who applied a 2 percent concentration of minoxidil for twelve months grew new hair and experienced a significant increase in the number of hair follicles. Others who received a 3 percent solution of minoxidil also experienced hair growth, but to a lesser degree. As of April 1987, the Food and Drug Administration was about to approve the drug for marketing as a treatment for hair loss. But this does not prevent physicians from prescribing minoxidil for baldness. Minoxidil is effective only as long as it is applied twice a day for the rest of your life. Treatment is expected to cost $20 to $25 a week.

A proven solution for baldness is hair transplantation, the grafting of tiny cylinders containing twelve to eighteen of your own hair roots from hair-bearing areas to cover a bald spot. A physician can graft only ten to twenty "plugs" at one session. You usually return at weekly intervals until the bald spot is covered. This may take an average of 175 grafts, or up to 400 for extensive baldness. Since new hairs do not grow in the donor spots, the total number of hairs on your head remains the same; they are just redistributed. The grafts usually "take" and last a lifetime. But hair transplantation does not work for everybody, it does not give you a thick head of hair, and it is expensive — about $15 to $25 per transplanted plug. Other techniques that work include grafting flaps of hair-bearing skin from the sides of the head to the bald area, and scalp reduction: the surgical removal of strips of hairless scalp so that hair-bearing areas stretch over once-bald spots.

The Food and Drug Administration warns against implantations of synthetic fibers to "cure" baldness. Unlike natural hair, these false ones cause pain and infection. Sometimes the entire scalp must be removed and replaced by skin from other areas. Another technique, in which real hair is sewn directly to the scalp, is almost as unsatisfactory. Most scalps react badly to the stitches and develop itching, discomfort, and infection. Hair implantation (as opposed to *trans*plantation) may improve in the future, but at present it is no answer to baldness. Weaving of tufts of hair in with hair growing on the scalp is impractical because hair must be rewoven as "anchor" hair grows out.

A painless and inexpensive remedy for baldness is a good wig or hairpiece. You also can tell yourself that bald is beautiful, that discriminating women are more interested in what is inside your head than what is on it, and that nobody falls in love with you to be close to your hair.

The Razor's Edge

Beards, like hair, are a sex symbol. A survey by a New York psychologist once showed that while men may complain about having to shave, very few would want to use a product — should one be developed — that would permanently remove their beards. In *Intimate Behavior*, Desmond Morris suggests a reason why: shaving leaves a masculine blue sheen on the lower face that men would not want to be without.

Men spend an average of one to two hours a week shaving. This daily ritual sometimes causes skin damage, especially in men who consider shaving a chore and rush to finish the job. They slap on shaving cream, pull their skin taut, and shave against the grain in long, impatient strokes. As the razor's edge passes over stretched skin, escaping hair retracts beneath the skin's surface, where it can become ingrown and inflamed. When this happens to hundreds of hairs the result is *pseudofolliculitis barbae,* or a face and neck that look like plucked-chicken skin. This disease often affects black men, as well as many white men who have coarse, curly beard hair.

The best remedy for *pseudofolliculitis barbae* is not to shave and to let ingrown hair grow free. If you *must* shave:

- Soften your beard with a hot washcloth for several minutes before shaving.
- Apply shaving cream and shave *with* the grain of hair growth.
- Do not stretch your skin or shave too close.
- Use short and gentle rather than long and pulling strokes.
- Brush your beard with a soft toothbrush to free hairs growing inward.

Skin Deep

Beauty may be only skin deep, but if your skin is dry, cracked, red, chapped, and itchy, it is decidedly unbeautiful. Skin, especially men's, is probably the most neglected organ of the body. Two common male skin problems, miliaria (prickly heat) and dry skin, are caused by too few baths or showers in summer and too many in winter. In the summertime, men tend to develop prickly heat: a red, itchy rash caused by temporary blockage of the pores because of prolonged sweating. If you unduly delay showering after hard physical activity, you are more prone to prickly heat because bathing cools the body and opens the pores. Acne conditions also might flare up if you unduly delay showering after vigorous exercise. Take time, however, to cool down (see chapter 2, p. 45).

Suppose you take a hot shower before work. At lunchtime you jog or play racquetball, jump into another hot shower, and lather with lots of soap. You may not realize it, but you are washing natural skin oils down the drain. The result is a dry, flaky, inelastic, "dishpan" skin that often starts around ankles gripped by elastic polyester socks. The itch may spread to your legs, waist, abdomen, chest, and back. Your skin may become so dry, with little red bumps oozing from scratching, that you may mistakenly think you are allergic to something.

Behind this passion for soap and showers is the myth that you must bathe daily or smell. Actually, daily sponge baths with soap applied only to the groin, underarms, and feet would prevent most apocrine odors that society finds offensive. (See the section on body odor, pp. 212–213.)

Too much soap can wash away skin oils, the body's natural barrier against loss of body water. When this occurs, water escapes through the skin at seventy-five times the normal rate. In self-defense, you can take tepid, soapless showers using a soap with a neutral pH on odor areas only. The dryer your skin, the more important it is to replace skin oils with a moisturizer *immediately* after bathing. Water is the world's best moisturizer, but it quickly evaporates from the skin's outer layer unless you seal it in with another moisturizer. Likewise, the finest moisturizing products are useless unless you first apply water to your skin — ideally by drenching dry areas for five to ten minutes.

A good moisturizing product contains oil — almost any kind will do. An oily preparation seals moisture or water in the skin and improves the feel and appearance of dry skin flakes by temporarily cementing them down. Bath oils are helpful but tend to get rubbed off on your towel. Petroleum jelly (Vaseline) holds water in your skin very well, but it is greasy and stains sheets and clothing. An oil-in-water emulsion is less oily but still works well. Products that contain aloe, which is a drying agent, are of benefit because of other oily ingredients. However, products that are unscented and lanolin-free are effective moisturizers and are least likely to cause reactions in sensitive skin. Baby oil works as well as many products with exotic ingredients and high prices.

Proper humidification may be the best way to prevent dry skin. The outer layer of human skin needs moisture to remain soft and supple. To achieve this, relative room humidity should be at least 30 to 35 percent. But the average relative humidity of the average American home is about 20 percent, less than that of the Sahara Desert. Forced-air heating is the worse offender in winter, and air-conditioning sucks moisture from the skin in the summer. Electric blankets, saunas, hot tubs, whirlpool baths, radiant heaters, and roaring fires all dry the skin, but who would want to live without them?

Prolonged exposure to sun and wind also "pull" water from the skin. Many people mistakenly believe that crow's feet around the eyes, vertical creases in the upper lip, and leathery furrows in the cheeks and neck are caused solely by aging. More often, premature aging of the skin is the avoidable result of solar damage from ultraviolet alpha (UVA) light rays. Too much exposure to the sun's ultraviolet beta

(UVB) rays also can lead to skin cancer (see chapter 6, pp. 176–177). Even if you do not burn, the sun damages your skin. Indeed, a suntan *is* the body's response to sun injury. Tanning is caused by melanin, a pigment that darkens the skin. There is no medical benefit from tanning. Although ultraviolet light helps the body make vitamin D, most people get all the vitamin D they need in their diet.

Myths about the Sun

- Dark-skinned and tanned individuals don't sunburn. (*False. Even blacks can sunburn if exposed long enough.*)
- Sunbathing in the early morning or late afternoon is not harmful. (*False. It may take longer, but early-morning and late-afternoon rays also can damage the skin.*)
- Only direct sunlight causes sunburn. (*False. The worst burns often occur on cloudy days. Even when sitting under an umbrella, you can burn from radiation reflected by beach sand.*)
- Sunlamps are not as damaging as sunlight. (*False. One minute under many sunlamps is equal to one hour under the sun.*)
- Some sun lotions or sunscreens "promote tanning" or give "longer-lasting tan." (*False:* The natural tanning process cannot be accelerated. These products merely let you tan more safely *if* you use them correctly.)

To prevent sunbeaten skin, treat the sun as your skin's worst enemy and use a sunscreen. Years ago, almost all suntan products were scented greases that offered little or no protection against the perils of sunbathing. Today sun worshipers can choose from dozens of sunscreens that block the UVB rays that cause most burning and skin cancer but admit UVA rays that cause tanning.

Today's sunscreens have an SPF (sun protection factor) rating. The higher the rating, the greater the protection, although there is no such thing as a total sunblocker.

- Individuals with very fair skin should use a sunscreen with an SPF of 15 or higher. This means they can extend safe exposure time in the sun by a factor of 15 before they will burn.
- Dark-skinned individuals need an SPF of 2 to 4.
- Apply sunscreens often and generously, and reapply after swimming or sweating.
- Begin tanning gradually. Most people take about two weeks to develop a full tan.

• Use a sunscreen under light summer clothing. A wet T-shirt exposes your skin to 20 to 30 percent of ultraviolet light.

Several other lifestyle factors may also affect skin appearance. Excessive alcohol intake can "age" the skin and cause rosacea: spiderlike red patches of enlarged blood vessels on the face. Heavy consumption of caffeine and hot spicy foods aggravate rosacealike skin. Smoking is thought to contribute to premature wrinkling because nicotine narrows the small blood vessels that nourish the skin. Wrinkles also can result from repeated facial expressions, such as squinting or smiling. Emotional stress also can "age" the skin, especially after prolonged periods of anxiety, depression, and tension. But youthful-looking skin depends most of all on heredity, climate, and protection from the sun. For an excellent discussion of plastic surgery for aging skin, see Curtis Pesman's *How a Man Ages*.

Athlete's Foot / Jock Itch

Athlete's foot, another common skin problem, affects men more than women, probably because many men encase their hot, sweaty feet in heavy, often airtight shoes. There moisture and warmth provide ideal growing conditions for fungi and bacteria.

Also known as *tinea pedis,* or ringworm of the feet, athlete's foot causes peeling, itching, and cracking skin, usually between the fourth and fifth toes. The infection can spread to the toenails, which turn yellow or brown, become brittle, and thicken. They tend to separate from the nail bed and are a source of infection for the rest of the foot.

Athlete's foot responds best to an antifungal cream, spray, or solution containing tolnaftate (Tinactin), miconazole (MicaTin), or undecylenic acid (Desenex). Treatment may fail unless you bathe your feet twice a day, dry them thoroughly — a hair dryer does this very well — apply medication, allow it to dry (again, with a blow dryer), then lightly dust with antifungal powder so that it does not cake. This infection may require four to six weeks of meticulous, twice-daily treatment. Many people stop treatment as soon as symptoms disappear, then wonder why they have recurrences.

If you mistreat or ignore a case of athlete's foot, you are apt to take notice when the same fungi infect your groin with a red, flaky rash known as "jock itch' or "crotch rot." Bacteria and chafing also can cause jock itch. Like athlete's foot, it strikes during warm weather, when heat and sweating from tight clothing (such as jockstraps) help fungi breed. Treatment for jock itch is the same as for athlete's foot: keep the affected area clean, cool, and dry, and apply a cream containing tolnaftate, miconazole, or undecylenic acid. *Warning:* in liquid form this medication can irritate the groin area.

The best way to prevent athlete's foot and jock itch is never to sit around in sweaty clothes after heavy exercise. In addition:

- Keep your feet and body clean and dry, especially between your toes and legs.
- Wear cotton or wool socks and cotton underwear, and change them often.
- Do not wear the same shoes two days in a row. Wear a lightweight shoe that lets air circulate. Avoid sneakers and rubber-soled shoes.
- Use a foot or body powder, but remember that too much can cake and cause irritation.
- Lose weight. Obesity makes you sweat.
- If you are fungus-prone, wear protective footwear in locker rooms, around swimming pools, and in other public places. However, it is more important to keep feet dry and maintain good foot hygiene every day.

Prostate Problems

Men may not even be aware that they have a prostate until it gives them trouble — usually after age fifty or sixty. This chestnut-sized mass of gland and muscle sits just below the bladder and contributes to the production of semen. The most common prostate disorders —infection, congestion, and enlargement— are not life-threatening. However, severe prostate disorders, if left untreated, can cause kidney failure. And prostate cancer, left untreated, can be fatal.

Prostatitis, or inflammation of the prostate, affects men of every age, from teenagers through the elderly. Acute prostatitis, a relatively unusual bacterial infection of the prostate, often is caused by bacteria from infections elsewhere in the body, including the urinary tract. Symptoms may occur suddenly and include fever, chills, pain in the lower back and groin, muscle and joint pain, and general malaise. A man may urinate more often than usual, and his urine flow may become weak and dribbly. He may feel like "going" but cannot. He may awaken several times a night to pass urine, yet have trouble starting the flow. He may feel pain and burning during urination, or notice blood and pus in the urine. Acute prostatitis usually responds to tet-racycline, penicillin, or other antibiotics.

Chronic prostatitis is a recurring, persistent inflammation. Most chronic prostatitis is not caused by any clearly identifiable bacterium. This makes it difficult to treat. Antibiotics relieve some cases, despite the absence of bacteria. In other cases, prostate massage may help. A physician (usually a urologist) inserts a lubricated, gloved finger into the rectum and uses rhythmic pressure to "milk" prostatic fluid from the gland.

There are many folk remedies and old-wives' tales surrounding the prostate. For example, zinc supplements are a controversial treatment for chronic prostatitis that may do more harm than good. The best policy is to check with a physician if you have symptoms, and never self-medicate.

Prostatodynia, a disorder common in younger men, causes pelvic pain or discomfort during erection and after ejaculating, but no urinary symptoms. For this condition, a physician may prescribe antiinflam-matory drugs and hot sitz baths. Irregular sexual activity can cause congestion of the prostate and lead to discomfort caused by seminal secretions accumulating in the gland. This condition is known as "sail-or's disease" or "blue balls" and is best dealt with by avoiding sudden changes in sexual habits.

Another common problem is enlargement of the prostate, or benign prostatic hypertrophy (BPH). Ordinarily, this noncancerous growth would cause no trouble. But the prostate gland's dense, fibrous tissues encircle the urethra, the tube through which urine passes from the body. When enlarged, the prostate can squeeze off or obstruct the flow of urine, reducing it to a dribble or damming it off entirely.

BPH affects about half of American men over age fifty, and about 80 percent of men over age eighty. Heredity, hormones, too much sex, not enough sex, and irregular sex have been blamed, but nobody knows what causes prostates to enlarge, only that the incidence of enlarge-ment increases with age.

Some of the symptoms of BPH resemble those of prostatitis. Many "quack" remedies — from pollen tablets to pumpkin seeds — purport to shrink prostates. But no medicine developed thus far can prevent or reduce an enlarged prostate. Prostatic massage helps in some cases. When an enlarged prostate restricts urine flow, part or all of it must be removed surgically. Otherwise, urinary tract obstruction and backup pressure from the obstruction can cause bladder infections and damage, dilate the two tubes (ureters) from the kidneys, damage the kidneys, and cause irreversible kidney failure.

Between 10 and 25 percent of men eventually need prostate surgery. The most common procedure, transurethral resection (TUR), allows removal of excess tissue from inside the prostate through a tube (cystoscope) inserted into the urethra. This surgery requires no incision, is extremely safe, and has a 98 percent success rate.

Perhaps the greatest concern of men facing prostate surgery is the fear that it will cause impotence. Postsurgical impotence rates run from 15 to 20 percent. But these figures include a great number of men who — thinking themselves incapable of sex because of their age — were not potent even before surgery. The only change most men notice is that they no longer visibly ejaculate because semen flows backward into the bladder. This retrograde ejaculation, or "dry orgasm," is caused by removal of prostate tissue that affects accessory sex glands near the urethra and affects muscles that prevent backflow of semen into the bladder. The resulting infertility is rarely a practical issue for men who are well into their fifties.

Studies show that impotence is less prevalent among men who are well informed about prostate surgery, healthy, sexually active, satisfied with life, secure, and optimistic, and who do not consider themselves "over the hill." One study showed that the most important factor in maintaining sexual potency after prostate surgery is a mate who is willing, healthy, understanding, and well informed about prostate problems. For more information on impotence, see chapter 3, pp. 72–77.)

Prostate Cancer

Cancer of the prostate is far less common than benign prostatic hypertrophy (BPH). For most men who develop cancerous prostates, the tumors will be small and dormant and will not cause serious illness or death. Still, prostate cancer is the second most common cancer and third leading cause of cancer deaths among American males. Prostate cancer is more dangerous when it affects men in their fifties and sixties than when it occurs in their eighties or nineties. The damage would be less extensive if more of these cancers were detected early. Ninety percent of prostate tumors can be felt during a rectal exam, which the American Cancer Society recommends that men over age forty have annually. When this slow-growing tumor is detected while still confined to the prostate, the five-year survival rate is about

77 percent. The rate is 39 percent if the cancer has spread to other organs and tissues.

Treatment of prostate cancer is often perceived as worse than the disease because of the effects on sexual functioning. In the past, nerves that control erection frequently were cut during surgical procedures to remove a cancerous prostate. In recent years, however, surgical methods have been modified to avoid injuring these nerves, allowing more than 70 percent of men who have prostatectomies to remain potent. For those who do not, special prosthetic devices surgically implanted in the penis restore their potency (see chapter 3, p. 75).

Prostate cancer also can be treated with radiation or with hormone therapy to reduce levels of testosterone, the male hormone that causes prostate cancers to grow. Physicians traditionally have treated advanced cases with varying combinations of surgery, plus radiation or large doses of the female hormone estrogen. The latter treatment can cause breast enlargement and blood clotting. Other approaches include drugs that reduce testosterone levels. These male-hormone-blocking drugs work as well as traditional treatments of advanced prostate cancer but eliminate toxic side effects and the need for surgical castration or female hormones.

There is no proven way to prevent prostate cancer, although studies of migrating populations suggest that environmental factors, such as diet and lifestyle, may affect the risk of developing this disease. Preliminary studies of several ethnic groups in Hawaii link prostate cancer to the consumption of animal fat and protein. Workplace exposure to cadmium during welding, electroplating, and the production of alkaline batteries may increase the risk of prostate cancer; rubber industry workers also may have increased risk. But none of these causes has been proved as yet.

The best protection is early detection by having a physician examine your prostate gland each year after age forty. Annual examinations are especially important for black men in the United States, who have the highest incidence of prostate cancer in the world. Men who have had surgery for an enlarged prostate (BPH) also should have annual rectal exams, since the part of the prostate that is not removed could become cancerous. A new male "PAP" test, which screens for prostate cancer by measuring blood levels of prostatic acid phosphatase, is unreliable because it misses too many cases of early prostate cancer. A digital examination of the prostate gland by a physician is a far more reliable test. In fact, there is no substitute for it.

Other Male Concerns

A number of conditions that are unique to men are not discussed in detail because they are relatively uncommon or do not threaten life. Men have higher rates than women of peptic ulcer, hernia, gout, paralysis, psoriasis, sebaceous gland diseases, and kidney stones. Kidney stones affect as much as 10 percent of the population — mostly middle-aged men — and can be treated with surgery or new nonsurgical use of shock waves to crush stones while the patient is under anesthesia. Men also have more orthopedic problems before age fifty to fifty-five. Women have more of such problems after that age because they tend to develop osteoporosis, a gradual thinning and weakening of bone that leaves hips and other bones fracture-prone. But older men, too, can develop osteoporosis even though they have more bone mass and do not lose it as rapidly as women. In addition to age and sex, the major risk factors for this disease include smoking, alcohol use, lack of weight-bearing exercise, a family history of osteoporosis, and immobilization (for example, from illness or injury) for several months. For men, the best ways to prevent osteoporosis are to stop smoking, cut down on alcohol use, consume 1,000 mg of dietary calcium daily (see chapter 1, p. 5), and engage in weight-bearing exercise, such as running, bicycling, walking, and weight training, *throughout life*. (Swimming is not a weight-bearing exercise.)

Many men's health problems, whether small or large, are made worse by the attitude that it is not okay for a man to be sick in this society. Illness makes many men feel passive, dependent, and out of control. Other problems arise because women do not know how to take care of a man — and he does not know how to take care of himself — when he is sick. A woman's attempts to "mother" a man, make his decisions, overprotect him, and assume responsibility for his health may cause a man to reject her efforts to take care of him. Yet a woman's care is what most men want and need, especially during illness.

Legitimate Requests from the Sick Room

The first man who read this list laughed, not in ridicule, he said, but in recognition. The list was developed by Dr. Donald S. Jewell, a psychotherapist in Washington, D.C., who notes that there are many appropriate ways to take care of a sick person who, silently or directly, is asking:

- Don't panic: your hysteria will make me feel even more helpless and afraid.
- Ease my mind: take care of routine household matters, deal with the medical bureaucracy, and don't let the bills pile up.
- Feed me.
- Relieve my loneliness: talk to me.
- Protect me while I am helpless.
- *Be there* with me, especially after surgery or when I am feeling pain.
- Encourage me to cry and complain.
- Accept my anger and jumpiness.
- Amuse me or help me to amuse myself: illness is boring.
- Make my surroundings pleasant and familiar.
- If my illness is serious, read and learn about it, but don't tell me unless I ask. Let me decide how much I want to know about my illness.
- Let the doctor be the expert: do not assume that role and tell me what to do.
- Be patient with me: even if I don't seem to appreciate what you are doing now, I will appreciate it later on.
- Remember that illness brings out the best and worst in everybody.
- Tell me you love me.

9

Love and Other Addictions

This chapter explores the premise that addiction — whether to drugs, such as alcohol, cocaine, and nicotine, or to unhealthy sex/love relationships — often begins with unmet, unconscious needs, not for the euphoria of the substance or activity itself but for

- anesthesia for emotional pain and grief caused by major losses, especially of loved ones
- relief from short-term anxiety and fear
- escape from long-term depression, boredom, isolation, loneliness, and feeling unloved

The escape, however, is temporary, and eventually the pain relievers, because they are so powerful, become masters instead of servants. Then comes the agony of addiction itself: guilt, shame, fear, anxiety, interpersonal conflict, and injury to health. Alcoholism and drug addiction are described in chapter 7 as indirect self-destructive behavior. The same can be said of addictions to nicotine, "crazy love," food, gambling, or whatever else fills these unconscious needs.

The Way We Drink

Of all addictive substances, alcohol is the most visible and socially acceptable. Films and television portray America as a nation of drinkers. The per capita consumption in the United States is about 2.75 gallons of pure alcohol per year. Yet one-third of the population claims not to drink alcoholic beverages at all; another third consumes fewer than three drinks a week. The remaining third drinks 95 percent of all alcohol consumed, according to a 1985 study, *Alcohol in America*, by the

National Academy of Sciences. This group includes the estimated 14 million Americans — two-thirds of them men — who have alcohol problems, including alcoholism, driving while intoxicated, drinking illegally, or drinking just to get drunk.

Despite the prevalence of social drinking and alcoholism, few Americans know much about alcohol, or even whether these statements are true or false:

1. You are less likely to become addicted to alcohol if you drink only beer. (*False.* Beer, wine, and distilled liquor all contain ethyl alcohol, the addicting substance.)
2. If you are depressed, a drink may cheer you up. (*False.* Alcohol may cheer you up for a while; then it tends to make you more depressed.)
3. Sex is better after several drinks. (*False.* As Shakespeare said in *Macbeth,* drink "provokes the desire, but it takes away the performance.")
4. Most alcohol abusers are skid-row bums. (*False.* Most have jobs, families, mortgages, and respectability.)
5. More men than women are addicted to alcohol. (*True.* Two out of every three persons with alcoholism are men. However, many women hide their disease because of social disapproval.)
6. Drinking shortens your life. (*True.* If you drink heavily over a long period of time, drinking can shorten your life expectancy an average of twelve years.)

It all seems so harmless at first. Many Americans first taste alcohol by age ten, usually in a watered-down experimental sip at home with their parents. Young people start to drink to have a good time, experiment, rebel against parents, and be "adult." Many, prompted by messages from the media, equate alcohol use with manliness, success, sex appeal, popularity, and good times. People also drink to celebrate, enjoy the taste, relieve physical pain, unwind, relax, lower inhibitions, or reward themselves for a good day's work. Whatever the reasons, one person out of every thirteen who begin to use alcohol eventually develops alcoholism, usually in stages that take about fifteen years.

For years scientists thought that environmental influences produced alcoholism, because sons and daughters of alcoholic parents so often became addicted. Scientific evidence now suggests that alcoholism can be inherited. Adoption studies show that children of alcoholics have a higher rate of alcoholism, even when adopted at an early age, than adopted children of nonalcoholic parents. Sons of alcoholic fathers have particularly high rates of alcoholism, whether they were raised by their biologic parents or by adoptive parents. Still, "both heredity and environment are involved in the making of most alcoholics," says Dr. Robert G. Niven, former director of the National Institute of Alcohol Abuse and Alcoholism (NIAAA).

What Is Alcoholism?

Alcoholism is difficult to define, but most experts agree that it is a treatable illness marked by impaired health, work, and personal relationships, and by loss of control over the use of alcohol. The definition does not include how much a person drinks, how often, or when. Although individuals in the early stages of alcoholism often tolerate large quantities of alcohol without appearing drunk, many persons with late-stage alcoholism tolerate far less alcohol than nonalcoholics. Many alcoholics alternate binge drinking with periods of abstinence. And many maintain the myth that they are not alcoholic as long as they never drink before 5:00 P.M.

Early warning signs of alcoholism include drinking routinely to relieve tension; preoccupation with alcohol; going to work intoxicated; feeling uncomfortable when no alcoholic drinks are available; driving while drunk; and drinking to escape loneliness, a sense of failure, or job, marriage, money, sex, and other problems.

Alcoholism then progresses to habitually "getting tight," blackouts or loss of memory while still awake, gulping and sneaking drinks, and chronic hangover. As the disease becomes more serious, a person can refuse to start drinking, but cannot stop drinking once started. A single drink is likely to trigger a chain of events leading to complete intoxication. Symptoms include elaborate alibis for drinking, morning drinking to ease increasingly painful hangovers, drinking alone, guilt, remorse, depression, antisocial behavior, loss of job or friends, and often futile attempts to change this pattern. The person who drinks may seek help at this point, but seldom receives lasting benefits because he refuses to admit the extent of the problem.

In advanced alcoholism, a person must have alcohol however and whenever he can. Symptoms include drinking to escape problems created by drinking, going on benders, tremors or "shakes," desperate efforts to keep supplied with alcohol, hostility toward others, nameless fears and anxieties, and — if recovery is to occur — admission that drinking is totally out of control.

A simple test to help physicians tell that a patient has an alcohol problem has been developed by Dr. John A. Ewing of the University of North Carolina School of Medicine in Chapel Hill, North Carolina. His CAGE Questionnaire asks:

1. Have you ever felt you ought to Cut down on your drinking?
2. Have people Annoyed you by criticizing your drinking?
3. Have you ever felt Guilty about your drinking?
4. Have you ever had an Eye-opener drink first thing in the morning to steady your nerves?

Answering "yes" to only two of these questions identified all the acknowledged persons with alcohol problems, and nearly all of the acknowledged heavy drinkers, according to several studies evaluating the questionnaire.

Alcohol and Health

Alcoholism can damage virtually every organ in your body and is involved in at least six of the ten leading causes of death for men. According to the National Academy of Sciences report *Alcohol in America*, alcohol may be involved in about one of every thirteen deaths in the United States. Of more than one hundred health problems caused or aggravated by alcohol, many affect even the social drinker. These include sexual impairment, overweight, automobile accidents, side effects from medications, problems concentrating, slowed reflexes, reduced productivity, irritability, emotional disturbances, fatigue, and loss of skin tone.

The digestive system often is the first casualty of continued heavy drinking. Damage takes the form of inflammation of the stomach, pancreas, or liver. The latter can lead to cirrhosis, one of the ten leading killers of men.

Chronic alcohol consumption can severely damage the heart, and alcohol can mask pain that might otherwise warn of a heart attack. Heavy drinking also is statistically associated with high blood pressure, a leading risk factor for heart attack and stroke. A recent study of 8,006 men in the Honolulu Heart Program, noted in chapter 7, page 192, showed that those who drank heavily were three times more likely than nondrinkers to have hemorrhagic stroke.

Cancers of the mouth, tongue, pharynx, esophagus, and stomach are more common in persons with alcoholism than in nondrinkers.

Some epidemiological studies also link rectal and lung cancers with alcohol consumption.

Alcohol is a lubricant for violence. Between one-third and one-half of all adult Americans involved in automobile and other accidents, suicide, homicide, deaths from fires and falls, spouse and child abuse, barroom belligerence, and various crimes had been drinking alcohol at the time they committed the act, according to the NIAAA.

Impotence and reduced sex drive occur in at least half of men with alcoholism. Recent findings suggest that the feminized appearance (loss of facial hair and breast enlargement) characteristic of alcohol-induced cirrhosis may be caused by estrogenic substances in alcohol. Drinking a pint or more of hard liquor daily for five to eight years may cause loss of sexual function entirely. Even drinking enough to occasionally cause a hangover may accelerate the liver's destruction of the male sex hormone, testosterone. Moreover, sexual dysfunction and infertility can occur at a comparatively early age. Studies at Presbyterian–University Hospital in Pittsburgh have revealed symptoms of alcohol abuse in young men complaining of infertility.

Prolonged alcohol abuse can cause loss of nerve cells in the brain and impair brain function: forgetfulness, confusion, inability to concentrate or think abstractly, difficulty speaking, and decreased coordination. About 10 percent of alcoholics may suffer from "chronic brain syndrome," a condition usually considered irreversible.

Alcoholism can cause nutritional deficiencies, dehydration, skeletal muscle damage, internal bleeding, gout, osteoporosis, insomnia, and increased susceptibility to infections. It also can cause adverse reactions to tranquilizers, barbiturates, painkillers, antihistamines, aspirin, and other drugs. In pregnant women, drinking alcohol can produce low-birth-weight babies who may be retarded or deformed. Alcohol taken in combination with Valium is the leading drug-related cause of emergency room visits and deaths. Yet most of the damage, even to the brain, can be arrested or reversed if drinking stops and if related medical problems, such as malnutrition, are corrected.

Kicking the Habit

Alcoholism is the most underdiagnosed, untreated, yet treatable condition in the world today, according to Dr. Morris E. Chafetz, a leading authority on the subject. But recovery depends upon admitting the problem, accepting help, and giving up the idea of ever drinking again. The first step in treatment, admitting to alcoholism, often is the most difficult since denial is a prime defense for people addicted to alcohol. Step two involves a medical examination to assess the degree of addiction and of health problems that often accompany alcoholism. Next comes detoxification, or ridding the body of alcohol. This can be done on an outpatient basis if the person is mildly addicted; otherwise hospitalization is necessary. Still, detoxification is not a cure in itself. Step four involves *staying off* alcohol. The best strategies involve individual, couple, and family psychotherapy, often with the continuing support of AA (Alcoholics Anonymous). Step five, periodic follow-up, is crucial since many people with alcoholism attempt to resume moderate drinking. Treatment of alcoholism, in other words, is a continuing process that takes years of commitment. AA and most professionals in the field maintain that although alcohol addiction can be arrested, it can never be cured, and that any amount of alcohol can trigger a relapse. Scientific studies continue to confirm that prospects of successfully returning to moderate drinking are extremely dim. Moreover, many alcoholism experts say further drinking will impair the recovery of tissues that have been damaged by alcohol.

Traditionally, experts believed that only those who volunteered for treatment of alcoholism could be helped. Now it appears that many workplace programs that require treatment for alcoholism may be as effective as voluntary programs. The threat of losing a job is a powerful incentive for many alcohol abusers.

Compassion and support from family members are of great value, but sometimes they are difficult to enlist. Family members suffer from the effects of another person's alcoholism even though they themselves do not drink. Many children of alcoholics, for example, live by the "rule of three": don't trust, don't talk, don't feel. The calming effects of alcohol make it easier to live with certain addicted individuals. Sometimes when a person stops drinking, others in the family — who may unconsciously aid and abet the addiction — lose the moral high ground they once occupied as nondrinkers. Or family members may find the alcohol-free personality so uncomfortably different that they prefer the status quo. In addition, they not only have their own problems, they may — unless aided by counseling — create additional ones for the person trying to stop drinking.

Family members should never ignore or minimize the problem, express rage, convey pessimism, condemn or punish the person with alcoholism, make excuses for his destructive behavior, assume his responsibilities, hide or dump bottles, shelter him from situations where alcohol is present, argue with him when he is drunk, or feel responsible for his disease. Attempts by spouses to persuade the person with alcoholism to stop drinking (for example, to "save" the marriage) often are doomed to failure. Alcohol aggravates — but seldom causes — problems in a relationship. Nor does one person "drive" another to drink.

The message from family members should be "We are concerned about your body's reaction to alcohol and think you need help." They should let the problem drinker know they are learning about alcoholism, and attend Al-Anon, Adult Children of Alcoholics, or other organizations designed for the concerned nonalcoholic. Family members can get help from a physician, a member of the clergy, or a friend who has experienced alcoholism personally. It also helps to remember that alcoholism takes a long time to develop, and that recovery, as AA says, must take place "one day at a time."

Drinking Intelligently

Despite its dangers, alcohol can be beneficial in moderation. It can stimulate the appetite, enhance a meal or celebration, act as a mild sedative, and help you unwind. Statistically, moderate drinkers appear to live longer than teetotalers and alcohol abusers. A number of studies show that one or two drinks a day may even lower the risk of heart attack. But until research results are more conclusive, the American Heart Association does not recommend moderate drinking as a way to prevent heart disease.

Sometimes a fine line separates the moderate drinker from the abuser. Susceptibility to alcohol depends on how fast you drink, how recently you have eaten, type of beverage, and your weight, body chemistry, sex, current mood and attitude, and drinking experience. To drink moderately:

- Eat high-protein and fatty foods and relax or nap before drinking. You tend to drink more when you are hungry, tired, tense, and angry.
- Snack throughout the evening to slow the rate of alcohol absorption, but avoid salty foods. They make you want to drink more.
- Mix wine or liquor with water or fruit juice rather than carbonated beverages. The latter speed alcohol absorption.
- Drink slowly: do not exceed 1½ ounces of liquor, one beer, or

one glass of wine per one to two hours. Alternate alcoholic with nonalcoholic beverages.

- Count drinks, and realize that "fill it halfway" may be the least honored request in America.
- Avoid unfamiliar drinks, and choose wine or beer rather than hard liquor.
- Beware of noisy, crowded parties. They are stressful and tempt you to seek relief with alcohol.
- Be a responsible host. Push snacks, not drinks, to make your party successful.
- Serve an attractive nonalcoholic beverage.
- Limit drinking to once a day, and do not drink a week's quota all at once.
- Beware of tranquilizers, antihistamines, cough and cold remedies, and other medications that can enhance the effects of alcohol.

Two recent books on responsible drinking are Allan Luks's *Will America Sober Up? A Dramatic New Approach to Healthy, Moderate Drinking*, and Leonard Gross's *How Much Is Too Much? The Effects of Social Drinking*.

The Addiction Research Foundation of Toronto, Canada, developed this chart, which applies to healthy adult men weighing about 155 pounds.

	Average number of drinks per day (1½ oz. whiskey or 5 oz. table wine or 12 oz. beer)
PROBABLY SAFE (consumed over 1 or 2 hours)	1 to 2
CAUTION—Increased health risk from long-term consumption	3 to 4
HAZARDOUS—Danger of addiction/psychological dependency	5 to 6
HARMFUL—Serious health risk (cirrhosis, heart disease, cancer); seek help	7 to 8
EXTREMELY DANGEROUS—Life expectancy may be reduced 10–12 years; professional treatment needed	9 to 10

Hangovers

A hangover is one of the many prices you pay for drinking too much. The charges include a cat-stomping headache, dehydration, nausea, vertigo, fatigue, general malaise, anxiety, depression, remorse, and guilt.

The amount of alcohol required to produce a hangover varies enormously and has little bearing on whether you felt "high" while drinking. Some people develop hangovers even though they never feel inebriated. The amount you drink, spread over an evening, adds up to an overindulgence hangover.

The most effective remedy for a hangover is rest and the passage of time. Expect recovery to take about twelve hours. It may help to rehydrate yourself, before retiring and after awakening, with several glasses of water or tomato juice taken with soda crackers or a salty snack. Salt helps readjust your electrolyte balance so your body can absorb water. Some people take vitamin C, B-12, or other nutrients for a hangover. What their bodies crave most, however, is restored fluid balance, not vitamins.

Aspirin is a traditional hangover remedy, but sometimes it can irritate your stomach, especially if taken with coffee. Take aspirin instead with a large glass of water or antacid to dilute its corrosive effect. Or try aspirin with enteric-coating that does not dissolve until the drug passes beyond the stomach into the intestines. A buffered aspirin does nothing to protect your stomach. Mild tranquilizers, sedatives, and antihistamines, like alcohol, are depressants and intensify the effects of a hangover. Finally, hair-of-the-dog remedies for hangovers may relieve immediate symptoms, but they also can lead to alcohol dependency. The best solution to hangovers is to drink moderately and keep alcohol in its place — as servant, not as master.

Cocaine

Persons who abuse alcohol often abuse other drugs, and vice versa. Drug abuse is any nonmedical use of a drug, whether prescription, over-the-counter, or illicit. Some of the most abused drugs include narcotics (heroin, codeine, opium, morphine), depressants (tranquilizers like Librium and Valium, barbiturates, methaqualone), hallucinogens (LSD, mescaline, and phencyclidine or PCP), cannabis (marijuana, hashish), and stimulants (amphetamines, cocaine). Synthetic versions constantly lengthen the list. One of the most widely abused drugs is cocaine, which is increasingly popular with teenagers and adults alike. For years cocaine has enjoyed the undeserved reputation of being relatively safe and nonaddictive. Yet it is one of the most powerfully addictive and dangerous illicit drugs known, according to *Cocaine Use In America,* a report published in 1985 by the National Institute on Drug Abuse.

Cocaine lore emphasizes the euphoric pleasures more than the dangers of this drug. Although it was not isolated until the mid-1800s, cocaine has been around for centuries as a constituent of the leaves of the coca plant that grows primarily in the Andean mountains of South America. Indians from that region have chewed raw coca leaves or brewed them in tea since at least the sixth century A.D. Although the leaves contain only about one-half to 1 percent cocaine, coca-leaf addiction is prevalent throughout the high Andes, particularly among the lower socioeconomic classes. The plant, according to an Incan myth, was created by the god Inti to lighten the labors of the people. Gradually coca-leaf chewing became the Andean equivalent of the coffee break. It made work bearable.

By the late nineteenth century, cocaine was isolated from coca leaves and won attention in scientific circles. In 1884 Sigmund Freud praised cocaine's euphoric effects so lavishly — in a research project he hoped would earn him success so he could get married — that his scientific reputation was nearly destroyed after colleagues accused him of sloppy research. Still, cocaine's medicinal properties became established as it came into use as an anesthetic in eye surgery and as an ingredient in patent medicines, suppositories, ointments, nose powders, and throat lozenges. The drug was seldom abused during the era of coca patent medicines. But as cocaine increasingly replaced coca, the former became up to two hundred times more concentrated, and the Incan prophecy that cocaine would destroy the white man came closer to fulfillment.

Cocaine was the "champagne of drugs" during the 1970s when only the rich and the famous could afford it. As prices dropped, usage increased until, according to recent surveys, more than 20 million Americans have tried cocaine, and at least four million are regular users. The most dramatic increases in cocaine use have occurred in the teenage and young adult populations of the United States. The typical user tends to be an employed, middle-class, educated white male between eighteen and thirty-five years old. Many users deal in drugs to support their addictions.

In recent years, emergency room visits, overdose deaths, and cocaine-related health problems have risen dramatically. Users employ more dangerous ways of administering cocaine, and many risk dual addiction by taking other drugs concurrently to alleviate unpleasant aftereffects of cocaine use. Modern methods of cocaine administration include sniffing or snorting, injection, and "freebasing." The latter involves cocaine powder that has been converted chemically to a purified form that can be smoked. Known as "crack," an increasingly popular form of cocaine that is typically smoked in glass water pipes, it is potentially more addictive and dangerous than the powder form. It can cause death from heart or respiratory failure, brain seizure, and paranoid psychosis. Users often combine cocaine with heroin in "speedballs" or use alcohol or other sedatives to ease postcocaine jitters. This can result in dual addiction.

Cocaine, even when it does not kill, does not treat the body kindly. In addition to addiction, it can cause sleep problems, chronic fatigue, severe headaches, chronic cough and sore throat, nausea and vomiting, increased heart rate and blood pressure, seizures, and loss of consciousness. Those who inject cocaine can contract hepatitis, AIDS, and other diseases from dirty needles. Those who snort it often develop nasal sores, bleeding, and collapse of the nasal septum (the cartilage that separates the nostrils). Those who smoke it can develop chronic cough with black or bloody sputum. Increasingly, evidence shows that cocaine can worsen preexisting heart disease, and heavy use can lead to acute hypertension, cardiac arrest, permanent brain damage, and fatal convulsions.

Psychologically, cocaine can cause depression, anxiety, irritability, apathy, inability to concentrate, memory problems, loss of sexual interest, paranoia, hallucinations, and panic attacks. Drug-induced psychoses (major mental disorders involving paranoia, hallucinations, and other losses of contact with reality) have been reported with long-term use. In addition, cocaine causes personal losses of jobs, spouses, friends, and fortunes. A national survey of five hundred cocaine users in 1983–84 revealed that serious health and personal consequences can result regardless of how much or how often cocaine is used, and regardless of whether it is snorted, smoked, or injected.

Because cocaine does not cause physical withdrawal symptoms like those of alcohol, opiate, or barbiturate abuse, a generation of Americans mistakenly believes that cocaine is not addictive. Actually, cocaine use leads to loss of control over the amount used, plus severe cocaine craving or compulsion to seek and use the drug constantly. Some users experience depression or "cocaine crashes" after extended periods of use, which may cause them to crave even more cocaine for relief.

Any cocaine user who cannot stop or significantly cut back, despite problems arising from drug use, is addicted and needs help. Unfortunately, cocaine induces a sense of well-being that may keep the user from seeking treatment. No one treatment program works for everybody; many are based on alcoholism programs and emphasize relapse prevention, lifestyle change, abstinence training, and follow-up. Many programs emphasize stopping *all* drug use since cocaine users often use alcohol, sleeping pills, tranquilizers, or marijuana as well. The user must recognize the dangers of cocaine and other drugs and be motivated to give them up forever. Only then can individual, group, and family counseling help an addict control impulsive behavior, avoid cocaine sources, and understand the role cocaine has played in his life.

Drug treatment for cocaine users is still experimental. Methylphenidate hydrochloride and lithium carbonate may help in the same way methadone helps opiate abusers. Some treatment programs prescribe aerobic exercise, which seems to help reduce cocaine hunger and anxiety. The greatest single cause of relapse is the user's belief that he can return to controlled use of cocaine.

For information, help, and referral to a treatment source, call the toll-free National Institute on Drug Abuse (NIDA) hotline, 800-662-HELP, or a privately operated hotline, 800-COCAINE. Cocaine Anonymous, which follows the same principles and twelve-step program as AA, helps many cocaine abusers, although it is not as widely available as Alcoholics Anonymous or Narcotics Anonymous. Since many cocaine addicts abuse other drugs as well, membership in AA and NA may be helpful.

Marijuana

Many Americans consider marijuana a harmless indulgence, a weed they smoked at parties during the 1960s and 1970s, and a drug that probably ought to be legalized. More than 50 million Americans are estimated to have used marijuana at some time in their lives. Today marijuana is a popular illicit drug among young adults, but it is not the same "pot" their parents used. The potency of marijuana in the United States has increased markedly in recent years. Average concentrations of the psychoactive ingredient, THC (tetrahydrocannabinol), are 4 percent in Colombian marijuana and more than 5 percent in California marijuana, compared to concentrations of 1 and 2 percent or less in the late 1970s.

Only recently has the harmful potential of marijuana been recognized. It can produce physical tolerance (as opposed to dependence), and its active ingredients remain in the body much longer than alcohol, according to *Correlates and Consequences of Marijuana Use,* a 1984 report published by the National Institute on Drug Abuse. Marijuana use is the major predictor of cocaine and other illicit drug use. A report called *Marijuana and Health: 1980,* published by the U.S. Department of Health, Education and Welfare, further notes the following:

- Daily marijuana use leads to lung damage similar to that caused by heavy cigarette smoking.
- Marijuana use over many years *may* eventually be shown to cause lung cancer in humans. Already, there is strong evidence of this in animals.
- Marijuana use may alter the reproductive functions of men and women and may affect the unborn child. In men, sperm counts have diminished as marijuana use increased, and the sperm of some chronic users are abnormal. In addition, some chronic users have lower levels of testosterone, although they return to normal when marijuana smoking stops.
- Marijuana use can negatively affect learning and motor coordination.
- Marijuana users are overrepresented in fatal highway accidents.
- Recent studies in mice suggest that high doses of marijuana suppress the functioning of the immune system.
- A report compiled by the Addiction Research Foundation of Ontario, Canada, and the World Health Organization warns that marijuana use may be especially dangerous for people with high blood pressure, cardiovascular disease, diabetes, epilepsy, or mental illness.

Reactions to marijuana often are unpredictable. The drug typically causes a heightened sense of sight, sound, and touch, and a lowering of inhibitions, which users consider desirable. But marijuana intoxication also causes a distorted sense of time, fragmented speech, disjointed thinking, and a tendency to lose one's motivation and train of thought. In some people, the drug may trigger confusion, panic, hallucinations, and aggression.

Smoking

The cigarette labels that warn about lung cancer, emphysema, and heart disease do not mention the addictive aspects of smoking. But any smoker who has tried to quit is aware of withdrawal symptoms. Nicotine, the psychoactive constituent of tobacco, is six to eight times more addictive than alcohol and is in the same dependence-producing league as morphine and cocaine. In a study at the Addiction Research Center of the National Institute on Drug Abuse (NIDA), drug-experienced subjects believed the nicotine they were receiving in unlabeled injections was cocaine. Dr. William Pollin, former director of NIDA, has called cigarette smoking "the most serious . . . widespread form of addiction in the world." Another NIDA-supported study shows that tobacco is a "gateway substance" that may lead to experimentation with alcohol, marijuana, and other drugs.

Spanish explorers introduced tobacco smoking to Europe in the sixteenth century. Early users, including Jean Nicot, the French ambassador to Lisbon after whom the tobacco plant *Nicotiana tabacum* was named, thought the leaf had useful medicinal properties. In the seventeenth century, Tobias Venner, an English physician, disagreed:

> Tobacco drieth the brain, dimmeth the sight, vitiateth the smell, hurteth the stomach, destroyeth the concoction, disturbeth the humors and spirits, corrupteth the breath, induceth a trembling of the limbs, exsiccateth the windpipe, lungs, and liver, annoyeth the milt, scorcheth the heart, and causeth the blood to be adjusted.

In the early nineteenth century, Dr. Benjamin Waterhouse added:

> *Tobacco is a filthy weed,*
> *That from the devil doth proceed.*
> *It drains your purse, it burns your clothes,*
> *And makes a chimney of your nose.*

In 1982 the U.S. Surgeon General called cigarette smoking the "chief, single, avoidable cause of death in our society and the most important public health problem of our time." By 1986, at least thirty thousand research reports had implicated smoking as a major cause of

- coronary heart disease, including sudden cardiac death
- cancers of the lung, esophagus, larynx, mouth, and throat
- emphysema and other chronic obstructive lung diseases

- stroke
- blood vessel diseases
- peptic ulcers
- premature births, low birth weights, high perinatal mortality
- heart attack and stroke among women using oral contraceptives

Smoking also causes bad breath, shortness of breath, impaired athletic performance, cough, high carbon-monoxide levels in the blood, increased miseries from allergies, and bronchitis and pneumonia in infants exposed to passive smoking. Even nonsmokers have an elevated risk of lung cancer from breathing someone else's smoke, whether from cigarettes, cigars, or pipes. In total, more American lives have been lost through smoking than through all the wars this country has fought in the twentieth century. A man of twenty-five who smokes two packs of cigarettes a day can expect to live, on the average, until age sixty-five, but a nonsmoker of twenty-five can expect to live until age seventy-three, a difference of *eight years*.

Despite the known dangers, nearly one-third of all adults in the United States smoke. Although male smokers still outnumber female smokers, the proportion of adult male smokers in all age groups has decreased markedly since 1964 — the year the U.S. Surgeon General declared war on cigarettes. Smaller decreases have occurred among women. As a result, lung cancer is a leading cause of death from malignancy in women, although men's rates of death from lung cancer still are higher.

"Smokeless tobacco" (snuff and chewing tobacco) increases the risk of cancers of the mouth and throat, oral leukoplakia (white patches on the oral tissues) that could transform into malignancy, and long-term nicotine dependence. The problem is particularly severe among teenage boys, whose use of smokeless tobacco increased during the 1980s (see chapter 6, p. 175).

Most smokers know that smoking is deadly. Most know that the risks of lung cancer and heart attack almost disappear within ten to fifteen years after quitting, even for people who have smoked for decades. Still, about three out of four heavy smokers who try to quit or cut down fail. Smoking is more than a bad habit. It is an addiction listed as Tobacco Dependence Disorder in the American Psychiatric Association's diagnostic manual of mental disorders. The habit is hard to kick because the nicotine addict — in addition to suffering withdrawal symptoms of irritability, anxiety, restlessness, insomnia, increased hunger, and nicotine craving — may be surrounded by smokers in his daily environment.

Yet more than 30 million regular smokers have stopped during the past twenty years. How have they done it? There are many ways to quit. In Japan, some smokers go to a Shinto shrine and toss their cigarettes into a fire. A priest offers his blessing and the smokers promise never to light up again. In the United States most people stop on their own; a minority receive help from doctors and treatment programs. The latter, according to studies sponsored by the National Institute on Drug Abuse, are more likely to maintain abstinence. Unfortunately, no one technique works for everyone. Quitting requires more than willpower; it requires strong, personal motives for wanting to stop. This inner decision to stop smoking — plus awareness that stopping will probably take several attempts — is far more important than the method employed. Thus any approach to quitting should incorporate why you smoke:

- For stimulation?
- For something to do with your hands and mouth?
- For relaxation?
- To reduce tension and other bad feelings?

If smoking is a crutch, it may be difficult to give up unless you deal with the needs and feelings that underlie smoking.

Because of the complex nature of nicotine use, a combination of quitting techniques often works well. A program might combine aversive therapy (rapid smoking to the point of illness) with nicotine chewing gum. Aversion therapy is unpleasant and potentially dangerous if you have cardiovascular disease, high blood pressure, or diabetes. Nicotine gum eases withdrawal symptoms, but it can cause unpleasant side effects and is not recommended for people with certain forms of heart disease. Some physicians recommend switching to cigarette brands with increasingly lower nicotine and tar content. By the time you reach a cigarette with very low nicotine, you are probably ready to give up. (Do not switch to cigarettes to which cloves have been added. They can cause serious lung injury.) Numerous drugs that appear to reduce the craving for cigarettes are being studied, but none has been found effective by the Food and Drug Administration.

Even if a "stop smoking" pill existed, it would not reduce craving for other aspects of smoking. Many smokers experience a sense of loss when this cherished habit disappears from their lives. Dr. M. Therese

Southgate, deputy editor of the *Journal of the American Medical Association*, observes that recent ex-smokers undergo the five stages of grief: denial, anger, depression, bargaining, and acceptance. The most dangerous stage is bargaining, or telling yourself that an occasional cigarette cannot hurt. For ex-smokers, one cigarette is too many and a thousand are not enough. Psychological counseling and relapse prevention programs teach new fitness and eating habits to combat fatigue and weight gain, and ways to handle "the crazies" that can cause backsliding.

A stop-smoking film titled *We Can't Go On Like This* suggests that smoking is like a love affair gone sour. Produced by the National Heart, Lung, and Blood Institute, the film shows the first thrilling moments, the blossoming of the relationship, the signs of trouble, and the pain of ending the affair. The smoker laments, "How can I go it alone when I see you in other people's faces? . . . We've been together thirty times a day. There's nothing I've done more than that. . . ." His point is that the smoking habit is "learned" bit by bit and takes a long time to unlearn. The reward comes when you no longer view smoking as a way to cope, but view *not* smoking as a way of living well.

Stop-smoking programs are listed in telephone books under "Smokers' Treatment and Information Centers." Information also is available from the following:

- American Cancer Society
  4 West 35th Street
  New York, NY 10001
- American Heart Association
  7320 Greenville Avenue
  Dallas, TX 75231
- American Lung Association
  1740 Broadway, P.O. Box 596
  New York, NY 10019
- Office of Cancer Communications
  National Cancer Institute
  Bethesda, MD 20895

Or call the Cancer Information Service, toll-free, at 800-638-6070.

Love and Addiction

The most widespread — and least recognized — addiction is to another person, usually in the form of a sex/love relationship that is based on dependency and neediness rather than on respect and caring. "We turn to each other out of the same needs that drive some people to drink and others to heroin. And this kind of addiction is just as self-destructive as . . . those other kinds," write Dr. Stanton Peele and Archie Brodsky in *Love and Addiction*. Addiction, in this view, is not a chemical reaction but an experience that an addicted individual finds so safe and reassuring, he cannot be without it.

When is a love relationship unhealthy? According to Dr. Peele, when one person serves as the sole means of satisfying the other's need for security and perhaps even survival. One or both partners have not learned to accomplish things they regard as worthwhile, harbor a deep wish to be taken care of, and need to fill a void in themselves.

The symptoms of addicting love include a consuming need to be constantly with your loved one and an inability to function when apart. In addition:

1. You feel as if your life began when you met ____.
2. It was love at first sight.*
3. You feel miserable when you are apart, even though you fight or bicker constantly.
4. You would like to end it, but you are hooked.
5. You feel jealous of your loved one's other involvements, even with friends and activities.
6. You increasingly see each other in order to satisfy a deep, aching need.
7. If it ends, you suffer withdrawal symptoms: you cannot eat, sleep, or concentrate; your heart speeds up for no apparent reason; and your stomach and intestines are in an uproar.
8. Your craving and pain are relieved only by returning to the person to whom you are addicted.
9. If you do manage to break away, you feel a sense of relief once the shock of withdrawal wears off.
10. You immediately begin looking for a new love.

    * Erich Fromm, in *The Art of Loving*, wrote that the intensity and speed with which love develops between two passionately attracted people "may only prove the degree of their preceding loneliness."

When you are love-addicted, you tend to have relationships with partners who withhold love and are painfully unattainable because they already have, do not want, or are incapable of having a committed relationship. Usually, these relationships are dead-end, lack what you want and need, and/or are battlegrounds for anger and abuse. Nor is love addiction always one-on-one. An addict may form simultaneous or successive relationships because he cannot tolerate becoming fully involved or cannot find a partner who completely accepts him.

In a healthy relationship, by contrast, you reach out to your partner from strength rather than weakness, you allow time for love to develop from shared experiences and feelings, you do not spend all your time together, you maintain other friends and interests, you feel free to grow and change, you are not threatened by growth and change in your partner, you do not force your feelings — even loving ones — on him or her, and you never lie in order to avoid making your partner feel bad or less loved. Most important, you are relaxed in the knowledge that no single relationship can give you life or take it away from you.

Every love affair or marriage contains some elements of addiction. The key is whether it is *predominantly* addictive. Fewer addictive relationships might develop if decisions regarding them were more rational, starting with choice of a mate. A study concluded in 1981 that the majority of thirty-eight thousand engaged couples did not seem to agree with, or know much about, their intended partner's views on child-raising, money, politics, or leisure activities. The couples responded to a 143-item premarital inventory that Charles Kirk Burnett, a psychologist specializing in family matters, developed with two clergymen to help engaged couples.

Thus it appears that many people, particularly the love-addicted, consider it more important to *have* a mate than to *choose* a mate. Yet if you were in business, would you merge with another company just because that company wanted to merge? Would you first do some personnel work and see what the other company had to offer? Would you insist on truth-in-advertising?

In *How to Break Your Addiction to a Person*, Howard M. Halpern suggests twenty-five addiction-breaking aphorisms, beginning with "You *can* live without him/her (probably better)" and ending with "If you end this bad relationship, you will be opening your life to new possibilities."

Building Better Relationships
- Recognize whether or not you are hooked.
- Form friendships with the opposite sex. They are addiction-breaking.

- Emphasize *loving*, not *being loved*.
- Build self-esteem, or the reputation you have with yourself, because low self-esteem destroys relationships and makes you susceptible to addicting ones.
- Learn to genuinely enjoy single life before getting "involved" again.
- Do not get hitched to avoid a bad home environment, a failed relationship, loneliness, or an unsatisfactory life.
- Stay out of bed until you are sure what is under it. (See the sections on sexually transmitted diseases in chapter 3, pp. 86–99.)
- Recognize that deciding to live together is just as significant as deciding to marry.
- Evaluate your relationship constantly, and find ways to talk about things you would like to improve but are afraid to mention.
- Remember that the best alliances are between people who think well of themselves and who therefore are capable of thinking well of and trusting another person.

Studies of happy couples reveal that they are strong as individuals, share power, accept conflict, allow one another independence and privacy, do not fear change in the other, share emotions, take an interest in each other's jobs and activities, do not try to be exactly alike, do things that please one another, look out for each other, share a confidence in their love, and exude tranquility in each other's presence.

The Heaven and Hell of Dependency

"All I can think about is ＿＿."

"Everything else seems unimportant except ＿＿."

"I want more and more of ＿＿."

"I even neglect my job, family, and personal welfare in order to have ＿＿."

These statements were made by a cocaine addict. But you can just as easily fill in alcohol, heroin, tobacco, or the name of the person to whom you are addicted. You also can be addicted to food, caffeine, compulsive gambling, compulsive sex, reckless driving, television watching, or even religion. The euphoria following the first drink, the first puff, or the first kiss in an impossible romance feels wonderful until you realize you no longer have a choice, just a need you cannot control. As you increasingly depend on one of these escapes as your sole source of gratification and happiness, you sentence yourself to the heaven and hell of dependency.

Millions of Americans — most of them men — suffer and die from brain and body slavery to alcohol, drugs, and cigarettes. Addiction to unhealthy relationships may be even more prevalent and destructive. These and others addictions are characterized as slow suicide in Dr. Norman Farberow's *The Many Faces of Suicide.* (See chapter 7, pp. 200–201.)

Addictions are difficult to treat because people who are hooked either deny it or believe — in thinking characteristic of the addict — that they are "cured" and in control of how much alcohol, cocaine, or other substances they use. Their denials — compounded by the collaboration of spouses and partners who themselves are addicted — ensure that millions of addicts go undiagnosed and untreated.

The addicted need help overcoming their specific addictions and underlying problems as well. Support groups exist for almost every kind of addiction. Most use modified versions of the twelve-step Alcoholics Anonymous program. They assume that dependency is a family affair, and that support from all its members will greatly help the addicted person learn to live again.

Becoming Your Own Best Friend

It is said that 10 million Americans would like to stop drinking, 48 million cigarette smokers would like to quit, and 80 million people would like to diet. But how? Many habits that jeopardize your health, career, or personal life do not necessarily require professional treatment, yet are serious problems that you would like to overcome. The Behavior Change Method, described in the film *For a Change: Breaking Old Habits and Making New Ones,* suggests that you begin by being realistic, flexible, and kind to yourself rather than setting up intolerable pressures to change. For example, do not try simultaneously to diet and leave your lover. The premise is that behavior is learned and, with concrete skills, can be unlearned. For example, you were not born smoking. The way to stop is to do the following:

1. *Increase motivation:* Are your reasons for changing vague? Do they depend on other people?
2. *Keep records of your behavior:* You can then face facts and discover causes and consequences.

3. *Set specific objectives:* Do not try to "lose weight"; plan instead to attend three exercise sessions per week.
4. *Take action:* Avoid triggers, substitute competing behaviors, and periodically reward yourself.
5. *Maintain the new behavior:* Remember that permanent change cannot come from willpower alone. Seek support from friends and family, and avoid people who practice the self-destructive habit you are trying to break.

For further information about the Behavior Change Method or the film, write to Spectrum Films, Inc., P.O. Box 801, Carlsbad, CA 92008.

Help for the Addicted

In *Megatrends: Ten New Directions Transforming Our Lives,* John Nesbitt identifies self-help groups as one of the major emerging trends across the country. Among those that help with addictions are

Alcoholics Anonymous
Al-Anon Family Groups (including Alateen and Adult Children of
    Alcoholics)
Cocaine Anonymous
Narcotics Anonymous
Smokers Anonymous
Overeaters Anonymous
Gamblers Anonymous
Checks Anonymous
Emotions Anonymous
Neurotics Anonymous
Battered Wives Anonymous
Sex Addicts Anonymous
Love Addicts Anonymous
Fundamentalists Anonymous (for people trying to recover from ad-
    diction to a rigid religion)

❧ III

THE BOTTOM LINE

❧ 10

Growing Older and Better

Male Menopause?

Male menopause is a relatively new concept that describes a time of shaken self-esteem and self-realization said to occur during a man's forties or fifties. The term actually is a misnomer because it suggests physical changes comparable to the end of a woman's menstruation, the literal meaning of menopause. No such transformation occurs in men. The male sex hormone, testosterone, diminishes gradually beginning at about age twenty, but the decline is so gradual that healthy older men produce sex hormones at levels comparable to those found in younger men.

During the transition, better named "male mid-life crisis," past successes seem meaningless, economic burdens overwhelming, and the future bleak. Confusion and despair dim the bright promise of youth. In *Crisis Time: Love, Marriage and the Male at Midlife*, Dr. William A. Nolen describes symptoms of insomnia, excessive drinking or drug use, job and career dissatisfaction, family and marital discord, sex problems, and fear of illness or death. Dr. Herb Goldberg, in *The New Male*, considers the crisis even more pervasive:

> I personally do not accept the rationalization that the "male menopause" is simply the result of panic over declining potency, biological changes, the fast pace of modern life or the breakdown of traditional values. To my mind it is the noise of the male organism shattering under the weight of oppressive, dehumanized conditioning. . . [and] years of repression and emotional denial.

Male mid-life crisis does not necessarily occur in middle age. This transition may occur earlier, or later, or never. It may dawn slowly over many years, or suddenly — upon losing a game of tennis to a son or daughter, losing a promotion to a younger competitor, or losing an erection in the midst of lovemaking. Some men do not experience a mid-life crisis at all. This may be especially true of men who are healthy and emotionally well-adjusted and who do not fear growing older.

Myths about Aging

Most Americans are not especially enlightened about aging. In his Pulitzer Prize–winning book, *Why Survive? Being Old in America*, Dr. Robert N. Butler explores myths and realities about growing older. The ruling misconception is that aging means physical and mental decline. Yet there is no immutable rule that says you cannot remain creative, productive, healthy, and sexy well into your seventies and beyond.

Myth: Many people believe senility is an inevitable consequence of aging. Actually, only 5 to 10 percent of people over age sixty-five, and 25 to 30 percent of people over eighty-five, are mentally impaired by Alzheimer's disease or multiple minor strokes, both of which cause widespread loss of brain tissue. Many older people suffer instead from more than one hundred different conditions that mimic the confusion, serious forgetfulness, and other changes in personality and behavior that commonly are mislabeled as "senility." These conditions — most of them reversible — include adverse reactions to drugs, depression, high fever, hypothyroidism, congestive heart failure, alcoholism, minor head injury, poor nutrition, dehydration, loss of self-esteem, loneliness, and boredom.

Myth: When you turn a certain age — sixty-five usually is the magic number — you automatically are "old." Yet there are people in their thirties and forties who are older in body and spirit than many individuals collecting Social Security. People who look younger than their age often are physically closer to someone much younger. Their biological — as opposed to chronological — age is associated with lifestyle, health, and possibly genetic endowment.

Myth: The typical older person is unproductive, inflexible, withdrawn, cranky, and hypochondriacal. According to Drs. Paul T. Costa and Robert R. McCrae of the National Institute on Aging's Gerontology Research Center in Baltimore, Maryland, more than one thousand subjects in the Baltimore Longitudinal Study of Aging — a research project that, since 1958, has documented how normal people age throughout their lifetimes — show no evidence of age-related personality changes. Personality is a unique characteristic that is formed by early adulthood and remains remarkably stable over time. This accounts for the finding that volunteers in the study show wide individual differences as they age. As for hypochondria, "The individual who makes excessive and exaggerated [medical] complaints in old age," the investigators add, "is probably the same person who has made them all of his or her life."

Myth: Old people lose interest in sex. The research of William Masters and Virginia Johnson long ago established that sexual activity need not decline with age, although many medications can impair the sexuality of older people. The greatest handicap older people face —according to Dr. Robert N. Butler and Myrna I. Lewis, authors of *Sex After Sixty* and *Love and Sex After Forty* — is the attitude that grandmothers should make cookies, not love, and that a young man's "lust" is an old man's "lechery." Studies at the Gerontology Research Center show that men in their seventies and eighties who maintain their love lives also maintain or increase their sex hormone levels.

Myth: Old people lose their ability to reason and remember. Research at the Gerontology Research Center and elsewhere shows that reasoning power usually declines only after age seventy-five or eighty, if then. The intellectual changes of normal aging do not become apparent until some time between ages sixty and eighty. They consist of decline in ability to learn new things and to make quick judgments of complex issues, neither of which is incapacitating. Crystallized intelligence — which depends on education and experience — usually improves throughout most of adult life and tends to decline only very late in life.

Often it is not intellectual functioning but eyesight and hearing that decline with age. Many of these sensory failures occur because of age-related diseases and disabilities that can be corrected. (See pp. 260–262.) Memory tends to decline with age, but not for everybody. Although most people in their fifties or sixties state that their memory "isn't what it used to be," objective testing seldom documents any decline. Older people who perform well on memory tests, research shows, are comparatively more active and emotionally stable than those with low scores. Studies show that older people can improve their memories, particularly for names and recent events, by learning mnemonic techniques.

Myth: Old age means inevitable decline in physical health. Actually, the physical and emotional problems people attribute to aging often preexisted in mid-life. Old age *does* introduce some new health problems and causes different reactions to certain diseases and drugs. Still, nine in ten elderly persons describe their health as excellent, good, or fair. About 20 percent of the elderly — mostly women in their eighties or older — live in nursing homes and other institutions, usually because of loss of intellectual functioning. The rest live in the community. Even in the over-eighty-five group, less than half are limited to some degree or unable to carry on major activities because of chronic illness.

Myth: Retirement is devastating to physical and emotional health. A series of studies at the Veterans Administration Outpatient Clinic in Boston shows, to the contrary, that the average retiree stands no greater risk of health problems than the employed person. Investigators there found that even compulsory retirement and living on a reduced income were not statistically associated with increased health complaints. These studies did not include men who retired for health reasons. Because that group is far more likely to report serious health problems, disability retirements may cause many people to associate retirement with declining health. Retirement also has a potential for psychological damage when a person who is not ready to retire is forced to do so. With people living longer and retiring earlier, Americans in the year 2000 will spend about one-fourth of their lives in retirement.

Myth: Nothing can be done about the negative aspects of aging. Yet the man who enjoys healthy living throughout life will enliven his future as well. The real enemies are not disease and decline, but *fear* of disease and decline. When you believe that the best part of you is buried at mid-life, the person you are shooting in the foot is your future self.

Ageism (prejudice against the old) is a hangover from the early 1900s, when most people died before age sixty-five and senior citizens represented only 4 percent of the population. For decades, older people have represented the fastest growing segment of the population. Soon after the year 2000, one in three Americans — most of them baby boomers — will be age fifty-five or older. If prejudice proceeds from minority status, ageism will soon become both unfashionable and unwise.

Healthy Aging

At the turn of the century, infections and acute illnesses were the major causes of illness and death among the elderly. Today, the major killers of people over age sixty-five are chronic diseases such as heart disease, cancer, and stroke; influenza and pneumonia; accidents (especially traffic accidents); and lung and liver diseases. The leading causes of physical disability — as opposed to death — in the elderly are arthritis, hypertension, hearing impairments, heart conditions, orthopedic problems (hip, back, leg, and spine), chronic sinusitis, vision problems, diabetes, varicose veins, hemorrhoids, chronic constipation, urinary problems, foot problems, hay fever, and abdominal hernias.

To be sure, some aspects of aging cannot be modified. Prostates enlarge, arteries become more rigid with age, nerve impulses travel more slowly, muscle mass and strength decline, the body's temperature-regulating mechanisms become less reliable, and hair may thin and turn gray.

On the positive side, the body at age sixty-five runs a little more slowly, not worse. The heart pumps blood at about the same level at age eighty as at thirty. And many — if not most — physical problems that occur are caused not by the aging process per se, but by the health choices of earlier years. Even when health problems occur, they are not necessarily limiting. Atherosclerosis, emphysema, cirrhosis, lung cancer, wrinkles, loss of stamina, muscular weakness, stiff joints, weight gain, varicose veins, hemorrhoids, constipation, and sexual changes can be prevented or modified, as can age-associated losses of teeth, vision, and hearing.

Teeth

The average twenty-year-old has only thirty of an original thirty-two teeth. By age fifty, the average person has twenty-two teeth; by age seventy, only seventeen. Teeth usually are lost to dental caries (tooth decay) — which affects almost every American at one time or another — or periodontal (gum) disease, which affects almost everybody past age thirty-five. The villain in both conditions is plaque: a whitish, almost invisible film that sticks to tooth surfaces and contains millions of bacteria. The longer plaque remains in place, the greater the likelihood of developing tooth decay and gum diseases: gingivitis, which causes bleeding, inflamed, tender, and swollen gums, and periodontitis, which can eventually lead to loss of tooth-supporting structures. Dental calculus (hard deposits of tartar) also leads to peridontal disease because plaque nestles in the nooks and crannies of calculus where it is harder to remove. Bleeding during toothbrushing is one of the earliest signs of gum disease. To prevent tooth loss:

- *Use fluorides to prevent tooth decay.* If your drinking water is not fluoridated, use a fluoride toothpaste or mouthwash, or have a dentist apply it topically.
- *Cut down on sugar,* especially between meals. How much sugar you eat is less important than how often.
- *Brush your teeth with baking soda and floss your teeth* at least once a day to remove plaque. Brush every exposed tooth surface and use dental floss in a gentle scraping motion up and down the surfaces between each tooth. The American Dental Association also recommends brushing your tongue to remove mouth bacteria.
- *Have a dental examination every six months.* Only a dental professional can remove hardened plaque and calculus and detect problems that can lead to decay, gum disease, and tooth loss.

Eyes

Cataract and glaucoma are two of the most common and controllable age-related eye disorders. Glaucoma, a leading cause of blindness, is characterized by high fluid pressure inside the eyeball. Symptoms usually do not occur until late in the disease and include trouble adjusting to darkened rooms and poor side vision. Glaucoma can be treated with drugs that relieve eye pressure, surgery, or laser beams. The disease tends to run in families, and blacks develop it at several times the rate of whites. Also at risk are people who have diabetes or high blood pressure. The most important risk factor, however, is age: one in fifty Americans over age forty-five has glaucoma. To detect the disease early, eye specialists recommend an eye examination at least every two years for people over forty. Eye examinations can detect diabetes, high blood pressure, brain tumor, diseased arteries, certain cancers, intestinal disorders, and a wide range of eye disorders, including cataracts.

Cataract is a cloudiness of the lens of the eye that can lead to blindness. Symptoms include blurring or dimming of vision, especially at night. About 60 percent of people over age sixty-five have some evidence of cataract formation. Of these, less than 10 percent require surgery, a procedure that is outstandingly successful. The surgery generally is done on an outpatient basis. Over 90 percent of patients choose to have intraocular lens implants rather than wear thick glasses to compensate for removal of the natural lens of the eye.

Another eye disease that occurs — usually in mild form — in millions of older Americans is age-related macular degeneration (AMD). It affects the macula, a structure at the back of the eye that provides sharp central vision needed for such activities as driving and reading small print. Usually AMD does not develop until age sixty-five or older, and most of those affected continue to have almost-normal vision throughout their lives. Even severe AMD does not cause total loss of sight and can be compensated for with low vision aids that use special lenses or electronic systems to produce enlarged images of nearby objects.

One age-related change that is not a disease, but a normal and gradual decline in the eyes' focusing ability, is presbyopia. The lens of the eye — which in a young person changes shape to accommodate for near and distant objects — hardens and cannot focus on close objects clearly. This hardening begins early in life. By age forty to forty-five, it may cause vision at the usual reading distance to blur. By age fifty, most people need reading glasses or bifocals to compensate for presbyopia. Aging also causes the pupils of your eyes to become smaller and less adaptable to changes in light, and causes the lacrimal glands to secrete fewer tears, a condition known as "dry eye." Older eyes may not adapt to glare as rapidly as they once did, especially during night driving on poorly lighted roads, and they may need more light for most tasks.

Ears

Presbycusis is hearing loss from cumulative damage to the delicate hairlike cells in the inner ear that allow you to hear high-pitched sounds. The damage results from disease, side effects of medications, and — above all — lifelong exposure to loud noise. Thus most of the presbycusis that affects about half of men and women by age sixty-five is not caused by aging per se. Before age sixty-five, men have higher rates of hearing loss than women, probably because of repeated exposure to occupational and recreational noise. The degree of damage depends upon sensitivity to noise, duration of the noise, and its loudness.

Zero decibels (dBA) represents the lowest level of sound your ear can detect. At 30 dBA you can hear a whisper five feet away. Because the decibel scale increases logarithmically, each additional 10 dBA seems twice as loud. At around 90 dBA, your ears may start ringing, a sign that your hearing is being irreversibly damaged.

	Approximate decibel levels
Quiet room	40
Conversation at three feet	60
Vacuum cleaner	70
Apartment near freeway	80
City traffic/baby screaming	90
Woodworking shop	100
Thunderstorm	110
Rock band, amplified	120
Discotheque	130
Aircraft carrier deck	140
Gunfire or firecrackers	125–160
Crew area of heavy artillery	160–180
Blast zone of exploding bomb	190

While hearing loss can result from a single exposure to a very loud noise or explosion, most noise-induced hearing loss takes place over time. Even moderate noises made by vacuum cleaners, portable radio headphones set above 4, and power mowers can damage your ability to hear and understand speech under everyday conditions if exposure is continuous. Whenever you stand at arm's length from a person in a noisy place and cannot be heard without raising your voice, the sound level is unsafe. Either get away, wear earplugs or ear protectors, or place a piece of Kleenex or a finger in each ear as an emergency earplug. Soft reusable wax earplugs that can be molded to fit inside your ears are comfortable and allow you to hear conversation or the hum of an engine while reducing harmful noise.

Most hearing loss is painless. For years you do not notice the damage because it affects both ears. Then you have trouble understanding what is being said. You notice tinnitus (a ringing or buzzing in your ears), or you start turning up the volume on the television set louder than others would like. Many specialists recommend an annual hearing test after age fifty-five. Although the only treatment for presbycusis at present is the hearing aid (sometimes supplemented by lipreading), it is better to wear one — modern devices are barely noticeable and are constantly improving — than to lose contact with other people and events, and always appear confused or dumb.

Life Extension

Back in 1889, British scientists reported that long life depends upon good eyesight and hearing, healthy and long-lived ancestors, a lean figure, good digestion, sound sleep, moderate consumption of food and alcohol, intelligence, quiet temperament, and energetic activity. An Austrian researcher in 1911 recommended twelve rules for longevity, including exercise and fresh air, adequate sleep, stress-free living, and temperate use of alcohol and tobacco. He also recommended daily baths, a daily bowel movement, wearing porous underwear, and resting one day a week without even reading or writing — findings not borne out by subsequent research.

Scientists today distinguish between life expectancy and life span. The former is the probable number of years a certain group of people or animals, on the average, will live. Life expectancy varies among different populations, depending on how long your parents lived, your physical health, lifestyle, and environment. Life span refers to the maximum number of years of life *possible* for a given species. The longest documented human life lasted 114 years, which is assumed to be the present outer limit of human life span.

Among the many theories of aging, several suggest that aging is genetically programmed. The DNA damage theory proposes that the cell's genetic material is subject to cumulative damage over time. Dr. Leonard Hayflick hypothesizes that there is a limited number of cell doublings in the life span of a species, and that human fibroblast (connective tissue) cells double about fifty times before they begin to fail to grow and then die.

In the late 1950s, Dr. Denham Harman proposed the free-radical theory of aging. Free radicals are highly reactive chemical by-products generated when the body uses oxygen; they oxidize and slowly damage body tissues, especially cell membranes. Many people have expanded upon the Harman theory and maintained that large doses of antioxidants can neutralize the effects of free radicals. The authors of the popular book *Life Extension*, Durk Pearson and Sandy Shaw, for example, propose that people can double their life spans by consuming various diet supplements and food preservatives, especially those containing antioxidants. In *Maximum Life Span*, Dr. Roy L. Walford, a researcher in aging at UCLA, recommends a combination of antioxidants, undernutrition, and exercise to extend life, but he has not tested his theories in humans as yet.

Skeptics oppose the use of antioxidant supplements because a balanced diet contains all you need. They warn that oral supplements of antioxidants, such as SOD (superoxide dismutase), an enzyme produced naturally in the body, are useless since SOD is digested before body cells can use it. Moreover, extremely large doses of antioxidants can hasten, rather than retard, oxidation and cause more rapid aging. At this point, nobody knows the real relationship of antioxidants to longevity.

Diet studies show that the life spans of undernourished rats and mice can be extended up to 70 percent longer than normal. Dietary restriction, however, has not been extensively studied in humans. Moreover, research results are contradictory: some show that thin, underweight persons live longer; others show that the most underweight people have the highest death rates. Some researchers have rejuvenated the immune systems of rodents with immune deficiencies by means of dietary restriction or administration of hormones from the thymus gland. But thymosin and other such hormones have not extended the lives of animals with normal immune systems.

Among the substances that are said, but not proved, to slow aging are Gerovital (a mild antidepressant available only in Romania), centrophenoxine (a drug popular among Europeans for removing so-called age pigments), DHEA (dehydroepiandrosterone — an adrenal hormone that decreases with aging), Levodopa (a drug for Parkinson's disease that increases survival in mice), and supplements containing DNA (deoxyribonucleic acid, the substance of which chromosomes and genes are made), RNA (ribonucleic acid, a related molecule that translates DNA's genetic information into proteins), and various vitamins. Still other scientists are exploring the life-extending effects of lowering body temperatures.

No magic bullet yet exists that will conquer aging, says Dr. Edward L. Schneider, deputy director of the National Institute on Aging. Aging is such a complex process, he notes, that no single substance or technique will ever stop or reverse all its changes. Yet there are many proven — although less magical — ways to maintain health and extend life expectancy that people are not using fully. They include smoking cessation, good dietary habits, regular exercise, adequate rest and relaxation, stress control, seat-belt use, good safety habits, control of addictions to alcohol and drugs, regular health checkups, proper medical care, and other measures mentioned throughout this book.

According to the theory of "organ reserve," proposed by Dr. James

F. Fries of Stanford University, the hearts, lungs, kidneys, and livers of young adults function at four to ten times the capacity required to sustain life. This organ reserve preserves health but begins to decline at about age thirty. The eventual result is natural death, even without disease, at the end of one's life span. But the human organism is not living to its full potential, because chronic illnesses such as heart disease, cancer, lung disease, and cirrhosis of the liver are accelerating loss of organ reserve. These chronic illnesses presumably can be postponed by changes in lifestyle, however, and compressed into a brief period of illness as late in life as possible. If sufficiently postponed, such diseases might never occur and people might simply die of "old age," ending up like Oliver Wendell Holmes's "one-hoss shay," in which everything falls apart at once and cannot be repaired. It is an attractive alternative to years of disability leading to lingering death.

Use It or Lose It

If a modern-day fountain of youth were discovered, inscribed on it would be the words USE IT OR LOSE IT. Premature heart, lung, joint, and other dysfunctions commonly are the result of underuse or misuse — not overuse — of those body organs and parts. Exercise has not yet been proved to increase longevity, but if it could be packaged into a pill, says Dr. Robert N. Butler, former director of the National Institute on Aging, "it would be the single most widely prescribed, and beneficial, medicine in the nation."

Exercise can improve heart and lung performance, strengthen bones, and protect against cardiovascular disease. It can also slow or reverse many age-related changes or declines in strength and motor performance.

	Effect of aging	Effect of exercise
Strength	Decrease	Increase
Muscular endurance	Decrease	Increase
Speed	Decrease	Increase
Power	Decrease	Increase
Balance	Decrease	No change
Muscular efficiency	Slight decrease	No change
Fine motor skills	No change	No change
Gross motor skills	Decrease	Increase
Reaction time	Decrease	No change

According to a Gerontology Research Center study of 120 extensively trained athletes aged fifty-five or older — many of whom run or race walk fifty to sixty miles a week — most have aerobic capacities similar to those of healthy twenty-five-year-old athletes. Investigators report that these individuals also have better overall health, fewer restrictions of their daily activities, lower blood pressures, less body fat, lower weight, fewer cases of diabetes, better cholesterol profiles, more agility and strength, more confidence and self-esteem, and less depression than their age-matched sedentary counterparts.

"Use it or lose it" applies also to the mind and spirit. Too often the mental decline said to occur with age stems from expectations that intellect will do just that. Research shows that people who lead active lives in middle age remain stable or improve their mental abilities after age sixty. Those who have unstimulating lives show a marked decline. For example, a study in the 1950s and 1960s of men and women listed in *Who's Who in America* shows that achievers of both sexes outlived their peer group by 29 percent on the average. While this may prove only that some characteristics associated with accomplishments may also be associated with long life (like being made of high-quality clay), it also is possible that the stresses of striving and competing may have lengthened, rather than shortened, their lives.

"Using it" applies also to sexual and social activities. Aging, as noted in chapter 3, does not lessen your ability to enjoy sex, and much of the reported decline in sexual activity is caused by alcohol, drugs, and poor attitudes such as "What do you expect at *your age?*" Although aging lengthens the amount of time needed for arousal and satisfaction, many older people report increasingly satisfying sex lives because of deepening emotional involvement and compatibility with their mates. It is also important to maintain a network of intimates throughout life. A person who flops, at any age, in front of the television and rarely talks to family or friends may flicker out long before his time.

Benjamin Franklin and thirteen of the other fifty-five men who signed the Declaration of Independence lived into their eighties: about thirty years beyond the average life expectancy in those days. They led active lives, as did Bertrand Russell, who organized international peace drives at age ninety-four; George Bernard Shaw, who wrote plays at ninety-three; and Pablo Casals, who gave cello concerts at eighty-eight.

In modern times the natives of Vilcabamba in Ecuador, the Hunzas of Pakistan, and the Abkhasians of the Soviet Union are renowned for their apparent good health in old age. Although it is difficult to document their actual ages, the inhabitants of these areas appear to live longer than usual. Studies of the Abkhasians, for example, have shown that they eat sparsely and well, exercise, work hard, remain sexually active, and live with their families into old age. It is not unusual to find among them an eighty-nine-year-old shepherd, a ninety-seven-year-old vineyard worker, or a hundred-and-one-year-old carpenter.

Several decades of research on aging have shown that people whose lives are varied and complex — who exercise, read, enjoy friends, learn, love, play, and help others — tend to outlive their peers who lead dull lives. As Shakespeare said in *Love's Labour's Lost*, "A light heart lives long." It also helps to have long-lived parents, but this advantage can be offset by pursuing unhealthy lifestyles.

The changes that occur with aging are not as adverse as many Americans think. Most are under your personal control.

Aspects of aging	Counterefforts
High blood pressure	Control weight; exercise
Heart-lung capacity	Exercise; stop smoking
Memory	Practice; memory training
Physical strength/endurance	Exercise; control weight
Reflex time	Training; practice
Serum cholesterol	Exercise; eat well
Social contacts	Stay active
Sexuality	Practice, practice, practice!

Your body thrives, in the fullest sense, on use. You can wear out or rust out. Many people who choose to remain healthy, creative, productive, and happy well into their later years have — perhaps as a result of mid-life crisis — examined their values and adjusted their attitudes about aging. Benjamin Franklin once wrote, "Wish not so much to live long as to live well." One of the essential tasks of middle age is to prepare for the realities of aging and anticipate its unexpected pleasures. Practicing the art of living well is not only the best way to live, but the surest way to live longer.

❧ 11

Why Men Die "Young" or How to Add Eight (or More) Years to Your Life

The Longevity Gap

The last time men and women in the United States could expect to live about the same number of years was in 1900, when the life expectancy of women was forty-eight and that of men was forty-six. Throughout this century, the longevity gap between men and women has widened, although it equalized briefly just after the 1918–19 flu pandemic, and has narrowed slightly during recent years. In 1984 the average woman lived 78.2 years, the average man 71.2, or 7.0 years fewer. Moreover, women live longer than men in all industrialized countries in the world.

According to current projections, life expectancy at birth in 2050 will be 81.0 years for women and 71.8 years for men. Some scientists predict that as more women smoke and enter the work force, their health patterns and life expectancies will approximate those of men. So far, however, there is little evidence that this is occurring.

Why Men Die "Young": Biology?

Why have women in industrialized countries during this century lived longer than men? The answer begins before birth, when more male than female fetuses are lost through miscarriage, making the sex ratio at birth about 106 males for every 100 females. Mortality rates, mainly from genetic and respiratory ailments, are higher for boys than for girls during the first year after birth, and this trend continues, although the life expectancy gap narrows after age fifty to sixty. Thus, even though males and females are born in roughly the same numbers each year, and even though women tend to develop more chronic physical and mental diseases resulting in longer periods of illness, female life expectancy surpasses that of males.

Some research scientists hypothesize that genetic differences make men the weaker sex. They note that at conception a child receives a complete set of forty-six chromosomes, half from the mother and half from the father. Female cells have two X chromosomes, while males have an X and a Y chromosome. Few genes are located on the male Y chromosome other than one that causes the development of testes. The X chromosome, by contrast, carries many defective genes that may cause a person to inherit any of hundreds of diseases. According to Dr. Estelle R. Ramey, professor of physiology and biophysics at Georgetown University in Washington, D.C., females are stronger than males from conception. A woman who carries an abnormal gene on the X chromosome has another X with a corresponding normal gene. If the latter gene dominates, she does not develop the disorder even though she is a carrier. Males, by contrast, lack a normal gene to counteract the effect of an X chromosome that carries an abnormal gene. The extra X chromosome of women, Dr. Ramey says, also may strengthen their immune systems and make them more resistant than men to infectious diseases such as influenza and pneumonia.

Studies by Dr. Ramey and colleagues at Georgetown University have shown that maleness is linked to blood clots that cause heart and blood vessel disease. Many years of animal experiments have demonstrated that the male sex hormone testosterone fosters the development of arterial thrombosis, or clots that damage the heart and circulatory systems, and that the female sex hormone estrogen hinders development of these clots. These animal, as well as human, studies suggest one reason why men have a higher incidence of heart attacks until later in life when women undergo menopause and lose the protective effect of estrogen.

Men's bodies also react more intensely to stress and produce higher levels of certain stress hormones, Dr. Ramey says. These hormones cause the "fight or flight" responses during which the blood clots faster, the heart beats more forcibly and — if the man is not in shape — faster, blood pressure rises instantaneously, and red blood cells increase and cause the blood to become thicker. "Beginning with puberty, men incur cumulative cardiovascular damage because of the intensity of their stress response," Dr. Ramey says. "About fifteen years later, or at about age thirty, comes the first rise in the number of heart attacks in men." Women's sex hormones, especially estrogen, protect them from heart disease until after menopause, whereas women without ovaries have the same incidence of cardiovascular disease as men. In addition to damaging the cardiovascular system, Dr. Ramey says, stress hormones damage the immune system, the gastrointestinal system, and virtually every cell in the body since these hormones are transported in the blood. All this happens, she adds, because females are designed to get pregnant and ensure the survival of the species. Males of all mammalian species need the "fight or flight" response to protect the pregnant female.

Human males, in addition, have a physiological handicap that affects their behavior, Dr. Ramey says. All human fetuses develop as girls during the first six weeks of life. Then the Y chromosome causes the production of testosterone and male genitalia. This design change also slows the physiological development of the male brain, compared with the female, and causes young boys to engage in more random behavior and what parents call "hyperactivity." In addition, social conditioning encourages boys to be more active and to take risks that eventually raise their rates of fatal accidents and other violent deaths. Meanwhile, girls are "programmed" both physiologically and by society to be more calm and cautious. Dr. Ramey concludes that "it is no coincidence that the question of why men die earlier than women has been largely ignored by male researchers." Dr. Ramey, who has studied the biological differences between males and females for more than twenty years, concludes that the gap in longevity could be narrowed by studying why female biochemistry produces greater longevity and by learning how to bypass the worst effects of testosterone while preserving its best effects on masculinity.

Why Men Die "Young": Behavior?

Many research scientists hypothesize that longevity is far more than a matter of biology. Dr. Ramey notes that although significant biological differences contribute to the longevity gap between men and women, about half of the "gap" — or three to four years — could be eliminated by behavioral changes in men, including taking an aspirin daily to reduce the risk of heart attack (see chapter 6, p. 167).

Biologist Ingrid Waldron of the University of Pennsylvania suggests that complex interrelationships between biology and behavior may account for most of the excess mortality of men. Male mortality, she

notes, exceeds female mortality by 100 percent or more for seven leading causes of death. The two greatest risk factors leading to these seven
killing diseases involve behaviors that predominate among males:
smoking and drinking. Cigarette smoking contributes to heart disease,
emphysema, and lung cancer, and excessive alcohol consumption contributes to motor vehicle and other accidents, cirrhosis of the liver,
suicide, homicide, and, recent studies show, heart disease and stroke.

These seven causes of death account for three-fourths of the sex
differential in mortality in the United States today, Dr. Waldron concludes. Heart disease alone accounts for about one-third of the longevity gap. In terms of behavior, she says, cigarette smoking accounts, on
the average, for about half of the adult sex difference in mortality. Men,
she notes, have more hazardous smoking habits than women because
men smoke more cigarettes per day and inhale deeply. In addition to
smoking and drinking too much alcohol, other behaviors that society
encourages in men and that elevate adult male mortality rates include
unsafe driving, especially while drinking; accident-prone behavior;
employment in jobs involving exposure to carcinogens and other physical hazards; use of illegal drugs; use of guns; hostile Type A coronary-
prone behavior; and poor self-care.

It is often said that men die "young" because — directly or
indirectly — they are self-destructive. But Dr. Waldron believes that
rather than being self-destructive, many men either are unaware of
healthy ways to cope with stress and take care of themselves, or are
aware of what to do but cannot motivate themselves to make healthy
changes. "In practicing self-care, men do what fits male stereotypes
and women do what fits female stereotypes," she says. "It would be
better if both did what fits each other's stereotypes."

Masculinity and Mortality

In *The Hazards of Being Male,* Dr. Herb Goldberg wrote about destructively rigid male conditioning or living according to traditional male
"blueprints." Cultural pressures, he said, have programmed many
men to accept a long list of "givens": early marriage, fatherhood, and
hasty career choices and other major decisions that lock many men into
a job, mortgage, and lifestyle without having considered the options.
Unquestioning acceptance of the roles of husband, father, provider,
and protector has caused many men to become angry, frustrated, isolated, bored, and defensive. Such men tend to be out of touch with
their feelings and their bodies, to deny their weaknesses, and to

engage in protest or "macho" masculinity in the form of physical violence, accident-proneness, and other life-threatening behaviors. To
such a man, Dr. Goldberg concludes in *The New Male*, care of the body
means:

1. The less sleep I need,
2. The more pain I can take,
3. The more alcohol I can hold,
4. The less I concern myself with what I eat,
5. The less I ask anybody for help or depend on them,
6. The more I control and repress my emotions,
7. The less attention I pay to myself physically, *the more masculine
   I am.*

In the best sense, "masculine" describes a self-sufficient, strong,
steady, uncomplaining, adventuresome, fearless, risk-taking hunter/
warrior upon whom women and children depend to feel safe, cared
for, and protected. The problem lies not in these traditional male vir-
tues per se, but in what growing up as a male in today's society does
to undermine men's well-being and survival. There are signs that men
are becoming aware of what the self-destructive aspects of rigid male
conditioning are costing them. Increasing numbers of men are making
healthier lifestyle choices by stopping smoking, exercising more, eating more fiber and less fat, using seat belts, and guarding against
sexually transmitted diseases. Men now need — if they are to live
longer — to learn to live in harmony with other men, women, and
especially with themselves.

The American male tends to be a lonely creature. Male-to-male
bonding has traditionally occurred while engaging in drinking bouts,
watching football games, or repairing cars. These kinds of ties help
men maintain their male identities and sense of masculinity, according
to Dr. Lionel Tiger, professor of anthropology at Rutgers University
and author of *Men in Groups*. But these activities produce proximity,
not intimacy, and do not begin to employ the untapped inner resources men can offer one another. To satisfy the need for closeness,
men need to forsake their suspicion of and competitiveness toward one
another, and acknowledge their universal concerns.

Male-to-female connections would vastly improve if women would
stop believing that men are the privileged sex and learn more about the
difficulty of men's lives. If women would stop regarding men as success objects, perhaps more men would stop regarding women as sex

objects. Women might better view men as "health objects" and ask, "How well does this man take care of himself?"

Much of the trouble between men and women stems from unhealthy dependence upon one another. Although many modern men want a woman who is economically self-supporting, they may not want one who is truly independent. Such a woman has trouble finding a man who is unthreatened by her self-sufficiency. A man who fails is emasculated, the saying goes. A woman who succeeds is defeminized. Despite their differences and defenses, the sexes have much to offer and learn from one another. In particular, men could learn much from women about living longer.

To be in harmony with themselves, men need to acknowledge their vulnerabilities, respect tenderness in themselves and other men, and stop viewing healthful activities as primarily feminine. Men need to separate masculinity from smoking cigarettes, drinking to excess, eating steak and eggs, and waiting until they are physically and emotionally disemboweled before asking for help. Above all, men must stop looking for external explanations of their physical and emotional ills and start examining what *they* contribute to their problems. Only then can they hope to arrive at a new and life-giving definition of masculinity.

Toward Living Well

Many people know how to stay healthy but do not use that knowledge, according to a survey in 1985 of more than thirty-three thousand U.S. households by the Department of Health and Human Services. Many people want to make changes but do not know how. Still others do not really want to change, especially when habits such as smoking and drinking afford positive reinforcement and pleasure. Some engage in running or dieting so obsessively that their efforts are more destructive than healthful. And some people set up intolerable pressures to make many vaguely defined health changes at once. When they fail, they become debilitated by guilt. They might succeed if they made only one change at a time and waited until the change became second nature before moving to the next.

Sadly, some men will not even try. "It's too late to change," they say. "Why bother? I have to die of *something!*" The answer is: "Yes, but *how soon* and *of what?*" Such men might consider whether they would rather expire slowly — and perhaps prematurely — from disease, or drop dead of old age as late in life as possible.

Psychologist Carl Rogers, in his book *On Becoming a Person*, describes personal growth and change as a process you never quite complete. The object is "getting there," not being there. Consider the case of a man in his late forties. Although he has been divorced for three years, he shares most of the concerns and vulnerabilities of men who are married. His first step toward better health, after his marriage ended, was to stop smoking. "I knew that most women wouldn't want anything to do with me if I smoked," he says. He runs three mornings a week and often takes thirty-mile bicycle rides on weekends. His diet includes more fat- and cholesterol-laden food than he would like, because he eats in restaurants so often. He has not learned to cook. He does not know his blood cholesterol level and has not seen a doctor since his preemployment physical when he was thirty-eight. He has cut his drinking down to a glass of wine per day or less. Occasionally he "falls off the wagon" but knows he will always climb back on. He sleeps regularly and well, and takes naps when he needs them.

After his divorce, he had a series of brief affairs. He learned in psychotherapy, while his marriage was breaking up, that he had a pattern of choosing extremely dependent women whom he would ultimately reject, and of avoiding competent women who might reject him. He is trying to break that pattern by taking "time off for good behavior" and cultivating nonsexual friendships with women.

He works sixty- to eighty-hour weeks because he loves his job, and because it fills time that might otherwise be spent feeling lonely. He takes "mental health" days off when he needs them. He worries that his job might someday disappear because his skills have been overtaken by technology, and because younger people are already vying to replace him.

He sees his children frequently and feels closer to them than when he was married. Although he sometimes feels the blackness of depression, he has a network of supportive friends with whom he shares feelings. He would like to have more male friends but does not know how to go about finding them. He supports his supporters by sponsoring frequent parties and bicycle trips.

He has a great sense of fun. He rewards himself by buying things he would never have indulged in while he was married. When he is alone, he is never bored. Sometimes he feels lonely, but he knows the feeling will pass. He has become slower to accept heavy responsibilities and to make important decisions, because he wants to write his own game plan.

He worries about aging and sometimes calls himself the "old man" even though he has the flat-bellied body of a thirty-year-old. His greatest fear is that he will never find someone to love, but, deep down, he knows that eventually he will. He has learned that if he does not take care of his body, nobody else will. He is, in every sense, in the process of becoming a person.

Change is frightening, but it is also an exhilarating process of becoming things worth being. If you can risk it, you probably will never again return to self-destructive patterns. You may backslide along the way, but your general direction will be from self-destructiveness to self-caring, from passive acceptance to taking charge of your health.

It takes so much time to adopt new habits that many people become discouraged. It might help to adopt Carl Rogers's view that you *are* what you are becoming, and to

- start slowly
- set achievable goals
- keep records of your progress
- expect bumps along the road
- reward yourself as you achieve interim goals
- ask your family and friends to support your efforts

Inner Listening

The health philosophy of too many men remains: "If it ain't broke, don't fix it!" But they tend to ignore body signals that indicate something might be "broke" until they are no longer early warnings but last gasps. Many men take better care of their cars than of themselves. They can hear when their engines need a tune-up, but when their stomachs, heads, and hearts ache, they do not listen.

Inner listening means paying attention to the signals your body transmits from time to time. Suppose you have a pain in the stomach and chest area. Do you tell it to "shut up," or do you ask: What kind of pain is it? When does it hurt? What makes it worse? If the pain occurs after a heavy meal and feels better after trying a mild antacid or simpler foods, it probably is heartburn. If it occurs after exercising and radiates into your arms, it may be a more serious warning of heart attack. Abdominal pains, shortness of breath, headache, dizziness, and even agitation and anger are part of a biofeedback system that tells you when to look for an underlying physical or emotional problem. Sometimes simply deciphering a symptom can relieve it. Sometimes, as Lewis Thomas notes in *The Lives of a Cell*, "most things get better by themselves. Most things, in fact, are better by morning." The point is to watch for symptoms such as weight loss or pain that persist or grow worse. When a symptom is particularly severe despite efforts to remedy it, the message is: Check it out.

Choosing and Using a Doctor

Many men do not have their own doctor, so they end up with their wife's or girlfriend's. This immediately places men in "her" territory and adds to the psychological discomfort of going to a doctor. In the examining room, men are faced — often for the first time — with their mortality in the form of an M.D.eity who usually is a male. Another problem is the lack of a male "ologist" to compare with a woman's gynecologist. Men have fewer problems involving the reproductive organs that so often send women to doctors. When men do have such problems, they usually consult a urologist, general practitioner, or internal medicine specialist (internist). While GPs can handle most situations, an internist has more specialized training in preventive medicine and can better deal with serious health problems, especially heart disease and other major illnesses of men.

To find your own doctor, ask someone you respect or a local hospital (preferably affiliated with a medical school) or medical society for the names of *three* physicians. Since doctors are in oversupply, you can pick and choose.

Many people choose a doctor on the basis of geographic convenience. There are other important considerations:

- What is his or her specialty?
- From what medical school did he graduate?
- How long has he been in practice?
- Is he board certified, that is, has he completed three to five years of training in a medical specialty such as cardiology or urology?
- Can he fit you into his practice?
- Is he affiliated with a hospital?
- How much does he charge?
- How does he handle emergencies, that is, does he have a

twenty-four-hour telephone service and another physician to cover when he is away?

- Do you feel he is concerned about you as a whole person, including your emotional self?

Find a physician who inspires your confidence and with whom you will want to continue. Continuity of care leads to greater patient satisfaction, shorter hospitalizations, and fewer emergency hospital admissions, according to research reported in the November 2, 1984, *Journal of the American Medical Association.* This study of 776 men aged fifty-five and older showed that continuity of care also helps eliminate duplicative or conflicting treatments, especially those involving drugs, and helps ensure better care, especially for more complex illnesses.

Before visiting a doctor, be prepared to describe in detail how you feel physically and mentally. During your initial visit, recount your past medical history, your family's health history, and your habits and lifestyle. If you are depressed or anxious, say so. Let your doctor know what you want. Doctors often underestimate their patients' desire for information, and patients are afraid to ask. Otherwise, the doctor-patient relationship may end up like a bad marriage, with unrealistic expectations on both sides.

One of the most sensitive doctor-patient issues involves second opinions about surgery. A surgeon recommending an operation is offering an opinion, not an indisputable fact. You can get a second opinion with or without the surgeon's knowledge. But most doctors do not object and will even refer you to a specialist. Indeed, second opinions are so accepted today that many health insurance companies provide coverage for them. To help you make an informed choice, the Department of Health and Human Services has published a booklet, *Thinking of Having Surgery? — Think About Getting a Second Opinion.* For a free copy, write to Surgery, HHS, Washington, D.C. 20201.

Which Tests Do You Need?

Doctors themselves seldom undergo routine annual physical examinations, mainly because nobody has yet proved that these exams have much value, except possibly for people over age sixty. Studies comparing patients who have had annual "physicals" with those who have not consistently show no statistically significant differences in incidence of death or chronic disease. Nor have health screening tests —

such as those performed at shopping malls and health fairs — proved valuable. For most people, diabetes tests and other routine screening procedures may do more harm than good. They are expensive and — if their results are "false positive," that is, incorrectly indicate that something is wrong — cause needless worry leading to even more expensive and sometimes risky tests. Annual chest X rays and EKGs (electrocardiograms) are no longer recommended because they do little to detect lung and heart disease. Still, certain medical examinations are vitally important at various times during your life.

Many men avoid medical tests because they might convey bad news or confirm the need for treatment. While diagnostic tests may be unsettling, consider the trade-off. When you give your car routine maintenance, you do not expect — or usually find — problems because you know that checking the oil and tuning the engine will prevent problems. Ostriching will not make car or health problems disappear. It could make them worse. Therefore, many physicians and leading health groups recommend the following:

Healthy Men under Forty Should Have:

1. *A baseline physical examination* and electrocardiogram (EKG) during your twenties or thirties at the latest. In 1981 the American College of Physicians declared the annual checkup unnecessary.
2. *Blood pressure checkups annually.*
3. *Dental examinations every six months.*
4. *A routine blood cholesterol checkup* during your twenties. If normal (below 200), check your cholesterol at least every five years until age forty unless you are in a high-risk group (see chapter 6, pp. 160–161). Abnormal blood cholesterol should be treated by a physician and checked regularly.
5. *A cancer-related checkup every three years* during your twenties to forties (including examinations of the mouth, thyroid, skin, lymph nodes, prostate, and testicles). A *monthly self-examination of your testicles* also is advisable (see chapter 6, pp. 171–172).

Healthy Men over Forty Should Have:

1. *A physical examination every one to three years* or more often if you have a hazardous job or family history of heart disease or cancer.
2. *An eye examination to detect glaucoma every two years.*
3. *A digital rectal examination* to detect colon and rectal cancer *every*

year. After age forty, *an annual stool occult blood test* to detect colorectal cancer, and a more thorough *sigmoidoscope examination of the colon every three to five years*.

4. *A blood cholesterol checkup every two to three years* as part of a regular physical examination.
5. *An annual prostate examination*.
6. *After age sixty, a physical examination annually*.

NOTE: Men of all ages should examine their skin monthly for changes in moles.

Handling Drugs with Care

Some men avoid taking drugs of any kind, under any circumstances. This instinct can be healthy, since many drugs are overprescribed and even the most innocuous can be misused. At times, however, medication is vital. High blood pressure drugs are a case in point.

Americans tend to disregard doctors' instructions for taking prescribed medications, sometimes with tragic results. Too many people stop taking a medication as soon as they feel better. This may cause the original problem to flare up. Or they swap prescriptions with a friend because their symptoms are similar. Or they take leftover medicines, which can be extremely dangerous and can make a condition more difficult to diagnose. Others hoard drugs for years and dose themselves with dangerously outdated prescriptions from their private pharmacies. People over sixty-five need to take extra care because they tend to react to drugs differently from younger people.

As a health care consumer, you should know

- what drug you are taking — its brand and generic names
- why you are taking it
- how much to take, how often, and for how long
- how to recognize possible side effects, especially serious ones
- how the medication mixes with alcohol, certain foods, and other drugs
- what to do if you forget a dose

For everything you ever wanted to know about prescription drugs, a good source is the latest edition of Dr. James W. Long's *The Essential Guide to Prescription Drugs*.

The Bottom Line

Conventional medicine too often emphasizes disease and death instead of prevention and wellness, and tends to provide too much care too late. The average physician, moreover, is poorly trained in issues concerning nutrition, fitness, sexuality, and mental health. But a health movement known as holistic medicine considers a person a functioning whole rather than a collection of separate parts. It views health not merely as the absence of disability and disease, but as total physical and emotional well-being and as an attitude toward life itself. Throughout the United States, centers for holistic medicine offer an array of nontraditional healing methods. Although the movement attracts marginal practitioners and tends to overemphasize vitamins and other products sold in health stores, it aptly stresses achieving greater levels of positive wellness, even when you have no specific complaints. More important, the holistic concept treats you not as a patient, but as a health care consumer, client, and active partner in your own self-care.

"All right, what's the bottom line?" you might ask. "What do I have to give up?" Although giving up smoking is the surest way to close the longevity gap — depending on how early you quit, it could add as many as eight years to your life — you might better ask, "What do I have to *do?*" Most health behaviors involve *doing* something, not giving something up.

Studies have long shown that men could add eleven years and women seven to their life expectancies if they adopted certain health practices. In the early 1970s, Dr. Lester Breslow, dean of the School of Public Health, UCLA, recommended no smoking, moderate or no use of alcohol, regular and moderate eating, moderate exercise, and seven to eight hours of sleep each day. This study showed that about seven thousand men and women who followed these practices enjoyed better physical health — defined as high energy levels with no chronic diseases or symptoms and less self-reported severe disability. Furthermore, as Dr. Breslow and Nedra Belloc reported in the August 1982 *Preventive Medicine*, these habits had a cumulative effect. People who reported all or many of the good practices were in better physical health than those who followed only a few of the practices, regardless of economic status, age, or sex. Research scientists have since confirmed and expanded upon Breslow's concept of positive health.

Every chapter in this book points to these conclusions about respecting your body:

1. Do not smoke.
2. Eat defensively: more fiber; fewer calories; less cholesterol, salt, and sugar; and, above all, less fat.

3. Exercise regularly and vigorously.
4. Get enough sleep, rest, and recreation.
5. Learn how to relax and manage stress effectively.
6. Improve communications with supportive friends and family; learn how to listen.
7. Take an aspirin daily (see chapter 6, p. 167).
8. Wear seat belts.
9. Drink in moderation or not at all.
10. Never drive while drinking.
11. Avoid addictive drugs and relationships.
12. Think positively, especially about aging.
13. Listen to your body's signals.
14. Get regular health checkups.
15. Take care of medical problems such as high blood pressure.

The bottom line is to enjoy life. Good health need not be an ordeal of self-denial. Indeed, it may have more to do with a perception of being in control of your life and with doing something every day that makes you feel happy and involved.

In the eighteenth century, the French philosopher Voltaire said, "The art of medicine consists of amusing the patient while nature cures the disease." Today, science has proved that while doctors, drugs, or even nature can help, you can no longer rely solely on them to make or keep you well. Much — if not most — of the mortality from heart disease, cancer, accidents, stroke, emphysema, and other killing diseases can be traced to personal lifestyle. Thus any increase in male (or female) life expectancy will depend not on the medical system, but on *you*.

The best way to close the gap between male and female life expectancies is to extend men's lives, not to wait for women's to become shorter. Perhaps life expectancy should be redefined as expecting not only more *years* of life, but more out of life.

To improve your health, you must improve your very self. Once you make a commitment to begin this momentous undertaking, you will probably keep it. Good health is not a gift; it is a personal achievement. And a healthy man is not only attractive, but masculine in the best sense of the word.

Author's Postscript

During the week before the final manuscript of *The Healthy Male* was to be submitted to the publisher, the following happened:

- The National Institutes of Health announced a decline in death rates from cancer in the U.S. population under age fifty-five.
- One group of scientists reported a development that will speed research on an AIDs vaccine, and another described a new theory about why cancer cells resist drugs used in chemotherapy.
- A research scientist told the author that he would be reporting on a new drug treatment for impotence within the next year, and that it would not involve surgery or injections.

Such announcements are good news for readers, but less good for authors who hope to keep their books up-to-date. No doubt by publication date, the list of new discoveries will lengthen, and some of the information herein will be rendered obsolete by the amazing gifts we receive daily from medical research.

Index